Conflict Management in the Family Field and in other Close Relationships

– Mediation as a Way Forward

Published with support from
Dreyer's Foundation

Edited by Pia Deleuran
Illustrated by Sisse Jarner

Conflict Management in the Family Field and in other Close Relationships
– Mediation as a Way Forward

DJØF Publishing
2011

Pia Deleuran (ed.)
Conflict Management in the Family Field and in other Close Relationships
– Mediation as a Way Forward
First Edition 2011

© 2011 the Author and DJØF Publishing

Cover: Bo Helsted
Print: Narayana Press, Gylling
Binding: Jysk Bogbind, Holstebro

Printed in Denmark 2011
ISBN 978-87-574-2303-7

Sold and distributed in Scandinavia by:
DJØF Publishing, 2100 Copenhagen, Denmark
Email: forlag@djoef.dk
www.djoef-forlag.dk

Sold and distributed in North America by:
International Specialized Book Services (ISBS), Portland, OR 97213, USA
Email: orders@isbs.com
www.isbs.com

Sold in all other countries by:
The Oxford Publicity Partnership Ltd, Towcester, NN12 6BT, UK
Email: djof@oppuk.co.uk
www.oppuk.co.uk

Distributed in all other countries by:
Marston Book Services, Abingdon, Oxon, OX14 4YN, UK
Email: trade.orders@marston.co.uk
www.marston.co.uk

Jurist- og Økonomforbundets Forlag
Lyngbyvej 17
Postboks 2702
2100 København Ø

Telefon: 39 13 55 00
Telefax: 39 13 55 55
e-mail: forlag@djoef.dk
www.djoef-forlag.dk

Index

Outlining the Idea of the Book   7
By Pia Deleuran

Foreword   11
By Anja Cordes

Chapter 1. '(Naughty) Departures': Expertise, Orthodoxy and the Role of Theory in the Practice of Mediation   15
By Barbara Wilson

Chapter 2. Guerilla Mediation: The Use of Warfare Strategies in the Management of Conflict   37
By Robert Benjamin

Chapter 3. Managing Courtroom Communication: Reflections of an Observer   51
By Joanna Kalowski

Chapter 4. Mediating High Conflict Couples   59
By Henry Brown

Chapter 5. Family Mediation and Children   75
By Lisa Parkinson

Chapter 6. Family Violence and Family Mediation in Australia   93
By Dale Bagshaw

Chapter 7. Mediation as a Process for Healing   109
By Greg Rooney

Chapter 8. Neighbour War and Peace on Danish TV   127
By Camilla Emborg

Chapter 9. Interview with Fay Weldon about Sex and Gender Issues in Conflict Situations   135
By Sabrine Mønsted

Chapter 10. Negotiation Styles and Strategies: The Influence from Sex and Gender Dynamics   143
By Tina Bolbjerg Winther-Nielsen

Chapter 11. Silencing the Self: Inner Dialogues and Outer Realities   151
By Dana Crowley Jack

List of Authors   175

Outlining the Idea of the Book

By attourney and mediator Pia Deleuran

The ideas and ethos of mediation and different techniques used in mediation have gradually become better known and more highly valued in the legal system. This has taken some time and many of the professionals involved in the development of mediation find it surprising that this way of managing conflict and resolving disputes is not welcomed more readily.

Mediation may be seen, after all, as a form of assisted negotiation in which the parties are helped to consider their interests and needs in a creative and problem-solving way, instead of putting forward claims as in traditional litigation. Many lawyers have considerable experience and understanding of the often entrenched disputes that many people get into when conflicts occur in the family field and in other close relationships.

Many professionals worldwide find that mediation's benefits are so huge, that they persevere in trying to convince others that many opportunities for the parties are lost if mediation is not considered as an appropriate means of dispute resolution. The loss is seen as a loss for society as a whole and also for those unable to resolve the conflicts or disputes on their own.

Voluntary participation remains, however, one of the corner stones of the mediation process. It creates a special dynamic in enabling people to recognize and take up the opportunities that mediation offers to them.

There is a huge need to increase awareness and understanding of mediation among lawyers and other professionals, so I am one of those who find it relevant to go on spreading "the mediation message". This is one of the main purposes of this book.

I have heard so often the question posed in workshops and seminars: "Are you for or against mediation?" Let me suggest that we should instead reframe the question as: "How can we as societies benefit from mediation's philosophy and methods without restricting access to justice and guarantees of fair outcomes?" We all know that the courts are important institutions in democracies that guarantee that disputes can find a peaceful and non-violent resolution and the ambition is that there is a transparency which is seen as a protection against abuse of power. This is a constant struggle to uphold these ideals and we need to consider how the use of mediation where you have confidentiality as another of the corner stones will have an effect on the system and vice versa. Getting more insight into such issues will help us improve the systems the best possible way.

I hope this anthology will encourage reflections on these important questions, bearing in mind that people are often capable of finding imaginative solutions when inspired and supported in doing so, and that we have to encourage this ability. At the same time we have to develop systems that protect people from violence and abuse and do not create unrealistic expectations to mankind. It is crucial to find and maintain this delicate balance. Mediators need to have a sound and realistic approach towards conflict management and dispute resolution and be able to use knowledge drawn from different disciplines. We too need to work in co-operation with other professions in developing cross-disciplinary approaches when situations are as complex as they often are in family conflicts and in many other conflicts involving close relationships.

Who does this book address and what is the structure of the book?

As in all human endeavours, theory and practice alternatively inform each other and grate against each other. No conflict management practitioner can competently work without some organizing frame that helps them think about where to begin and how to proceed in managing complex issues, yet many dismiss theory as a largely unnecessary abstraction. Likewise, it is not realistic that a competent academic or theoretician can posit a competent hypothesis about the nature of conflict without some exposure to experience.

I therefore hope that the book will inspire to further exchanges between the fields.

This book is therefore a collection of texts from experts working in many different fields and in different countries around the world: Australia, U.K., US and Denmark. This sharing of experience and ideas helps us all to reflect on ways of improving systems currently in operation in our respective countries.

The target group of this anthology is mediators and other professionals i.e. lawyers, psychologists, social workers, child-experts and others who work with parties to help them manage and resolve the difficult situations. It is my hope that some of the texts as well can inspire people who are "just" interested in conflict management and resolution.

In the first three chapters in the book it is considered how conflicts can be dealt with efficiently and what expectations we can have in that respect. Do we do what we think we do when we mediate? Are we realistic in our approaches and how do we most effectively use the language? These are some of the questions being dealt with.

In chapter four to six we learn about the family mediation-field. How to approach high-conflict-cases, how children's perspective can be included and what implications for family mediators family violence has.

The next chapters – chapter seven – it is explained how a mediation process can provide healing and in chapter eight a Danish television program "Neighbor-War" from 2010, where mediation was used to calm the parties and get a dialog about their conflicts, is referred to. In the last three chapters – nine to eleven – the authors write about sex and gender issues and how they influence the mediation setting.

The anthology is one out of four books in the Danish project called "Mediation as a Way Forward" – in Danish "Mediation som mulighed" – the other three books are mainly in Danish and cover

1. The role of the lawyer in mediation
2. Mediation in the IT-field,
3. Mediation in cases about real estate and in the construction field.

Acknowledgments

As you will know by now a group of mediators and other experts, who work with conflict-issues in different ways or deal with issues relevant for the mediation process have written the essays in this book. Without them there would be no book and no input to reflect from. I therefore so much thank each of the authors.

Since this book is inspired by the contact I have with lawyers and other professionals – among them the other trainers and participants at the Trinity-courses – I would link to thank all for the pioneer spirit and the enthusiasm shown.

Without my family, friends and good and helpful colleagues who have been involved at all levels in this process it would not have been the same. So thank you so much for helping me giving birth to the project.

Then there are Djoef publisher where I have had a close contact to Editor-in-chief Vivi Antonsen and production manager Per Kjæmpe. From them I have received an immediate understanding of the concept and a great help to carry the project through. I am very thankful for that. The Dreyer Foundation has again supported a mediation-initiative what has been valuable. The Foundation has from the very start been open-minded towards this new and advanced way of resolving conflicts that can be seen as a future oriented approach for which I am thankful for.

Finally, I want to thank photographer Sisse Jarner for the fantastic cooperation we have had again. The book is decorated with colorful and expressive illustrations made by Sisse Jarner. They provide us with inspiration. Following the true spirit of creativity that mediation is a provider of. Works of art can sometimes touch us in a different way than the written word. We hope that the combination of text and illustrations will create a synergy that aids more lawyers and others who work with conflicts getting interested in knowing more and helping to reflect on how to improve the way we think about conflicts and resolutions.

You are welcome to visit the webpage www.mediationtouringexhibition.com where you can see all illustrations presented in this and the other three books.

Foreword

By president of the Danish Family Lawyers, attourney and mediator Anja Cordes

During the early 90's the Board of the Association of Danish Family Lawyers (FAF) took the initiative to invite two British mediators, Henry Brown and Felicity White, to Denmark. During 1997-1998 they conducted a training programme in mediation with the participation of 25 family lawyers. The courses were tailored to Danish conditions. Subsequent virtually all the participants undertook additional commercial and business mediation training in London.

Our Association has also offered various training and mediation courses in the form of workshops and participation in conferences. This has contributed to the formation of a Danish group of mediators of a high professional standard, who continually update and further develop their skills. New mediators have joined the group by completing the mediation training program offered by the Association of Danish Law Firms (Danske Advokater). This program is composed of seven training days spread over three months and divided into three modules.

The Family Law Mediator Group has its emphasis on members' ethical standards and practical training.

In order to promote awareness of mediation the Family Law Mediator Group collaborated with the Copenhagen City Court (Københavns Byret) from February 2002 until the end of January 2003 in offering mediation in family matters brought before the court. 15 Family Law Mediators from the group made themselves available for the experimental project.

A working group of judges and mediator lawyers from FAF outlined the framework for the project and prepared a brochure that could be handed out to the parties and their lawyers in the respective cases. It was agreed that mediation could be offered for cases dealing with marriage, separation and divorce, child custody, division of property and injunctions.

The project took longer to become established than expected due to the fact that there was very little awareness of the mediation option. Initially many of the solicitors and party advisers were quite skeptical, but their attitude became more positive as the results began to emerge.

In approximately half of the cases a settlement was reached through mediation. Remarkably, three out of four cases were settled in situations where an injunction had been issued to give one of the parents access to their child. Such cases are typically considered to be extremely conflict-ridden. Before the experiment it would have been very difficult for people to believe that mediation could be applicable in such cases. The actual results of the experimental project provided a different picture.

When the pilot project with the Copenhagen City Court was completed the mediation process and program were taken up by five other local courts spread across the country. This second phase of the pilot program was initiated in collaboration between the Association of Danish Lawyers (jeg ville mene der skulle stå The Danish Bar and Law Society?) (Advokatrådet), the Ministry of Justice and the Court Administration.

It ran from 1 March 2003 until 1 February 2007. During this period, virtually all civil proceedings – including family cases – could be referred to mediation. The results of the pilot program were evaluated in an interim report, and users, party lawyers and legal agents were overwhelmingly satisfied. On average, agreement between the parties was reached in about two-thirds of the referrals to mediation. The Ministry of Justice made an evaluation of the project, which can be read on the Ministry's website. When this evaluation was available it became clear that mediation was a good way to get warring parties into dialogue about solutions to their issues.

Mediation was adopted by law with effect from 4 January 2008 and is now offered in litigation in all district and city courts, the High Courts and the Maritime and Commercial Court. More information is available on the website www.domstol.dk.

Danish Family Lawyers share a long and strong tradition of sharing experiences and updating their knowledge, methods and techniques.

With this background we greatly appreciate this new publication. It provides us with unique access to new insights and knowledge as to the deliberations and experiences of other mediators and professionals.

'(Naughty) Departures': Expertise, Orthodoxy and the Role of Theory in the Practice of Mediation

By mediator Barbara Wilson

This paper discusses the nature of mediator expertise and whether skilled practitioners' implicit knowledge can be elicited and made available to others. Regardless of setting, a considerable body of research suggests that experts do not necessarily behave according to the conventions of their field, or 'by the book'. Although expertise is generally acknowledged as domain-specific, some authorities trace sufficient similarities across disciplines in order to propose a general theory of expertise and expert performance. This general theory may be extrapolated to provide valuable insights into understanding and supporting the practice of experienced mediators, as well as training new practitioners.

Also touched upon here are mediation orthodoxy and ideologies, the findings of research programmes involving mediators considered by others (i.e. case referrers) to be experts, and the notorious theory/practice divide. The paper concludes with a short discussion of the benefits and disadvantages of expertise models.

Keywords: mediation, mediator, ideologies, orthodoxy, expertise, expert, theory, practice.

Introduction

This paper concerns the nature of mediator expertise and whether skilled practitioners' implicit knowledge can be elicited and made available to others. The title borrows a somewhat provocative phrase from Hoffman & Lintern (2006, p.215), who are representative of researchers interested in the nature of expertise and its manifestation in different disciplines. Regardless of setting, Hoffman & Lintern contend that experts do not necessarily behave according to the conventions of their field, nor 'by the book'. They write:

> "... all experts who work in complex sociotechnical contexts possess knowledge and reasoning strategies that are not captured in existing procedures or documents, many of which represent (naughty) departures from what those experts are supposed to do or to believe ...".

Although expertise is generally acknowledged to be domain-specific, some authorities trace sufficient similarities across disciplines to propose a general theory of expertise and expert performance (Ericsson, 2006a, p. 9). For present purposes I shall refer to the extensive body of publications addressing expertise as the *expertise literature*. An 'expertise' study of civil mediators (attorneys and judges) was conducted in 1996 by Crandall et al. (summarised in Crandall, Klein et Hoffman (2006, pp. 83, 123-4)). They reported differences in strategies and practices attributed to expert and novice mediators, although their mediator subjects appear to have engaged in a form of med-arb: the skills reported in 1996 are not those which would necessarily be associated with the finesse and subtlety of present day mediator expertise. In Australia, the relevance of the expertise literature to mediators has been identified by Holmes (2006), to whose work I shall return, together with elements of Marshall's (2008) reported findings following her research with experienced mediators in the Melbourne area.

Also discussed are mediation ideologies, the outcomes of certain research programmes involving mediators considered by others (i.e. case referrers) to be experts (Carnevale et al, 1989, cited by Goldberg, 2005), the theory/practice divide (Honeyman et al, 2001, Wade, 2009) and issues of knowledge transfer. The paper ends with a short discussion of the benefits and disadvantages of expertise models.

Mediation is here understood to be a third party activity within the wider Alternative Dispute Resolution (ADR) spectrum. I accept that some of the terminology and discussion below is potentially problematic, although fuller discussion is beyond the immediate scope of this brief paper.

The meaning and study of expertise

Experts are people whose special knowledge or skill causes them to be an authority or specialist (*Shorter Oxford English Dictionary*). Although the term 'expertise' is often used to describe an individual's superior cognitive competence, Billett (2001, p. 431) points out that workplace, or vocational 'knowing in practice', is not a disciplinary abstraction; expertise is situational, the product of social participation and interactions between the individual and his/her vocation. Conversely, domain experts do not perform well when asked to do something outside their usual area of competence (Ross et al, 2006, p. 405). Despite different interpretations of what it is to be an expert, the general theory of expertise proposes that the majority of experts shares a number of generic features. There is no agreement as to what these might be, although Ericsson (2006b) suggests:

- The 10-year rule. People usually need at least about 10 years' experience to become experts (even Mozart – born into a famously musical household – did not demonstrate true originality until his teens, and Bobby Fisher undertook nine years of intensive chess study before he was recognised as a grand master at the age of 16) (p. 689).
- Extensive experience does not automatically lead to expertise. Many experienced people function at a pedestrian level throughout their working lives, and do not reach the highest levels of mastery (p. 683).
- Intensive training, study, support and a nurturing environment are essential for expertise to develop and flourish (p. 699).

- Expertise is deliberative – individuals seeking expertise consciously engage in 'raising their game' over extended periods of time (p. 699).

Expertise authority Klein (1999) has conducted numerous in-depth studies of skilled workers from different backgrounds, including firefighters, nurses, pilots and chess masters. His methodology is ethnographic in orientation, involving immersion with his subjects in order to study them under typical working conditions (known as naturalistic decision-making settings). His purpose has been to investigate and identify the factors which distinguish expertise. By studying his subjects as they go about their everyday duties, Klein has been able to research real-life experts, rather than running laboratory experiments with inexperienced participants. He writes:

> "Features that help define a naturalistic decision-making setting are time pressures, high stakes, experienced decision makers, inadequate information (information that is missing, ambiguous or erroneous), ill-defined goals, poorly defined procedures, cue learning, context (e.g. higher-level goals, stress), dynamic conditions and team coordination." (Klein, 1999, p. 4).

Klein's description of typical naturalistic settings seems highly relevant to mediation, although it does not sit comfortably with certain tenets of mediation orthodoxy, which often portray mediation as an essentially orderly phase process comprising several (usually at least five) stages. Conventionally, the parties and practitioner cycle through these stages, using rational choice decision-making strategies to reach an outcome. In reality mediation is likely to be far more untidy and labyrinthine than this rather idealised format suggests.

Klein concludes that experts think differently; they notice when familiar patterns are violated or departed from. They make fine discriminations and engage in mental simulation, drawing from past events to anticipate what is likely to happen in the future. They also have the ability to see their own limitations and know 'how to manage around these' (p. 149). Within the ADR framework, practitioner and researcher Holmes (2006) notes the contextual complexity, ambiguities and uncertainties of conducting mediation, the 'confounding variables that contribute to the effectiveness of work in this field' (p. 114). She identifies three main factors defining elite mediator practice, namely relational expertise, clinical judgment and the ability to engage in reflective practice in order to deal with the challenges of the work (p. 118). Holmes' findings are also compatible with Goldberg's research (2005), which is discussed below.

Naughty departures and mediation

One strand of the expertise literature posits that experts behave differently from novices, adopting different paradigms when they approach complex workplace problems (Benner, 1984). Novices are rule-governed (p. 21), whereas experts operate from a deep understanding of the total situation they confront. Though experts may still use rules and analytical tools, they do not engage these simplistically, but act instead with perceptual acuity and recognitional ability based on long experience (pp. 32-33). A summary of earlier research by Abdolmohammadi & Shanteau (1991, Table 1) indicates that experts go beyond mechanistic thinking and routines in their search for mastery. This is not because experts have no regard for directives and procedures (although they sometimes find them irksome); on the contrary, Shanteau (1992, p. 7) found experts often display a common set of psychological traits, one of which is a clear sense of responsibility and commitment to their decisions. An expert's knowing abandonment of rule-bound practices, the active pursuit of expertise, and the extensive experience necessary for this to be achieved may explain the naughty departures identified by Hoffman & Lintern (2006, p. 215).

Naughty departures in mediation have been observed for some years, notably as disparities between received mediation orthodoxy and actual behaviours (Honeyman, McAdoo & Welsh, 2001, Wade, 2009). Naughty departures are not wilful, unethical violations; they occur because skilled practitioners are endeavouring to perform optimally in complex situations, but have learnt from experience that following manuals will probably not help them to do so. I propose that there are broadly two types of naughty departures in mediation. First, experienced practitioners may engage in operational non-compliances, such as the discerning abandonment of instructions, procedures and protocols. The second form of naughty departure is ideological non-compliance – for example, where skilled mediators dissent from one or other of the various belief systems which dominate the ADR field, and which are typically embedded in codes of conduct and influential ADR texts.

This fine distinction between rules and ideologies is arguably somewhat artificial, since belief systems may drive practice, and practice may in turn influence beliefs. This is known as the heuristics and biases paradigm. Researchers sometimes interpret this paradigm as showing that experts are inherently biased, and will therefore misconstrue evidence to confirm their existing hypotheses (Klein, 1999, pp. 272-3, citing Kahneman & Tversky, 1973). Klein asserts that this interpretation of Kahneman & Tversky is a misunderstanding, as several studies have found that decision biases are reduced if the studies themselves are contextualised (i.e. they are conducted in naturalistic settings). He further contends that most common strategies of scientific research derive a prediction from a favourite theory which is tested to show that it is accurate, thereby strengthening the reputation of that theory. Klein wryly reflects that researchers undertaking this form of investigation simultaneously condemn any appearance of such self-confirming bias in the people they research, instead of attempting to disconfirm their own favourite theories (p. 273). In other words, researchers do not practise what they preach.

In my experience, mediators are extremely conscious of the possibility of bias, and are concerned that any biases of their own might operate to the detriment of the parties (see also Marshall, 2008, p. 28). The ability to deal with one's predilections requires a degree of self-awareness and self-management that goes to the heart of expert practice. One might suppose a mediator's biases would most readily be evidenced by the hypotheses they generate. Haynes et al (2004, p. 14) suggest that mediators constantly construct hypotheses about the range of issues, which they then test in the parties' early interactions, while Ross, Shafer, & Klein (2006, p. 408) identify the ability to hypothesise based on recall as a feature of general expertise theory.

Rooney (2008) adopts a different position from Haynes et al's, identifying the shortcomings of models driven mainly by the testing of a practitioner's advance hypotheses. Describing mediators' need to 'hold the space' (p. 250), he argues that, by sitting with uncertainty and even discomfort, mediators act as role models who help the parties to manage any discomfort of their own when faced with the uncertainties of decision-making (p. 252). The 'intuitive' thoughts which then occur to the mediator are receptive to this encounter, and can help the mediator to make sense of an event, decide on an intervention, or form a credible hypothesis. Responding reflexively to the parties' own awakenings and letting the process evolve is thus the antithesis of hypotheses-driven practice, whilst acceptance and tolerance of uncertainty and ambiguity are also reported in Marshall's research on experienced mediators (2008, pp. 171, 267).

Therapist Mason describes the shift from first to second order thinking in therapeutic practices which took place during the 1980s, when an emphasis on problem-solving shifted to a perspective of mutually (although not necessarily equally) influencing relationships. The latter involves genuine curiosity and the avoidance of premature certainty being displayed by the practitioner (Mason, 2005, p. 160).

Discussing the benefits of creating a therapeutic context which feels safe enough for those involved to explore their uncertainties, Mason defines a position of authoritative doubt as the ownership of expertise in the context of uncertainty (p. 163). Although the focus of this paper is not therapy (nor therapeutic forms of mediation), I consider Mason's 'safe uncertainty' to be a helpful construct for mediation practice in general.

Hypothesising at any stage of mediation requires prior reflection and mental simulation regarding the potential consequences of any hypothesis. In Klein's terms, mediators should seek disconfirmation of their favourite theories before testing them (1999, p. 273). Discussing hypotheses with the parties may lead to affirmation and movement, but may also trigger denial and challenge; hypotheses-testing can be a relatively high-risk strategy for mediators to pursue. Although successful hypothesis-testing may be instrumental in promoting progress, there are compelling reasons to avoid forming or offering hypotheses which could appear to display unintended bias on the part of the mediator. Where hypothesis-testing is contemplated as a useful strategy, one must be fairly confident that any attendant risks and benefits are first anticipated and thought through.

Naughty departures and operational non-compliances

Operational matters are often localised or determined by organisations in terms of that which is required of mediators. At the time of writing (2010), publicly-funded family mediation in this jurisdiction (England and Wales) is overseen by the Legal Services Commission (LSC). The LSC is an independent public body governed by a board of commissioners, but is expected to become an executive agency of the Ministry of Justice in due course, subject to primary legislation. Publicly-funded work is delivered via for-profit and not-for-profit franchises; both must comply with the LSC's Mediation Quality Mark Standard (MQMS). Franchises are subject to LSC audits, and non-compliance with the MQMS requirements can have serious consequences, such as disciplinary action or even withdrawal of the franchise.

Operational orthodoxies appear in ADR text books, sometimes uncritically or prescriptively. For example, Kovach (2005, p. 306) identifies 'opening remarks/statements by parties' as one of a number of 'important things that happen in most mediations', although she accepts that the mediation process is not linear. I believe the use of formalised opening remarks and statements by the parties promotes positional bargaining strategies, and thus encourages competitive rather than cooperative behaviours (as described by Deutsch, 2006, p. 24). An example of the problems which can arise from mismanagement of the 'who goes first' dilemma is neatly provided by Haynes, Haynes & Fong (2004, p. 11), while Patton (Patton, 2005, p. 288) observes that the first person to speak is likely to stake out high initial demands which are met by correspondingly high (or low) demands by the other disputant. Negotiations then usually take the form of a series of reciprocal trade-offs and concessions until agreement is reached or discussions break down.

By way of contrast, Jones' (1994, p. 28) considerably more refined conceptualisation of mediation stresses the importance of relational interdependence in contextualising the meaning given to the parties' text or behaviours. Meaning and relational context are thus mutually generative. Jones' argument for attention to situation and text is supported by the expertise literature; for example, Lipshitz, Klein, Orasanu & Salas (2001, p. 335) contend that expert decision makers are sensitive to semantic as well as syntactic context (citing Wagenaar, Keren & Lichenstein, 1998, Searle, 1995). Mechanistic views of communication in conflict necessarily de-emphasise relational factors and deny the evolutionary nature of conflict as a discursive process which structures context and communication interchangeably (Jones, 1994, p. 32). Even a mediation model focused on problem solving or distributive bargaining between non-repeat players takes place in a relational and dynamic context, however curtailed that context might be.

The parties must of course have ample opportunities to state their points of view, but I believe that a mediation model which emphasises the use of 'opening statements' is rather too reminiscent of litigious court processes. Furthermore, encouraging early position-taking probably hinders parties from negotiating as effectively as they might; it may also cement strategic advantage between them. My own practice mirrors a report by of one of Marshall's research subjects:

... "it's like riding a horse. You hold the reins tightly at the beginning, but not too tightly so that the horse might buck and not so loosely that that it will bolt. But firmly, to say who is in control here" (Marshall, 2008, p. 162). (emphasis original).

The mediator's control described here is one of 'power with' (Follett, 1924, xii-xiii). Coactive power is the antithesis of coercion, and the mediator's control is exerted in order to create a safe and empathic context for discussion. Inevitably, some mediations start and end as struggles between competing strengths and positions. The management of power and control is central to practice; if these factors prove too unequal between the parties, it may mean that negotiations are not possible. Nevertheless, I attempt to democratise the mediation process from the outset, relinquishing the reins as soon as possible. If it becomes necessary to again take up the reins at different points in the session, I still look for the earliest possible opportunity to slacken my hold; working knowingly with the parties in order to create Mason's (2005, p. 160) state of safe uncertainty allows for such slackening.

Another expertise authority (Weick, 2001, p. 333) endorses the need for certain operational guidelines, but is somewhat scathing about having more injunctions than are absolutely necessary in order to conduct difficult tasks. He argues that long checklists shut down improvisation, and that resilience is more important than the anticipation of events. It is critical that the ADR practitioner prepares for the unforeseen by reinforcing his or her personal resilience and expertise, rather than by simply following prescribed methods of practice. We therefore need to question the received operational wisdom in our field, and ask ourselves not only what we should do, but why we should do it.

Naughty departures and mediation ideologies

Claims that mediation is ideologically driven are not uncontroversial, especially if mediation is construed as an essentially rational response to conflict management and resolution. Mediation as an ideological project has been argued by Mayer (2004) and others, and criticisms of ADR as ideological have also fuelled some of its harsher critics (for example, Nader, 1991). Mediation's detractors sometimes appear oblivious to their own ideologies – for instance, there is evidence in their work that at least some commentators implicitly believe that consensus is bad and contest is good (which appears to be the vantage point of authors such as Fiss, 1984). Critiques of ADR may be based on an atomistic world view, in which people are not understood as essentially inter-related, rather as having overriding rights as individuals. This perspective drives the type of thinking that argues that disputes should only be dealt with by due (Western) legal processes, and that the demands of justice require resolution to be by trial or some other form of arbitration. Parallel concerns are also expressed about the need for the ongoing creation of legal precedents (Eisenberg, 1976) amid a diffusion of decision-making processes (Galanter, 2004), although other writers consider such anxieties to be based on a myth (e.g. Lande, 2005).

Conversely, the communitarian nature of many societies provides a very different perspective from that which is traditionally associated with Western constructs. Communitarianism conceives of people as social beings belonging to cohesive and interdependent groups. There is, of course, a risk in stereotyping human groupings, since these are self-evidently far more complex and diverse than such labels allow. One of democracy's greatest challenges is the balancing of competing worldviews regarding conflict and justice in the context of global migration and international cultural assimilation and difference. The dominance of a largely individualistic perspective in Western societies has been challenged by the introduction and promotion of ADR ideologies in many liberal jurisdictions. Without the challenge of ADR ideology, mediation processes would probably not be publicly available in the developed world, nor would they have become contemporary options for dealing with a variety of disputes in postmodern societies. The dominant legal framework nevertheless remains, captured in Mnookin & Kornhauser's (1979) much-quoted phrase 'bargaining in the shadow of the law'. Where ADR processes become conventional, it is questionable whether they can still truly claim to be alternatives to the courts: this has resulted in terminological adjustments, such as the substitution of 'appropriate' for 'alternative' dispute resolution in the ADR lexicon.

The ADR world is indeed ideologically driven, and is not represented by homogenous beliefs. Numerous debates have developed internally amongst its practitioners and academics, some of which are highly contentious. Mediation's moral validity, format, purpose, 'ownership', and relationship to the law have been argued at length in a canon far too extensive to cite here. At first, these quarrels may seem surprising in a field devoted to conflict resolution – however, disputes amongst authorities are seen positively within the expertise literature, and understood as evidence of the challenges and complexities with which experts must deal. Shanteau (2001, p. 238) writes:

> "Investigators have overlooked the fact that in most real-world problems, unique solutions do not exist. Instead there are multiple solution paths ... It should not be surprising, therefore, to find experts disagreeing about which is the appropriate course of action to take."

Typical of controversies in the ADR sphere are issues of mediator neutrality and impartiality, to which texts such as Mayer (2004) are almost entirely devoted (see also Marshall, 2008, pp. 133-136). Strict adherence to concepts of mediator neutrality and impartiality in this jurisdiction raise issues of possible non-compliance with the overarching legal requirements that the welfare of minor or dependent children must be paramount in residence (custody) and contact (access) cases (Children Act, 1989). The welfare of the parties' dependent or minor children must also be the first consideration in matters involving property and finance distributions (Matrimonial Causes Act, 1973). Mediators must therefore make plain to the parties from the outset their duty with regard to the welfare of children (College of Mediators Code of Practice, 2008, 4.7). This obligation to focus on children's welfare does not imply that the practitioner should determine the terms of the parties' negotiated outcomes; nevertheless, the mediator's stated position regarding children is undoubtedly influential in practice, and may raise potential conflicts of interest between the practitioner and parties. This is a difficult and ethically challenging area in which there are often no easy solutions, and where expert practice is especially relevant.

In continuing to reassure people that we do not take sides – and are thus above the fray – it can sometimes feel as though we have painted ourselves into a corner from which it is difficult to escape. Adherence to the dominant discourse of neutrality and invisibility regarding mediator influence can make it hard to discuss what actually happens in mediation, and may result in practitioners instead reciting received orthodoxy regarding their role, purpose and casework. The hiatus so created is illustrated by Macfarlane (2002), who describes the ethical dilemmas and unconventional approaches of some of her own mediation work. Her paper provides thought-provoking evidence of the theory/practice divide, as well as of the enduring influence of mediation's 'neutrality' narrative over its practitioners. The pressures of mediation orthodoxy persist, but openly discussing naughty departures can be a means of illuminating mediator expertise, as Macfarlane's (2002) paper illustrates so well.

Orthodoxy pressure extends to the epistemological value of certain texts selected for mediator training. For example, an extensive negotiation canon (predominantly North American) is very influential in mediation pedagogy, and has provided some useful paradigms for understanding conflict. However, even a cursory review of the research data appearing in various cited studies in this canon shows that they often involve undergraduates or MBA students, acting in one-off laboratory experiments with relatively small cost/benefit consequences for those taking part. Such contrived, controlled scenarios are a far cry from the turmoil and high stakes of real life negotiation, whereas expert mediation practice demands theories that are domain-specific and applicable to the uncertainties and vicissitudes of ADR.

Practitioners have an important role to play in demystifying and validating their role through exposing their own skills and knowledge. One way to achieve this is for skilled mediators such as Macfarlane to write about their practice. Weedon (1997, pp. 106-107) calls this exposure and articulation 'reverse discourse', which she identifies as the first stage in challenging meaning and power. Without the contributory voice of those actually engaged in this work, mediator expertise will be defined mainly from the vantage point of external observers, who may (or may not) fully comprehend the topic they are critiquing. To my mind, this sometimes means our expertise is undervalued, misunderstood or 'lost in translation'.

Naughty departures and research on successful mediators

In February 2004, Professor Goldberg of Northwestern University, Illinois, conducted the first of three studies on 'successful' mediators. This section focuses on the outcomes of his first study, published a year later (Goldberg, 2005). Goldberg analysed the self-reported views of experienced mediators working in various dispute resolution settings; all had already been nominated to Goldberg as successful by those who had referred cases to them. Goldberg emailed an identical memorandum to 93 practitioners requesting that they account for their success as mediators, and also identify the skills and techniques which they thought enabled them to reach settlements. His memorandum also included the following request:

> "... That leads me to ask if you'd respond in writing to the above questions ... I certainly don't expect a lengthy response, somewhere between one paragraph and a page or two would be fine. I would, however, appreciate the most candid response possible, not necessarily what you would say for publication, but what you might really view as your essential strength(s) and technique(s)." (Goldberg, 2005, p. 366).

Goldberg subsequently kept to his 'experienced mediator' brief by eliminating five of the 35 responding practitioners on the grounds that the former had not mediated at least 50 disputes each. His analysis of the remaining 30 replies – reported in his summarising paper (Goldberg, 2005, hereafter 'Goldberg') – makes for interesting reading. In his results section (p. 366), Goldberg reports that over 75% of his sample attributed their success to their ability to develop a rapport with the disputing parties, and to foster a relationship of understanding, empathy and trust with the people with whom they were working. Other factors identified by this mediator group were creativity (including the ability to reframe), empathic listening, humour, patience and tenacity. Less tangible factors, such as a keen sense of timing and optimism, were also mentioned as important elements accounting for success.

Later in the same paper (p. 373), Goldberg cites an earlier study of mediator behaviours by Carnevale et al (1989), undertaken with a presumably different tranche of practitioners (hereafter 'Carnevale et al'). Goldberg notes that this previous research resulted in a taxonomy of 'successful' mediator strategies which differed considerably from his own findings. According to Goldberg's account of Carnevale et al's (1989) work, successful behaviours identified by their mediator subjects included their ability to:

- Keep negotiations focused on the issues
- Avoid taking sides on important issues in joint sessions
- Clarify the needs of the other party
- Let everyone blow off steam
- Attempt to move one or both parties off a committed position
- Help devise a framework for negotiations
- Help establish priorities amongst negotiators

The discrepancy between the two studies clearly created a problem of dissonance for Goldberg, which he raises in his paper (p. 374). Attempting to reconcile the data, he speculates that some disparities may have occurred because he asked his experienced group of mediators about the 'essential strengths and techniques' of their practice, rather than requesting them to identify 'all (sic) the tactics they use in mediation' (p. 374). Goldberg also observes that he asked his mediators to give relatively brief responses, leading him to question if this request might also have influenced the replies he received, and was thus a potential source of the incongruence between the studies. He wonders if, had he asked for longer replies from his own group, the outcome might have been more closely aligned with Carnevale et al's. Goldberg thus effectively attributes the difference between the findings to the wording of his own memorandum.

My own reading of the disparities is very different. I think the key to the two studies' anomalies is indeed to be found in the wording of Goldberg's memorandum, but for reasons other than those he identifies. The memorandum's brief to the mediators as cited above contains the following sentence: *I would, however, appreciate the most candid response possible, not necessarily what you would say for publication*' (emphasis added). This sentence seems to me to invite the mediators to say *what they actually do, rather than recite versions of what they are supposed to do*. Goldberg's request for candour appears to have been taken literally by his respondents, possibly resulting in naughty departure replies that are indeed honest and reflective, but not necessarily compliant with the received wisdom of the field.

According to my interpretation of his work, Goldberg himself is not impervious to orthodoxy pressures. In a footnote to his 2005 paper (footnote 1, p. 375), he is careful to clarify what he meant when asking the mediators about their 'success'. He states that – for his purposes – success should be defined as the resolution of party disputes, rather than other outcomes or goals such as personal transformation. In so writing, it is possible that Goldberg was anticipating potential challenges to his work from those who adhere to beliefs about mediation's transformative powers, whilst simultaneously taking the opportunity to set out his own ideological views about its moral value and purpose. The incongruities between the Goldberg and Carnevale et al studies – in particular, Goldberg's request that mediators should give their candid views, rather than those they would say for publication – raise vexed issues of mediators' tacit knowledge and the role of theories-in-use (Stempel 1997). To the seasoned practitioner, Carnevale et al's cited list of successful strategies looks suspiciously like a textbook version of 'how to mediate'. There is nothing inherently wrong with this list, although some elements are very debateable. For instance, it is questionable that encouraging people in conflict to blow off steam is helpful; Friedman et al (2004) in fact assert that this is not always a good idea.

Compared with Goldberg's results, Carnevale et al's cited list reads as formulaic, unyielding and lacking is dynamism and authority. Especially notable is the absence of any mention of the mediator's relationships with the parties (a factor noted by Jones, 1994, p. 31), whereas Goldberg's cohort identified building rapport as the most important factor accounting for mediators' success (described by over 75% of his respondents as the ability to develop understanding, empathy and trust with the disputants). The comments here should not be read as implying that Carnevale et al's findings are incorrect or unimportant. It is possible, however, that their respondents answered in ways which they felt might be expected as orthodoxy-compliant, which is why they perhaps did not reply with the candour legitimised by Goldberg.

I have no doubt that a mediator's relationship with all the parties is the most important factor in his or her work, and crucial to success, even if not automatically identified as such. Training programmes and the ADR literature often do not highlight this key element, focusing instead on maintaining mediator distance from the parties, rather than the benefits of engaging with them as sincerely, transparently and even warmly as possible. An example of such engagement is noted by Adler (2003, p. 75); this aligns with Goldberg's (2005) findings, and is cited elsewhere by Marshall (2008, p. 86). Describing his collegiate attempt to conduct a strategic analysis of some successfully mediated cases, Adler speculates:

> "... We deciphered the breakdowns, breakthroughs, and the windows of opportunity both lost and found. The participants in our cases had a very different view. What they recalled us doing was opening the room, making coffee, and getting everyone involved." (p. 75).

I offer an account of my own work, which perhaps echoes some aspects of Adler's with regard to how mediation practice can be perceived. Several years ago I undertook a mediation which was observed (with the parties' prior consent) by an unconnected third person, who did not participate save to exchange some introductory pleasantries. It was a child contact (access) case involving middle-management parents, who were verbally and intellectu-

ally very able. The level of conflict between them was not displayed by shouting or other emotional outbursts, but rather through a measured, 'professional' but nevertheless hostile debate demonstrating their familiarity with a number of psychosocial and child development theories. Within their somewhat arcane discussions were numerous clues indicating their high level of conflict, but also cues suggesting potential leverage points (Klein, 1999, p. 111). Because of the parents' deceptively calm conduct, these clues and cues were opaque, complex and subtle. Nevertheless, they eventually negotiated a settlement which comprised three pages, setting out detailed arrangements for the daily care and schooling of their child, the times to be spent with each parent during holidays, birthdays and other important occasions, contact with extended family members, and contingency arrangements in the event of future variables.

After the parents left, and to my – probably ill-concealed – dismay, the observer commented, 'well, that was easy enough, wasn't it?' The parties had achieved a successful outcome and avoided litigation, but I was left drained, demoralised and confused. I had experienced concerted and sometimes frantic paddling in order to avoid the numerous hazards in this case, most of which were well below the surface; my effort had been construed by the observer as an undemanding glide through relatively calm waters.

I have often thought about this family, and wondered whether the parents' proposals worked out for their child in the long term. At the time, however, I was also left with severe misgivings about my own abilities (Marshall, 2008, p. 183). Was this mediation really as easy as my observer thought, or did her lack of mediation experience mean that she could not see the many navigational problems I encountered? Would one of my fellow mediators have found the parents as equally challenging as I did? More worryingly – were all mediations actually a great deal simpler than I had come to believe? If I found something supposedly so 'easy' to be so difficult, should I not give up mediating altogether?

I have since countered these thoughts with observations of people carrying out expert activities in domains in which I have absolutely no knowledge or skill – an ice skater executing a triple Axel jump, my dentist interpreting my X-rays, a pilot landing a jumbo jet plane in appalling weather, and so forth. All demonstrate apparently effortless skill, expertise and even artistry. However, unless one has at least some understanding of the prerequisites essential to achieving such accomplishments, even these tasks can look simple.

Expertise and the theory/practice divide

Getting to grips with theoretical constructs can be a bewildering task for practitioners. Deutsch (2006, p. 33) believes that mediators must develop a 'mosaic of theories' relevant to the specific situation, but does not indicate the ethical basis on which such theories should be founded, nor which theories his mosaic should include or exclude. Much ADR thinking originates in systemic, decision-making or communication theories, although postmodernism is now influential in the form of narrative and other deconstructive approaches. Given mediation's multidisciplinary origins, and the galaxy of available concepts, views and published research, it is hard to know where to start. Nonetheless, nor is it good enough for practitioners to enthuse about the 'magic of mediation' without stopping to examine what they actually mean, or seeking to advance their knowledge and skills through deliberative study, reflective thought and openness to new ideas and empirical research.

In an insightful and frank paper, Honeyman et al. (2001) describe various factors which combine to defeat and discourage collaboration between conflict resolution scholars and practitioners. The authors make a number of constructive suggestions for narrowing the divide, but also bemoan the barriers which restrict the dissemination and adoption of potentially useful theoretical concepts. These include the pressures on academics to publish only in relatively inaccessible, elite journals, and their tendency to discount practitioner expertise. I think mediators have not helped themselves in this regard; Honeyman et al. suggest that practitioners want to learn only that which they can use immediately, accusing them of a frequently cavalier attitude towards professional enlightenment.

In some ways, Honeyman's allegation is understandable, and probably true. Quick rules of thumb – or heuristics – reduce the need for redundant thinking, and help people to function in everyday life, especially when they need to make rapid decisions in difficult circumstances. Unfortunately, a quick rule of thumb mentality also permeates mediation training and professional development, often in the guise of workshops and courses offering 'tools for your toolbox'. The heat of conflict makes huge emotional and cognitive demands on mediators, who need the best possible range of skills and techniques for the tasks they face; but, and as has often been said, everything tends to look like a nail if you only have a hammer. Having more tools in our metaphorical toolbox may indeed help us deal more effectively with conflict situations, although I think that the issue goes far deeper than this. The toolbox metaphor suggests that mediators are already fully competent and require only minor adjustments to complete their skill-set – analogous to the qualified plumber who decides s/he could probably do with another spanner (but of course s/he will remain a plumber). Bolting on conflict resolution techniques to our disciplines of origin does not make us expert mediators; as Yates (2001, p. 25) points out, it is possible for someone to demonstrate experienced incompetence (or even intractable incompetence) in his or her work.

I suggest there is a more profound understanding of what it is to be an expert mediator, which is linked to concepts of mastery and the expertise literature. This alternative understanding proposes that conflict resolution practitioners need to make a transition from their disciplines of origin, and that mediation is a discrete practice, not merely the addition of optional skill-sets to pre-acquired accomplishments and qualifications. Because of the inherent conflicts of interest and power issues that are axiomatic to mediation, practitioners must operate at optimal levels of competency and professionalism. I contend that mediation is a *moral project* – not in the sense of moralising or imposing one's values on the parties, nor seeking their personal growth, but because mediators are always dealing with the parties' competing interests, needs and wishes, and making justifiable judgments about why, how and when to intervene. Mediators must therefore think and act *qua* mediators, always aware of the complexities and contradictions of their role; the standards or practices of any discipline from which ADR practitioners originate are likely to prove impoverished for this task.

In opposition to this view is the argument that mediation is not a profession, since ADR generally lacks the distinctive hallmarks of professionalisation. Based on established professions such as law, medicine, veterinary science and architecture, these hallmarks may be briefly summarised as:

- Competitive entry to a dedicated, relatively lengthy academic/experiential training programme, followed by examination
- Subsequent command of a discrete body of technical knowledge and skills
- Eventual individual acceptance as qualified by an elite gate-keeping organisation which is publicly recognised
- Attendant benefits and restrictions that typically accompany regulation
- Career development, professional autonomy and/or marketplace advantage/preferment
- Potential high social status and earning capacity

Mediation certainly does not possess these hallmarks. Banks (2004, p. 25) writes of the rise of semi-, quasi- 'bureau' or emergent professions, and it may be that mediation properly belongs within one of these less elevated categories. Because mediation operates within so many contexts, including formal justice systems, it is highly unlikely that a single training programme or professional body will ever be established in any jurisdiction, even if this were desirable. These being absent, it is critical that we conduct ourselves according to the highest possible ethical and operational standards, regardless of whether we are members of a recognisable profession. We should also engage with theory in our pursuit of excellence, for which Honeyman et al.'s (2001) own work provides an excellent point of departure.

Naughty departures and creativity

A further thread in the expertise literature concerns idea generation and creativity (Herring, Jones and Bailey, 2009, p. 5) in the context of ill-defined problems. The authors argue that most texts regard creativity as a beneficial process and a vital area of research in a wide variety of disciplines. The practitioner's creative contribution to helping parties to generate options and think laterally is well-established, although Moore (2003, p. 288), notes that mediators need to ensure that they are not seen as unilateral advocates. Experience in executing naughty departures may assist in developing a mediator's creativity, since the expertise needed for naughty departures requires practitioners to think through not only what they are doing, but why they are choosing or rejecting certain courses of action or inaction.

There is a sense in which every mediation requires some form of dispute design; no amount of training or even experience can anticipate every move the parties might make, nor every response the mediator might need to consider. This is true of even relatively straightforward cases. There are also conflict circumstances which require unique dispute designs, because they have no immediately relevant or available precedents. In common with many mediators, I have worked in multi-party situations where I have had to think a great deal about whom to involve or omit, how and when to sequence the meetings, how to help the parties identify and deal with the issues, when to be highly active, and when to allow the process to unfold. Although I have made good use of consultations with other experienced mediators, there has never been a single right answer to the challenges of these cases. In such circumstances, even dispute design strategies (Ury, Bret & Goldberg, 1988) may not offer sufficient guidance regarding how to act, and I have been thrown back on my own resources, creativity and a constant pondering of the ethical matters involved, in order to know how to proceed. Even then, there have always been degrees of stress and anxiety, the inevitable consequences of working with the uncertainties of conflict (Marshall, 2008, p. 33).

Expertise, knowledge elicitation and transfer

The term 'tacit knowledge' originated with Polanyi (1967, p. 4), who wrote that 'we know more than we can tell'. This suggests it is possible to hold expert knowledge so deeply embedded and inaccessible that it cannot be expressed or transferred to others. Polanyi's claim was of its time, and has since been challenged, including by those who question whether knowledge that cannot be expressed really qualifies as knowledge in the first place – at least from a Socratic perspective.

Many experts refer to gut feeling or the power of intuition as functionally central to their skill, or 'a rich source of data' (Rooney, 2008, p. 248). Klein's work endorses the importance of intuition, although he expands the somewhat metaphysical descriptions of intuition offered by some of his research subjects. He comments (Klein, 1999, p. 31):

> "*Intuition depends on the use of experience to recognise key patterns that indicate the dynamics of the situation* (emphasis original). Because patterns can be subtle, people often cannot describe what they noticed, or how they judged a situation as typical or atypical. Therefore, intuition has a strange reputation. Skilled decision makers know that they can depend on their intuition, but at the same time they may feel uncomfortable trusting a source of power that seems so accidental."

Klein's description offers a helpful explanation of intuition – that it is the refined, discriminatory recognition of patterns and anomalies borne of long experience and observation. This opens up the possibility that intuitive practice can be articulated and shared with others in order to advance the field. To foster mediator expertise, Kressel (2006, p. 749) recommends interaction with colleagues and the persistent questioning of each other's tactical choices as a means of developing an explicit understanding of mediation theories in action – although such questioning must not be hostile, but empathic and encouraging. Likewise, conferences, practitioner gatherings, supervision and consultancy provide supportive fora to develop skills and knowledge. Within such opportunities to share practice, the expertise model warrants our attention, as it provides an investigative and supportive framework for identifying and disseminating domain knowledge.

Expertise – some final thoughts

A general theory of expertise is not unproblematic, and has been critiqued by decision scientists such as Yates (2001, pp. 9-33), who argues that – among other issues – some of its claims to originality and theorising are deficient. Pedagogist Eraut (1994) is cautious about theories of intuition, reflection and expertise, on the grounds that they do not always promote metaprocesses such as controlling one's own behaviours or exercising critical self-evaluation, although I think this criticism is debateable. He observes that work involving consultations with clients needs to be deliberative if it is to remain client-centred. Inductive knowledge and propositional knowledge are notoriously difficult in terms of knowledge transfer, and experts may exhibit cognitive bias and other failings, notwithstanding Klein's (1999) views to the contrary.

In this paper I have used the concept of naughty departures to highlight just a few of the problems I see arising from practising in a discipline that is still dominated by various prescriptive models of practice and strong ideological discourses. Whereas these existing constructs may be helpful and beneficial to the parties, their dominance may also makes it difficult for new concepts to develop, or even replace old concepts as our understanding of ADR evolves. Discussing naughty departures may help us identify some of the shortcomings of both the operational and ideological aspects of ADR. Domain knowledge bases evolve and benchmarks shift, with the result that standards previously accepted as demonstrating expertise and elite performance alter. The expertise literature may not provide all the answers we need, but might nevertheless move us beyond the toolbox mentality to one where mediator expertise is more clearly elicited, defined and taught.

Finally, and observing that even the most elite practitioners may plateau, stall or make mistakes, Eraut reflects '... [i]t is partly a matter of lifelong learning and partly a wise understanding of one's own fallibility' (1994, p. 155); evidently then, there is no such thing as accidental expertise.

An earlier version of this paper was presented at the 10th National Mediation Conference, Adelaide, September 2010.

The author is grateful for Professor Kenneth Kressel's initial signposting, Greg Rooney's editorial comment and Alastair Wilson's proof-reading. Any errors and omissions are her own.

References

Abdolmohammadi, M.J. & Shanteau, J. (1991). 'Personal Attributes of Expert Auditors'. Retrieved July 10, 2010 from http://www.k-state.edu/psych/cws/pdf/obhdp_paper91.PDF

Adler, P. (2003). Unintentional Excellence An Exploration of Mastery and Incompetence. In: D. Bowling & D. Hoffman (Eds.). 'Bringing Peace Into the Room How the Personal Qualities of the Mediator Impact the Process of Conflict Resolution'. (pp 57-77). San Francisco: Jossey-Bass.

Banks, S. (3004). 'Ethics, Accountability and the Social Professions'. London: Palgrave.

Benner, P. (1984). 'From Novice to Expert Excellence and Power in Clinical Nursing Practice'. Menlo Park, California: Addison-Wesley Publishing Company.

Billett, S. (2001). 'Knowing in practice: re-conceptualising vocational expertise'. *Learning and Instruction*, 11, 431-452.

Children Act 1989 (c.41). Retrieved July 20, 2010 from http://www.opsi.gov.uk/acts/acts1989/ukpga_19890041_en_2

College of Mediators Code of Practice (2008). Retrieved July 10, 2010 from http://www.collegeofmediators.co.uk/index.php?option=com_rokdownloads&view=folder&Itemid=19

Crandall, B. Klein, G. & Hoffman, R.E. (2006). 'Working minds: a practitioner's guide to cognitive task analysis'. Cambridge: Massachusetts Institute of Technology.

Deutsch, M. (2006). Cooperation and Competition. In: M. Deutsch, P.T. Coleman and E.C. Marcus (Eds.), 'The Handbook of Conflict Resolution: Theory and Practice'. (2nd ed.). (pp. 24-42). San Francisco, California. Jossey-Bass.

Eisenberg, M.A. (1976). 'Private Ordering Through Negotiations: Dispute Settlement and Rulemaking', 89, *Harvard Law Review*, 637-381.

Eraut, M. (1994). 'Developing Professional Knowledge and Competence'. London: The Falmer Press.

Ericsson, K.A. (2006a). An Introduction to Cambridge Handbook of Expertise and Expert Performance: Its Development, Organization and Content. In: K.A. Ericsson, N. Charness, P.J. Feltovich & R.R. Hoffman (Eds.) 'Cambridge Handbook of Expertise and Expert Performance'. (pp. 3-19). New York: Cambridge University Press.

Ericsson, K.A. (2006b). The Influence of Experience and Deliberate Practice on the Development of Superior Expert Performance. In: K.A. Ericsson, N. Charness, P.J. Feltovich & R.R. Hoffman (Eds.), 'Cambridge Handbook of Expertise and Expert Performance'. (pp. 683-703). New York: Cambridge University Press.

Fiss, O.M. (1984). 'Against Settlement'. [Electronic version]. *Yale Law Journal*, 93, 1073-1089.

Follett, M.P. (1924). 'Creative Experience'. New York: Longman Green and Co (reprinted by Peter Owen in 1951).

Friedman, R., Anderson, C., Brett, J., Olekahns, M., Goates, N. & Lisco. C.C. (2004). 'The Positive and Negative Effects of Anger on Dispute Resolution: Evidence from Electronically Mediated Disputes'. *Journal of Applied Psychology.* American Psychological Association, Vol. 89, No. 2, 369-376.

Galenter, M. (2004). 'The Vanishing Trial: An Examination of Trials and Related Matters in Federal and State Courts'. *Journal of Empirical Legal Studies*, Volume 1, Issue 3, 459-570, November 2004. Retrieved July 10, 2010 from http://marcgalanter.net/Documents/papers/thevanishingtrial.pdf

Goldberg, S.B. (2005). 'The Secrets of Successful Mediators'. *Negotiation Journal*, July 2005, 365-376.

Haynes, J.M., Haynes, G.L. & Fong, L.S. (2004). 'Mediation: positive conflict management'. Albany: State University of New York Press.

Herring, S.R., Jones, B.R. & Bailey, B.R. (2009). 'Idea Generation Techniques among Creative Professionals'. Proceedings of the 42nd Hawaii International Conference on System Sciences-2009. Retrieved July 20, 2010 from: http://www.computer.org/plugins/dl/pdf/proceedings/hicss/2009/3450/00/01-04-02.pdf?

template=1&loginState=1&userData=anonymous-IP%253A%253AAddress%253A%2B86.144.58.216%252C%2B%255B172.16.161.5%252C%2B86.144.58.216%252C%2B127.0.0.1%255D

Hoffman, R.R. & Lintern, G. (2006). Eliciting and Representing the Knowledge of Experts. In: K.A. Ericsson, N. Charness, P.J. Feltovich & R.R. Hoffman (Eds.), 'Cambridge Handbook of Expertise and Expert Performance'. (pp. 203-222). New York: Cambridge University Press.

Holmes, S.B. (2006). 'Becoming 'The Best Possible' Family Counsellor or Family Mediator: What Expertise Research Has to Say'. *Journal of Family Studies*, Volume 12, Issue 1, 113-122.

Honeyman, C., McAdoo, B. & Welsh, N. (2001). 'Here There Be Monsters At the Edge of the Map of Conflict Resolution'. Retrieved July 10, 2010 from http://www.convenor.com/madison/monsters.pdf

Jones, T.S. (1994). A Dialectical Reframing of the Mediation Process. In: J.S. Folger, T.S. Jones (Eds.) 'New Directions in Mediation Communication Research and Perspectives'. (pp. 26-47). Thousand Oaks: Sage Publications Inc.

Klein, G. (1999). 'Sources of Power How People Make Decisions' (Paperback ed.). Cambridge, Massachusetts: Massachusetts Institute of Technology.

Kovach, K. (2005). Mediation. In: M.L. Moffitt & R.C. Bordone (Eds.). 'The Handbook of Dispute Resolution'. (pp. 304-317). San Francisco: Jossey-Bass.

Kressel, K. (2006). Mediation Revisited. In: M. Deutsch, P.T. Coleman & E.C. Marcus (Eds.). 'The Handbook of Conflict Resolution'. (pp. 726-756). San Francisco: Jossey-Bass.

Lande, J. (2005). 'Replace the 'Vanishing Trial' with More Helpful Myths. 23 Alternatives to the High Cost of Litigation', 161, (2005). Retrieved July 10, 2010 from: http://www.law.missouri.edu/lande/publications/vanishing-trial-alternatives-west.pdf½

Lipshitz, R., Klein, G., Orasanu, J., & Salas, E. (2001). 'Focus Article: Taking Stock of Naturalistic Decision Making'.

Journal of Behavioural Decision Making. Volume 14, 331-352. Retrieved July 10, 2010 from http://download.clib.psu.ac.th/datawebclib/e_resource/trial_database/WileyInterScienceCD/pdf/BDM/BDM_4.pdf

Macfarlane, J. (2002). 'Mediating Ethically: The Limits of Codes of Conduct and the Potential of a Reflective Practice Model'. [Electronic version]. *40 Osgoode Hall Law Journal, 49*, 49-87.

Marshall, P. (2008). 'Stress and Coping among Professional Mediators: attributes and competencies'. Saarbrücken: VDM Verlag Dr. Müller.

Mason, B. (2005). Relational risk-taking and the therapeutic relationship. In: C. Flakas, B. Mason & A. Perlesz (Eds.) 'The Space Between: Experience, Context and Process'. (pp. 157-170). London: Karnac (Books) Ltd.

Matrimonial Causes Act, 1973 (c.18). July 20, 2010 from http://www.statutelaw.gov.uk/content.aspx?LegType=All&searchEnacted=0&extentMatchOnly=0&confersPower=0&blanketAmendment=0&sortAlpha=0&PageNumber=0&NavFrom=0&parentActiveTextDocId=1476183&ActiveTextDocId=1476202&filesize=15299

Mayer, B. S. (2004). 'Beyond Neutrality Confronting the Crisis in Conflict Resolution'. San Francisco: Jossey-Bass.

'Mediation Quality Mark Standard' (2010 edition). Retrieved July 20, 2010 from http://www.legalservices.gov.uk/docs/cls_main/MQM_Standard_Sep09_with_cover.pdf

Mnookin, R. & Kornhauser, L. (1979). 'Bargaining in the shadow of the law: The case of divorce'. [Electronic version]. *Yale Law Review*, 88, 950-997.

Moore, C.W. (2003). The Mediation Process: Practical Strategies for Resolving Conflict (3rd ed.). San Francisco: Jossey-Bass.

Nader, L. (1991). Harmony models and the construction of law. In: K.Avruch, P.Black & J.Scimecca (Eds.), 'Disputes Resolution: Cross cultural perspectives'. (pp. 41-60). Westport, CT: Greenwood Press.

Patton, B. (2005). Negotiation. In: M.L. Moffitt & R.C. Bordone (Eds.). 'The Handbook of Dispute Resolution'. (pp. 279-303). San Francisco: Jossey-Bass.

Polanyi, M. (1967). 'The Tacit Dimension'. New York: Anchor Books.

Rooney, G. (2008). 'The use of intuition in mediation'. *Conflict Resolution Quarterly*, Volume 25, Issue 2, 239-253.

Ross, K.G., Shafer, L. & Klein, G. (2006). Professional Judgments and 'Naturalistic Decision Making'. In: K.A. Ericsson, N. Charness, P.J. Feltovich & R.R. Hoffman (Eds.), 'Cambridge Handbook of Expertise and Expert Performance'. (pp. 403-419). New York: Cambridge University Press.

Shanteau, J. (1992). 'Competence in experts: The role of task characteristics'. *Organizational Behaviour and Human Decision Processes*, 53, 252-266. Retrieved July 10, 2010 from http://www.k-state.edu/psych/cws/pdf/obhdp_paper91.PDF

Shanteau, J. (2001). What Does it Mean When Experts Disagree? In: E. Salas & G. Klein (Eds.), 'Linking Expertise and Naturalistic Decision Marking'. (pp. 229-244). Mahwah, NJ: Lawrence Erlbaum Associates, Inc.

Stempel, J.W. (1997). 'Beyond formalism and false dichotomies; the need for institutionalizing a flexible concept of the mediator's role'. *Florida State Law Review*. Retrieved July 10, 2010 from http://www.law.fsu.edu/journals/lawreview/frames/244/stemtxt.html

Ury, W., Bret, J & Goldberg, S. (1988). 'Getting Disputes Resolved: Designing Systems to Cut the Costs of Conflict'. London: Jossey-Bass.

Wade, J. (2009). 'The Edges of Orthodoxy in Mediation – You Did What!'. *Bond University Dispute Resolution Centre Newsletter*, 31. Retrieved July 10, 2010 from http://epublications.bond.edu.au/cgi/viewcontent.cgi?article+1035&context=drcn

Weedon, C. (1997). 'Feminist Practice and Poststructuralist Theory'. (2nd ed.). Oxford: Blackwell Publishers.

Weick, K.E. (2001). Tool Retention and Fatalities in Wildland Fire Settings: Conceptualizing the Naturalistic. In: E. Salas and G. Klein (Eds.), 'Linking Expertise and Naturalistic Decision Making'. (pp. 321-336). Mahwah, NJ: Lawrence Erlbaum Associates, Inc

Yates, J.F. (2001). "Outsider:" Impressions of Naturalistic Decision Making. In: E. Salas and G. Klein (Eds.), 'Linking Expertise and Naturalistic Decision Making'. (pp. 9-33). Mahwah, NJ: Lawrence Erlbaum Associates, Inc.

CHAPTER 2

Guerilla Mediation: The Use of Warfare Strategies in the Management of Conflict

By mediator Robert Benjamin[*]

Introduction – conflict mediation as a fanciful idea or realistic option

The real test of the acceptance of professional mediation in our society will be the sustained and regular use of those services by a substantial number of people to manage conflicts that arise in their personal and business lives in the private market.

The use of mediation in the public sector, exampled by the rapid proliferation of court programs and legislation that encourage and legitimate mediation, is helpful but cannot be taken as competent evidence that people in general have accepted negotiation as a viable means of conflict management. Even so, many mediators are waiting for or actively lobbying legislatures or courts to enact or implement mediation programs in the belief that they will deliver mediation work to their doorstep; however, a steady stream of mediation business has not materialized for many mediators. In fact, ironically, some court sponsored mediation programs have engendered an unintended consequence – an increased resistance to mediation, especially from those people who have felt coerced to participate. Anecdotal reports hint that an increasing number of people are voicing resentment at being forced to mediate.[3] In any event, the private demand for mediation services remains underwhelming in most of the country with only a few areas and contexts being of modest exception. For the most part, people in our culture remain leery of negotiation as a means of settling disputes.

Some suggest mediation is underutilized because the marketing of those services has been minimal. While that may hold some truth, it could also be that the marketing message of many mediators is ineffectual. Mediation is often portrayed as the 'kinder-gentler' alternative. The common operating assumption is that if people knew about the mediation process and how it could save time and expense and give them greater control over their lives, that consumers as thoughtful and rational people would prefer mediation over the more traditional process – reliance on lawyers, judges, and other experts – for the settlement of disputes. The presumption is that consumers, faced with conflicts, will apply a cost/benefit analysis and act out of their self interest to choose the most efficient means of dispute resolution. Some do. Many do not.

It should come as no surprise that logic alone does not necessarily sell even the best product. If people were to act based purely on objective data, none would smoke, all would wear seatbelts in their cars, none would be entrepreneurs, many would not marry, and not many would have children. Few purchases, whether it is a car, a house, or a doctor's, lawyer's or mediator's services are made solely on a rational basis. A strictly rational marketing approach often fails to effectively reach many prospective consumers.

Marketing experts have long appreciated the importance of taking into account human nature and emotion in sales and advertisement. A significant part of any promotional strategy is deciphering how the service/product enhances consumer self image or alleviates fears and insecurities. Choosing to mediate a dispute remains for many, a non-traditional, untested and risky business. When faced with conflict, the emotion many experience is fear, specifically, their fear of being taken advantage of or being played for a fool if they negotiate for themselves. The rational reasons to mediate do not easily overcome that overriding fear and an effective marketing message must address that underlying emotion directly.

Beyond just selling a product however, marketing strategy reflects how mediation is professionally understood and practiced. Currently, many mediators view their work as a thoughtful, humanistic enterprise intended to help others resolve conflict; their process relies on trust and good will. Some well-intentioned practitioners even find marketing distasteful or unseemly. However, while human beings have the capacity to act rationally and collaboratively, they don't necessarily start there when faced with a conflict. The resistance to negotiation and mediation is long standing and deeply seated in our culture.

There are two significant sources of resistance to mediation. First, the idea of mediation or negotiation of a conflict is a difficult one for many people to accept, especially in our culture where there is a strongly ingrained sense of being right and a belief that the truth will prevail. Case in point: John Wayne, a cultural icon, who never negotiated in any of his many and varied movie roles. He remains a hero for many people and professionals alike, who have taken from his modeling the belief that to negotiate is to compromise, 'give-in,' or even sell-out your principles. As a general rule, Americans dislike negotiation; bargaining is thought to be an unseemly activity. Many prefer to pay a set price for a Saturn rather than dicker over the purchase of a car.[6] Note that the resistance to mediation follows directly from the resistance to negotiation; mediation is merely a negotiation between three (or more) people. The mediator essentially negotiates his or her authority with each of the participants. For all intents and purposes, the terms 'negotiation' and 'mediation' are interchangeable, mediation being only a more formalized, third party facilitated negotiation process.

To consider mediation requires a break with traditional thinking patterns as a means of managing conflict. Mediation, like negotiation, requires that people take responsibility for their own decisions. Many people are afraid, or simply do not want that responsibility. They prefer to believe, or are conditioned to think that professionals – lawyers, judges, doctors, therapists, etc. – know more and are better able to make decisions for them.[6]

There has, however, been some breakdown of this resistance, albeit slowly. People are becoming more aware that conflicts are complex and that there are not simple, formulaic right answers. As well, people are increasingly cautious, skeptical and critical of professional services, advice and directives.[7] This is reflected in the increased use and availability of alternative sources of information, products and services in both health care and law. The Internet is, no doubt, a significant contributor to this dynamic.

The second source of resistance is more troublesome because mediators themselves often bear responsibility. Mediation is often presented in an overly simplistic manner that makes it all the more difficult for prospective consumers to take seriously. Mediation is described in misleading and Pollyannaish terms, such as: "a win/win process," or as "a collaborative problem solving process." The implicit suggestion is that all parties will be satisfied with the outcome, respect each other or even be friends. Many mediators see themselves as peacemakers and mediation as a healing or "transformative" process.[10] While that might occur on occasion, it is by no means the rule and in any case not the purpose of mediation.

There is a still greater risk: the expectations of the mediation process are, by those simplistic descriptions, set unrealistically high and in many cases unobtainable. The terms belie a quasi-utopian vision that conflicts can be, not just managed, but finally and completely resolved. The result may be the increased likelihood of failure, which in turn can generate even greater resistance to mediation. Many parties already do not consider mediation because they believe the process requires a level of trust, reasonableness and goodwill that they have predetermined the opposing party lacks. Common refrains heard from consumers in ruling out mediation are: "(s)he is not trustworthy" or "I'm reasonable, but (s)he is not." The risk is exacerbated by the presentation of the mediation process in fanciful and idyllic terms.

Countering this resistance will require a shift in the thinking of mediators from a soft, idealized approach to conflict management to a more rigorous, strategic approach. To encourage the acceptance of mediation in the real world, it must pass the test of being cost effective, efficient and, most important of all, be safe. Mediation cannot be limited to those rarefied situations that rely and depend on all parties being reasonable, rational, acting in good faith, trusting or even trustworthy. If mediation services come to be viewed as applicable only to those matters where all parties concerned exhibit a collaborative, cooperative and humanistic demeanor at the same time, then mediation might as well await the simultaneous alignment of the stars and planets. The number of available cases susceptible to mediation will be reduced to a fraction of one percent. To flourish, the mediation process must be recast as good business that need not rely on trust or good will. Mediators must work in the real world, not in an idealized world of their own concoction.

The sources and rationale for guerilla mediation

For mediation to work in the real conflicts of everyday life and be accepted as a viable mode of conflict management, then the approach taken must be active, strategic and calculated to constructively redirect the energy of the conflict. Human nature must be confronted directly. Instead of hoping for, or expecting people to be reasonable and thoughtful in the face of conflict, mediators must non-judgmentally accept their more base motivations for power and control as well. While messengers (Machiavelli, Kissinger, et al.) and methods might be criticized, the primary postulate of 'realpolitik' is as applicable today as it has been throughout human history: "Those who desire peace should prepare for war." For mediators, the corollary axiom is "Those who pursue settlement should be prepared for conflict."[16]

Perhaps ironic, but not surprisingly, warfare strategies and tactics offer parallels in thinking and approach that are useful to a mediator. If conflict is understood as a lesser form of warfare that left unchecked can quickly escalate into open warfare, then the strategies and techniques effective in war may also be applicable in the negotiation of conflict. Only the purposes remain fundamentally different. Parties in conflict are not an enemy to be subdued or defeated; for the mediator, the purpose will be to carefully hone their thinking and skills to effectively manage the jungle of fears that seize many parties in conflict. The purpose of scrutinizing warfare practices is to strip out from that higher intensity conflict circumstance the thinking and strategies that are useful in order to apply them preemptively to avoid the escalation of conflict. What is common to both war and negotiation, and essential for success in either field of engagement is the recognition of the basic nature and behavior of the opponent or parties. In short, not to underestimate your opponent and to accept him on his own terms.

The term and concept of guerilla mediation are derived in some measure from the writing of Sun Tzu in *The Art of War*. He was a Chinese general who, by varying accounts, recorded his approach to warfare sometime between 500 and 300 B.C., and has been studied throughout the centuries up to and including the present. The principles he enunciated for the preparation for war apply to the management of conflict by other means, including negotiation and mediation. In fact, early on and often, Sun Tzu emphasizes that to fight and conquer is not "supreme excellence," that excellence is reserved for breaking the enemy's resistance without fighting.

While there could be some quibbling over the exact meaning intended in the phrase "breaking the enemy's resistance," the writing provides good instruction for the practicing mediator. It is neither cynical nor utopian, but instead is soberly realistic. He reflects an appreciation for the human rhythms of conflict: "in peace prepare for war, and in war prepare for peace." Not unlike the warrior, the mediator necessarily relies on strategic planning, tactics and maneuvering, observing the terrain of the conflict and the use of deception. Specifically, the analogy of mediation to guerilla warfare, as distinguished from more formalistic approaches to warfare, highlights the parallels between mediation and the non-traditional, more fluid and mobile form of combat that guerilla tactics conjure.[17] The mediator, as does the guerilla fighter, must creatively use the resources immediately at hand and cannot depend on outside reinforcements or the traditional sources of authority (e.g., a court) to impose an outcome on conflicting parties.

The risk of using guerilla warfare as a metaphor for mediation is for some perilously close to encouraging the combative and argumentative nature of many disputes that most mediators want to disavow and distance themselves from. In fact, Deborah Tannen gives a searing critique of the language of our culture that encourages argument instead of dialogue in *The Argument Culture*.[23] Yet, while her observations are valid and useful, they fail to sufficiently take into account the reality of our human circumstance. While human cooperation occurs and is evident to greater or lesser extent in many circumstances, war, violence and conflict are not likely to be extinguished any time soon by social engineering. The proof is in our history, biology and psychology.[9, 17, 18, 21] The extent to which conflict and warfare can be mitigated or averted, may be a function of looking directly at what war and conflict are about, not merely pretending it could be otherwise.

George Lakoff and Mark Johnson, in *Metaphors We Live By*,[20] observe that our ordinary conceptual system is metaphorical in nature; linguistics – our words and metaphors – are how we experience one thing in terms of another. In short, in disputes where argument is the preferred tactic, argument is a sub-species of war and while argument is not war, it is partially structured, understood, and performed in terms of war. A dispute is metaphorically structured as a battle; our language reflects this reality: one party 'attacks' another's position, a claim is considered 'indefensible,' or the comments are 'on target.' With the war metaphor so deeply ingrained, to pretend mediation is about peace and good will, when people are thinking in terms of war and distrust, disregards reality and is blatantly naive. The way to shift a dispute away from open warfare toward settlement is not to deny this reality and pray for peace but to strategically re-deploy and re-align our argument metaphors in ways that encourage constructive dialogue. The first step, however, is for the mediator to relinquish the notion that parties in conflict can be expected to be reasonable and trusting. Managing conflict in a hostile terrain requires all of the wit and wile a mediator can muster.[4]

For most people faced with conflict, mediation is not their first thought or a term on the tip of their tongue; in fact, even settlement is a remote idea, especially at first. More likely than not, they are thinking 'lawyer' and 'fight.' At the outset of a conflict, whether it is a personal or business dispute, the idea of settlement is an anathema, the mere suggestion of which is taken by them to be indicative of a lack of resolve in their position or a moral sellout of their principles.[6] Most people faced with a dispute of almost any kind or level of seriousness, take it personally; while negotiation may make perfect sense and be in their self interest, they have an abiding fear of being played for a fool which trumps rational thinking. Parties in conflict can move to a place where they are able to consider more thoughtfully what decisions make sense and how they want to handle difficult situations, but not until they feel safe. That safety is not gained by merely being told to trust the mediation process, or the mediator, and certainly not the opposing party; the process is, at least at the outset, an abstraction, and trusting the other party is simply too far a reach. The first task of the mediator, then, is to manipulate the situation in such a way that the parties need not be required to trust, but to believe they will not be left at a disadvantage.

Notwithstanding this reality, many mediators insist on presenting and approaching disputes out of preset principles and belief in reasoned discussion and collaborative values. They proceed to carefully and methodically analyze the interests and needs of the parties and try to explain to the warring participants why their positions are not sensible or in their self interest.[14] To read the literature in the field and listen to mediators discuss their craft, it is quickly apparent that many encourage and some even insist that the participants in mediation be reasonable, calm and collaborative if they are to negotiate successfully. Mediators often disregard that many people in conflict, when they are facing the loss of their dreams and life as they know it is disintegrating before their eyes, are not able to be calm and trusting on command. For a mediator to presume parties can or should be so is patronizing at best, and may be down right insulting. Few of us, mediators included, could maintain the equanimity seemingly required, when directly faced with a personal conflict.

The irony is that guerilla mediation, though the term may sound antagonistic and harsh, may well be more respectful of parties in conflict than the more conventional approaches to mediation. If there is an assertive sensibility to this approach, it is because the force and energy that most conflicting parties bring to a dispute must be met by a sufficient counter force if the energy is to be redirected constructively.

The basic tenets of guerilla mediation

There are three basic tenets of guerilla mediation: (1) respect for human nature as it is, not as we would like to believe it could be; (2) a realistic understanding and acceptance of conflict; and, (3) the effective use of strategic planning. Assuming the acceptance of these basic tenets, the techniques for implementation and the requisite skills necessary to accomplish the purpose of mediation, can be more readily clarified and applied. Notwithstanding the use of a warfare metaphor, the purpose of mediation and the role of the mediator remain to facilitate the substantially informed and consensual management of issues or conflicts by disputing parties.

Respect for human nature as it is, not as we would like to believe it could be

Borrowing from the principles of evolutionary biology and psychology, the human animal has ingrained multiple kinds of behavior patterns that are sometimes contradictory. Generally, humans can be (1) altruistic, good natured, and trusting[13]; (2) rational, analytical, and objective, acting more or less predictably out of self-interest[1]; and, (3) fearful, spiteful, deceptive, manipulative, and seemingly irrational, acting in ways that appear to be anchored in pure emotion. [22]

The most prevalent approaches to the mediation of conflict, the rationalistic and humanistic, are premised on the belief that parties in conflict are capable of being collaborative in the reasoned pursuit of an outcome that meets the needs of all parties. Humanists believe people are basically good at heart, rationalists believe they essentially operate out of predictable patterns of self interest. Short shrift is given to that part of human nature that is deceptive or manipulative and there is often attached an implicit negative moral judgment of that behavior. There is nothing wrong with the conventional approaches, they just do not systematically and holistically account for the whole repertoire of human behaviors that are commonly displayed in human interactions and especially in conflict.

To round out the field, there is the competitive/opportunistic approach to negotiation and mediation that most people popularly tend to associate with negotiation. This style is typified by the used car dealer; it is essentially Machiavellian, and operates from the belief that humans are basically evil, self-interested, deceitful and manipulative, and bent on the accumulation of power and control. Once again, it is not so much that this approach is inaccurate as it is incomplete; it fails to account for the prospect that humans are able to cooperate and might be able to negotiate collaboratively. In short, none of the prevailing negotiation approaches take into account the whole range of the human behaviors, and to the extent they do not, the approach will be found lacking.

The naturalistic/pragmatic approach to negotiation is premised on the belief that humans operate out of the full range of ingrained human behavior patterns. This approach is not intended to dismiss or denigrate the prevailing approaches, but rather to provide an integrative framework that includes them all to offer a more comprehensive view of humans' behavior in the negotiation of conflict. It is premised on the belief that to effectively negotiate issues or disputes, parties must be accorded the respect that they will be simultaneously desirous of reasoned communication and, at the same time, are likely to be fearful, deceptive and manipulative. Deception is a natural behavior common to all animal species, including humans, which has evolved over time to foster procreation and survival. It cannot be dismissed and should not be morally judged.[21] The naturalistic approach does not presume to dictate how people should behave for negotiation to proceed and takes full account of all human behaviors.

The naturalistic approach to negotiation is well suited to guerilla mediation, reflecting the same views of human nature and conflict. Thus, while communication and empathy between parties are necessary and important, and the reasoned analytical discussion of issues and options are helpful, both approaches are incomplete in themselves. The guerilla mediator, in sizing up the conflict terrain, does not rely solely upon reason, trust and good will to manage a dispute; he or she may well have to employ constructive forms of deception to accommodate and counter the anticipated fears and resulting manipulations of the parties. The mediator is obligated to accept the parties as they are, not how he or she would like for them to be.

A realistic understanding and acceptance of conflict

Conflict is part of the natural terrain and, unless one subscribes to the millennial belief that with the coming of the messiah where "the lion will lay down with the lamb," it is likely to continue to be so. Too often, however, conflict mediation is confused with peacemaking. Many mediators accept conflict only grudgingly in theory and are even less tolerant of its open expression in practice.

Conflict is a basic ingredient in our evolutionary biology and psychology; it is part of our human makeup and chemistry. Analogically, conflict is to the body politic what cholesterol is to body physiology; some cholesterol, the LDL, constricts the arteries, immobilizes the body and can ultimately kill. The other form of cholesterol, HDL, helps the body metabolize and function properly. Likewise, some forms of personal and social conflict are peripheral, unnecessary and destroy the body politic, while other conflict is substantive, that is, necessary and useful, encouraging the growth and development of society.

In our Western, techno-rational culture, there is a strong tendency to suppress and dismiss emotion in general and conflict in particular. The mind-reason/body-emotion dichotomy, postulated origi-nally by Plato and articulated by Descartes, reflects the traditional pejorative notion of conflict. The conventional wisdom posits that conflict results from the absence of reason and from being overrun by emotion. Many mediators of the rationalist persuasion use techniques derived from that view. For instance, establishing communication ground rules in mediation are ostensibly calculated to preclude or limit unhelpful emotional outbursts by a party which are thought to impede the calm discussion of substantive issues. The reigning conventional wisdom is that emotion unchecked will likely or even predictably lead to physical aggression. The technique may have the reverse effect: suppressing the expression of emotion may lead to an escalation of the conflict.

By contrast, the guerilla mediator accepts the expression of emotion as a natural and necessary part of the conflict, not to be suppressed but constructively managed. Ironically, current studies in neuro-biology suggest that reason and emotion stem from the same area of the brain and it is difficult, if not impossible, to separate the two; reason cannot be accessed without emotion.[12] In the same way physical pain or discomfort is symptomatic of an underlying body dysfunction or illness, emotion is the expression of underlying personal or interpersonal stressors. As health care providers are coming to understand, treating the pain without assessing the underlying circumstance makes no sense, nor does managing the illness without addressing the pain. Likewise, quashing the emotion in a dispute may serve to cosmetically cover up the underlying stressors without effectively managing the conflict.

The guerilla mediator redirects and uses the energy the conflict generates constructively. Conflict contains within it considerable natural force and energy. To liken some conflicts to a 'class 5' river (serious white water), the force of the water flow can easily sweep away the unprepared. In rafting that river, and negotiating the rapids, the pilot understands the necessity of bringing his or her own energy to bear on the river; if he puts the paddle down, he will be swept away. There is no quiet, calm way to face a wild river; the pilot will never control the river and there is no suppressing or containing the river's energy. The only hope will be to deal with the river on its terms, which means to paddle hard and fast enough to approximate the river's speed, thereby allowing the pilot to position him or herself to use the river's energy. The trick is to stay centered, off the rocks and out of the sinkholes. Like a good pilot reads the river and sometimes must calculate bouncing off of one rock to avoid a more perilous one or a worse situation, a good mediator reads the conflict between the parties and devises a strategy that effectively uses the parties' force and energy to negotiate the conflict.

The effective use of strategic planning

Strategic planning is the key to both winning wars and the effective negotiation or mediation of conflict. Curiously, the etymology of the word strategy is from the Greek, 'strategama,' translated as a trick or ruse, and still commonly defined as a military maneuver to deceive or surprise an enemy.[24] The notion of being strategic has also long been associated with business and negotiation, and carries with it a pejorative connotation. This is so especially in the Western cultural tradition where humanism and rationalism are highly valued. From the rationalist and humanist perspective, strategy is unnecessary if the argument is rational and the motives are, genuine; the power of logical reasoning, communication and empathy should theoretically, at least, obviate the need for tactical presentation.[6] Unsavory strategic devices are associated with 'spinning the story' in politics, or being disingenuous, inauthentic, or outright deceitful in personal relationships.

Ironically, despite the disinclination to accept the human necessity of being strategic, there is little doubt that most people, successful in managing their public and private affairs, are careful to consider how and when to most effectively present themselves and their ideas in pursuit of their goals and to obtain a desired result. Most mediators, as well, even those of the rationalist and humanist persuasion, as a practical matter, are forced to be strategic at some point. Therein lays the gap or incongruence between what they say is their approach to mediation and how they are observed in their actual practice.[19]

The naturalist/pragmatic mediator understands from the outset that he or she will not be likely to overpower the parties by the strength of argument, overwhelm them with a brilliant solution previously unconsidered, nor believe that talk alone will resolve difficult conflicts. Drawing from that understanding, the guerilla mediator must rely on finesse and other stratagems to redirect the conflict energy constructively toward settlement. There are countless examples of techniques that effectuate strategy in the negotiation/mediation of conflict. Three, in particular, are among the most basic: the use of confusion, the structuring of the process and, the use of time.

Far from being calm, rational and patient, the mediator must use "hit and run" tactics to confuse entrenched parties and undermine their belief that their cause is just and they are right.[5] If they are allowed to remain sanguine in their original entrenched positions, there will be little motivation to negotiate. People function less by rational calculation than by ritual and operative myths – stories they tell themselves to make sense of the world around them. Their myths of Justice, Truth, Rationality, Finality and Objectivity, disincline them to consider other alternatives to managing conflict. Most parties in conflict want to be vindicated in the belief that they are right and that any fair minded, impartial and neutral review of the matter at hand will so determine their cause to be just. The quest for the truth of the matter, however, is of little relevance in the mediation of conflict.[8]

A mediator must pierce that operative mythology. Sometimes reflective questions can do the trick, confusing and unsettling one or both parties' certainty that justice will prevail. For example, the reflective question, "Are you sure that your position can be proven and that the court will agree with you?" insinuates a measure of doubt into the discussion. The purpose is to throw them off guard and dislocate their thinking, to make just enough space for the consideration of other options that can possibly open the door for agreement.[2] By contrast, a frontal, straightforward logical statement, such as, "I don't think the court will agree with you," is likely to be viewed as confrontation or attack which sum- mons argument and rebuttal, "Yes, they will, it's the law, and I'll win." Logic, of course, is the least effective means of convincing anyone of anything. The mediator does not want to be caught in an argument, which is, by definition, unwinnable – even if you win, you lose. Thus, he or she merely plants the seeds of doubt and moves on – the hit and run.

In structuring the process, the mediator may strategically use deception to delay and avoid direct discussion of the key issues until the parties are ready. Many negotiations break down because people begin to discuss the ultimate issues too soon and negotiate out of fear, without sufficient or accurate information; they want to begin by discussing the hardest issues first, which may be self-defeating. Without a negotiation strategy, or game plan, it is common to 'cut to the chase' – 'what do you want/ what will you give.' Conventional wisdom and the logical approach often encourage direct discussion of the issues in the belief that the shortest distance between the problem and a solution in a dispute is a straight line. Few conflicts are that simple or linear.

In contrast to the conventional wisdom, a surreptitious, surprise approach may be more effective. Strategically, using paradoxical logic, the shortest distance in a dispute between the stated problem and possible outcomes is not a straight line. A more circuitous route allows time for the parties to reflect on their perspectives, to communicate with each other, and to assure all parties are working with sufficient and accurate information in preparation for the ultimate negotiation.[24, 2] The more complex and difficult the issues, the more important the structuring of the process will be in the management of the conflict. The mediator must build a solid foundation, first slowly gaining commitment to the process, next gleaning the story, then clarifying the issues, and finally assuring all options are available and considered. The mediator uses techniques that are calculated to delay and avoid the actual discussion of key issues until the parties are ready – 'no conflict before its time.' By initially sidestepping the hardest issues in a dispute, the mediator surreptitiously finesses what conflicted parties might think they want to do. This feint allows him to effectively sneak up on the hardest issues.

Finally, in mediation, as in warfare, time is of critical strategic value. For most disputing parties the conflict did not arise overnight and is not likely to be resolved quickly. Notwithstanding that reality, most expect the matter to be resolved immediately, and if not, to presume it cannot be resolved at all, let alone in mediation. With that thinking, it is easy to see how so many people slip-slide into the more traditional, formalized and extreme modes of conflict management such as litigation. Time allows for the parties to shift in their perspective and consider alternatives. Therefore, the mediator often stalls for time: parties cannot shift in their perspective faster than it takes for them to assimilate that change.[15] Thus, sometimes it is what the mediator does not do that is more important than what he or she does do. Setting the pace of the negotiation process, knowing when to stop a session after there has been some progress, but before the parties become too tired, are critical timing skills. The mediator must sense the point of diminishing returns; moving too quickly to 'close the deal' can unduly risk any progress that has

occurred, bring on 'buyer's remorse,' or even place the whole negotiation process in jeopardy. Contrary to conventional wisdom, 'holding people's feet to the fire' to obtain an agreement is likely to be counterproductive. There is a Zen aspect to negotiation: the less parties feel pushed to agree, the faster they may decide to settle in their own time.

A guerilla fighter does not seek to win the war in one skirmish. Likewise a mediator does not expect to reach agreement in one fell swoop. In fact, for the mediator, the purpose may not be for the parties to come to agreement at all – that is for them to decide. The purpose is to give parties every opportunity possible to reach an understanding, to remove obstacles – real or imagined – to a potential settlement. Often parties will trap themselves in a myopic belief system that is self defeating. The process, especially in difficult matters, must be drawn out to allow the parties sufficient time to re-appraise their negotiation perspectives. Time allows for them to save face and accept some measure of the reality that one does not necessarily win because they are right or lose because they are wrong. Settlements in hard cases are not so much forged as they are allowed to emerge in due course. Just as in guerilla warfare there are no clear victories, in mediation parties don't win or lose, they merely find a means to survive.

Conclusion – the promise and future of mediation

In the last quarter of this century, conflict mediation has gained a small foothold in the cultural and legal landscape of the United States and numerous other countries around the world as a means of managing conflict. At the core, the promise of the mediation process is the opportunity it gives people to settle their own disputes without the undue interference of government authorities or others. In an age where people often feel they are losing control over their lives, faced with an ever increasing onslaught of rules and regulations, and assailed by countless professionals who presume to know better about how they should live their lives, mediation is one way they can re-assert themselves and seize back some measure of control in the decisions that most effect their personal relationships and business dealings.

But the footing of mediation is precarious at best. If the success and acceptance of the mediation process are left to the courts and other public authorities, and mediators wait for it to be legislated into existence, then it risks becoming just one more cog in the institutional machine and the heart of the process may be fundamentally compromised.[3] Nor is it enough that mediation is a good and noble idea that holds promise. For it to flourish, the process must be functional, practical and safe.

To that end, guerilla mediation is not a regression to a primitive, 'win at all costs' approach to negotiation; nor is it in any way intended to suggest that the mediator should design the outcome of a dispute. It does, however, pointedly intend to suggest that for mediation to survive as a viable form of conflict management, then mediators must look directly into the heart of conflicts in the real world and manage them. Force fitting hard issues and stressed parties into mediation approaches that are based on wishful thinking about what human beings could become, does not sufficiently take account of the power and energy of human emotion. This limits and impairs the effectiveness and validity the mediation process could have in our culture.

Ultimately, if mediation cannot be demonstrated to work outside of hothouse conditions, where parties meet preset standards of reasonableness and cooperative demeanor, then the process will remain a marginal mode of conflict management or, worse, be relegated to history's trash heap of good ideas and good intentions that did not work or were not accepted. If mediation is to effectively become part of our cultural pattern of managing conflict, then mediators must adopt a rigorous, reality-based approach that can manage conflicts as they present themselves, not as we might hope for them to be.

Bibliography

* Originally posted at www.Mediate.com, August, 1999, http://www.mediate.com//articles/guerilla.cfm.

1. Axelrod, Robert. 'The Evolution of Cooperation', New York: Basic Books, 1984.

2. Benjamin, Robert D. 'The Constructive Uses of Deception'. *Mediation Quarterly*, vol. 13, no. 1, Fall 1995. Jossey-Bass Publishers, San Francisco, Calif.

3. 'Mediation as a Subversive Activity'. *DCBA Brief (DuPage County, Illinois Bar Journal)*, vol. 11, issue 2, September 1998; also published by Mediation Information & Resource Center (MIRC), www.mediate.com.

4. 'The Mediator as Trickster: The Folkloric Figure as Professional Role Model'. *Mediation Quarterly*, vol. 13,

no. 2, Winter, 1996. Jossey-Bass Publishers, San Francisco, Calif.

5. 'The Natural Mediator', *Mediation News*, Winter 1999, Vol 18., No. 1. Academy of Family Mediators.

6. 'Negotiation and Evil: The Sources of Religious and Moral Resistance to the Settlement of Conflicts'. *Mediation Quarterly*, vol. 15, no. 3, Spring 1998. Jossey-Bass Publishers, San Francisco, Calif.

7. 'The Physics of Mediation: The Reflections of Scientific Theory in Professional Mediation Practice'. *Mediation Quarterly*, vol. 8, no. 2, Winter, 1990. Jossey-Bass Publishers, San Francisco, Calif.

8. 'The Quest for Truth and the Truth of Lies', *Mediation News*, Fall 1999, Vol 18, No. 3. Academy of Family Mediators.

9. Bloom, Howard. 'The Lucifer Principle: A Scientific Exploration into the Forces of History', New York, Grove/Atlantic, 1995.

10. Bush, Robert. A. Baruch and Joseph P. Folger, 'The Promise of Mediation', San Francisco, Jossey-Bass Publishers, 1994.

11. Cleary, Thomas (Trans. with commentary). 'Sun Tzu II, The Art of War'. HarperSanFrancisco, 1996.

12. Damasio, Antonio R. Descartes Error. 'Emotion, Reason and the Human Brain'. New York: Grossett & Dunlap, 1994.

13. deWaal, Franz. 'Good Nature: The Origins of Right and Wrong in Humans and Other Animals'. Cambridge, Mass.: Harvard University Press, 1996.

14. Fischer, Roger, William Ury. 'Getting to Yes', (2nd ed.) Boston: Houghton Mifflin, 1991.

15. Haynes, John M. and Gretchen L. 'Mediating Divorce: Casebook of Strategies for Successful Family Negotiations'. San Francisco: Jossey-Bass Publishers, 1989.

16. Kagan, Donald. 'On the Origins of War and the Preservation of Peace', New York: Anchor Books, 1995.

17. Keegan, John, 'A History of Warfare'. New York: Knopf, 1993.

18. Keeley, Lawrence H. 'War Before Civilization'. New York: Oxford University Press, 1996.

19. Kolb, Deborah. 'When Talk Works: Profile of Mediators', San Francisco: Jossey-Bass Publishers, 1994.

20. Lakoff, George and Mark Johnson, 'Metaphors We Live By'. Chicago: The University of Chicago Press, 1980.

21. Niehoff, Debra, Ph.D. 'The Biology of Violence: How Understanding the Brain, Behavior, and Environment Can Break the Vicious Circle of Aggression'. New York: The Free Press, 1999.

22. Rue, Loyal. 'By the Grace of Guile: The Role of Deception in Natural History and Human Affairs'. New York: Oxford University Press, 1994.

23. Tannen Deborah, Ph.D. 'The Argument Culture: Moving from Debate to Dialogue'. New York: Random House, 1998.

24. van Creveld, Martin. 'The Transformation of War'. New York: The Free Press, 1991.

CHAPTER 3

Managing Courtroom Communication: Reflections of an Observer

By mediator, facilitator and judicial educator Joanna Kalowski[*]

In the highly structured courtroom environment, communication is a strange hybrid with unique features. The following article identifies these and suggests practical interventions for judicial officers to manage effective and courteous communication.

To understand what tips the balance in a courtroom (or an individual) from courteous and receptive to unreceptive or hostile is necessary to consider many factors:

- Litigants' expectations of courts, judicial officers and the hearing process
- The quality of understanding they have of their case, of the hearing process, and their role in it
- Their level of language competence and confidence
- Previous experience of courts in particular, and authority figures in general
- Their attitude to winning and losing, whether in or outside court
- The quality of their representation in court.

A litigant's state of mind is also a factor, and while a degree of tension and nervousness is predictable and normal, tension is dramatically higher in litigants without legal representation.

The people central to the purpose of the court (the litigants) are required to speak in a limited and formalised way, and often speak least of all. Those who speak on their behalf are in far more direct communication with the judicial officer than they are, a situation many find frustrating, even when prepared for it – and many are ill-prepared. While legal representatives know the applicable law, parties feel they know the fact situation better than anyone else, having lived it, and can be puzzled and irritated by the omission of details they regard as essential features of their case. This type of mediated communication is unusual in itself, and is usually reserved for people needing the services of an interpreter. In social settings, nothing is quite so irritating as having someone speak for you when you are present and perfectly able to speak for yourself.

The reverse, however, is worse. Unrepresented litigants do speak for themselves, but find themselves saying things inappropriately, either at the wrong moment or in the wrong way; they soon discover that underlying communication in court are some assumptions about process without which they quickly appear bumbling and incompetent.

Bumbling, incompetent, puzzled, frustrated, irritated: these are hardly descriptive of the state in which people do their best, and adults can be reduced to feeling like children. Add to this the shame adults feel when they are out of their depth, and it becomes obvious why comprehension declines in direct proportion to the rise of feelings of inadequacy.

Judicial officers, too, are in the unusual situation – from the communication point of view – of having to gauge levels of understanding without being able to rely on the usual tools: eye contact, direct interaction, mutual questioning. At best, judicial officers can ask if all is clear; but which adult is going to admit, aloud, in the presence of others who seem at ease with what is happening that they don't understand a process which is ostensibly about them?

It is this reality which provides the backdrop to the reflections contained in this paper, and the basis of suggested approaches, interventions and skills deployment.

Some safe assumptions about litigants judicial officers can make

The list of assumptions include:
- People believe legal representation largely evens out power imbalances between parties, and unrepresented parties are keenly aware of the unevenness of power relations, and of their level of disadvantage.
- This sense of being disadvantaged often makes them defensive or aggressive.
- It can also have the opposite effect, silencing them, making them passive in the face of much they do not follow. A feeling of helplessness frequently results, further impairing the capacity to understand and participate.
- Litigants will be anxious, even when represented, but far more so if they are not.
- Anxious people are more likely to seem hostile, even if they don't feel particularly hostile.
- People's capacity to understand and respond is reduced in direct proportion to their level of anxiety, yet litigants not unreasonably expect to understand everything that will happen around them. ("After all, it's my case.") As the case proceeds, and their understanding remains limited or declines, their resentment grows, further fuelling their inability to focus, follow and respond.
- Most litigants are poorly prepared for the court event, whether represented or not. Where lawyers are involved, litigants rely on them and behave quite passively. However, unrepresented litigants' more active participation can be equally unhelpful to the process unless they are among a tiny group of highly skilled and well-informed people who know how to conduct their matter in court.
- Litigants generally have high expectations that the process will be fair, and have preconceived, often unrealistic notions of what fairness entails.
- Their unrealistic expectations include the idea that the outcome will vindicate them, and resent-

ment can grow as they realise it is unlikely to happen. Not knowing how rare it is for a litigant to leave court feeling vindicated, they leave feeling cheated.

- This is the cycle that predisposes such a litigant to be even more difficult to deal with in future court hearings, whether related to the first event or not.

Judicial interventions aimed at reducing anxiety will lower the level of litigants' defensiveness and helplessness and raise their capacity to participate. Among the most effective are introducing the court event with a description of what is to happen on this occasion, and a summary of what previously happened.

What people know before they are familiar with a subject or a setting ("entry knowledge") deeply influences the way they act once they are in the setting or dealing with the subject ("entry behaviour"). Judicial officers and lawyers know the subject and the setting so well that they can easily overlook how strange it can be for litigants: how formal, how artificial, how unusual, how constrained and rule-bound.

Attempts to deal with this sense of strangeness by altering the physical setting have been partly successful, especially where litigants can sit next to their representatives instead of behind them. Doing away with all ceremony, however, may defeat the purpose, since parties to litigation have twin goals, sometimes seen as inconsistent, but in fact quite compatible. They want input into their matter to be heard and taken seriously, but they want someone else, someone in a position of authority, to take responsibility for resolving their problem.

How does the ordinary litigant know what to expect

Judicial officers' use of language is crucial to ensuring litigants' understanding of stages in the hearing, and may also lower tension in the courtroom. The capacity to speak simply and clearly, using accessible yet not simplistic language is a daunting task where technical language is regularly used and widely accepted as the norm. It requires judicial officers to be able to paraphrase and explain common legal expressions, or to suggest others do so for the benefit of litigants.

Communication improves if judicial officers use active rather than passive voice, and avoid talking over parties or lawyers, double negatives and multi-layered questions. Judicial officers report they also propose these techniques as a solution when litigants fail to understand questions from counsel (listening for the "how" as well as the "what").

It is apparent that one aspect of judicial leadership lies in the ability to model the kind of communication that assists both the court and its users.

It really matters for those whose business is language clarity to stop and consider how, when and why they use particular forms of expression, and to choose consciously how they will communicate, and with whom.

English has a rich heritage, influenced by many other languages, but its primary influences are Germanic and Latinate. In workshops I offer judicial officers either a "hearty welcome" or a "cordial reception", and ask which they would prefer. Someone always (correctly) observes that they mean the same thing; and someone always adds that they feel different – and that is the point. The "hearty welcome" sounds immediate and comfortable, while the "cordial reception" sounds cooler, and more formal. The former is the Germanic, the language of the many, and creates a tone which the latter, in the language of the few, cannot. Only the clergy and the judiciary knew Latin, and used it in ways that reserved meaning and high purpose for a select group.

Those who study and love the language enjoy the by-play English permits, but rarely recognise that it is possible to retreat into unnecessary formality under pressure, because almost everything in English can be said in two "languages". That is not to say there is no place for the use of formal language, but it is unhelpful if the goal is to increase litigants' sense of participation and understanding. When judicial officers reproach parties who are having difficulty understanding an issue that "this is a simple proposition", the outcome can be quite difficult.

Under pressure from high case loads and increasing numbers of unrepresented litigants in complex matters, judicial officers are now faced with reformulating what they say to ensure the ordinary listener – quite literally the average person in the street – can follow and answer, query and respond. For judicial officers, this can be about simply reframing Latinate phrases into everyday English, or persistence in explaining a point to a litigant without feeling that this reflects poorly on themselves. On the contrary, litigants' respect for judicial officers grows in circumstances where judicial officers have gone to some lengths to ensure they understand and can follow the process.

As a stress management tool, it is of unparalleled benefit to judicial officers, too.

Expectations of courts in general and the judicial officer in particular

These expectations include:
- The buck stops here: this is the person who will sort it all out.
- The judicial officer is in control, and won't let me be overborne.
- The judicial officer will protect my rights.
- The climate here is serious, and I will be taken seriously.

The adversarial nature of most proceedings ensures that litigants will at times feel discomfort. If they perceive this, rightly or wrongly, as an assault on their rights, anxiety and tension result. At high levels, this can lead to hostile and unproductive behaviour on the part of litigants and tension in the courtroom. Paradoxically, it is sometimes when judicial officers are following due process scrupulously that litigants with unrealistic expectations of what protection of their rights looks and feels like may become aggressive.

It is of great value therefore, if judicial officers can explain procedural steps in simple terms along the way.

Realistic expectations of judicial authority

Realistic expectations include:
- Direction
- Stability
- Conflict management
- Maintenance of norms.

Authority, defined as the ascribed power to achieve an end or carry out a responsibility through others, is distinguished from influence, the capability to carry out a task with others "by recruiting their interest, energy and commitment to a common goal or purpose".

Recruiting the energy of others depends upon the conscious use of active listening skills, and being prepared to attend to a litigant's expression of emotion (obviously without overstepping boundaries) in order to ensure emotion does not swamp reason.

The purpose of an intervention aimed at managing emotion is to return the individual to the state in which he or she can best participate: a rational state rather than an emotional one.

It seems counter-intuitive that attending to a party's emotional state when it is impairing their capacity to participate will actually lower emotion and raise the level of cognition; many professionals ignore emotion in the hope that it will go away. Judicial officers themselves report that a range of interventions, from offering or calling a short adjournment to asking parties whether they feel able to proceed, assists parties to "pull themselves together" and function more appropriately from that point on.

Saving face is not only a cross-cultural phenomenon, but a human one, and is particularly important for adults, whose fear is that they will look foolish (childlike) if they are unable to conduct themselves appropriately in a given setting (like an inexperienced child). Feedback and interviews with litigants reveal that the judicial officer's status is actually enhanced by subtle interventions that restore digni-

ty and confidence. A phenomenon known as "locating people in their expertise" emerges from the understanding that no one knows more about a situation than those who have lived it. Judicial officers who adopt this view find parties are more likely to accept and follow instructions designed to assist them also to understand procedural or legal issues. It is the "also" which is the key here. ("You may understand the facts of the case; now let me help you understand how it will run and why so that you can participate more fully." This may not be stated, but litigants will "hear" it as an enabling message, since it will underpin much of what they experience in court).

A quick self-assessment using the four factors (direction, stability, conflict management, maintenance of norms) after a tense session in court can help judicial officers to identify whether today's difficult litigants were and possibly remained confused, and to reconsider the techniques used to manage them. More often than warranted, people jump to the conclusion that litigants behaving aggressively are querulants in the sense used by Lester et al.[1] More often than not, they were merely being difficult.

Considering what was done to create a sense of direction and stability, and what kind of interventions were used to manage conflict and maintain norms can reveal interesting gaps. Remembering that litigants, especially unrepresented litigants, are unfamiliar with the norms of conduct and procedure in court presents a raft of possibilities for intervention by the judicial officer. However, it goes without saying that not all judicial officers will feel comfortable with all possible interventions, and will probably deploy mostly those with which they are most comfortable themselves. The trick is to expand judicial officers' own comfort in order to acknowledge and manage the discomfort of litigants. This is best achieved by discussion and exchange of views among judicial officers themselves, not just skills training or practice.

A judicial educator, herself a judicial officer, identifies four factors which assist in maintaining the tone of communication in court:

Preparation + Knowledge → Politeness + Control

Preparation, she asserts, goes a long way to protecting judicial officers from being taken by surprise and assists judicial officers to remain in their comfort zone. It is fear of loss of status which may cause some to respond aggressively to a surprise issue, although undoubtedly such issues will arise, regardless of the level of preparation. If civility is a by-product of preparation, it will enhance both the function and the tone of the court, and prevent that downward spiral so difficult to reverse. (Here again, the same judicial officer says that if she feels herself losing her temper, she takes a short adjournment and on return apologises for speaking sharply – a good way of reframing the outburst and restoring calm).

At the heart of effectiveness in this area are some selfevident skills:

- Awareness of the importance of managing people in all situations
- Ability to define and describe a task and set limits up front
- Ability to build confidence and manage risk

- Capacity to stay with ambiguity for a time – easier for the judicial officer than for the litigant, who wants and expects everything to be clear from the outset, and can become agitated if this does not happen.

Anxious litigants can't manage themselves, are unfamiliar with the process as well as the judicial officer and his or her role, and they usually don't know the nature of the task or its limits. Building litigants' confidence in the process as it runs its course is one role the judicial officer plays: it is all but imperceptible to everyone in the courtroom, including many judicial officers who, upon hearing favourable observations, regularly express surprise that they achieved them, and in what ways they did so.

Key communication skills revisited
- Communicate clearly and simply
- Use accessible yet not simplistic language
- Involve litigants in the process – eyes and words
- Create a climate conducive to "participation" by
  - maintaining a focus on the issues
  - ensuring there is clarity about process
  - maintaining courtesy in the courtroom
  - listening, summarising, paraphrasing if necessary
  - asking questions, not statements disguised as questions
  - avoiding talking over litigants or lawyers
  - avoiding double negatives and multi-level questions
  - using active rather than passive voice

Interventions to settle litigants down

- Make opening remarks which indicate how the case will proceed today
- Acknowledge litigants as well as their representatives
- Tell unrepresented litigants what is expected of them, what they can and can't do
- Assure them they will be heard
- Let them know they will have a chance to speak, and indicate when and in what ways at the outset and as the case proceeds
- Use as wide a range of interventions as you comfortably can.

Six interventions defined by their purpose

1. Prescriptive: purpose – to be directive, for example, "You must answer 'yes' or 'no' to the question"
2. Informative: purpose – to instruct, make an observation, for example, "You look uncertain about that"
3. Confrontative: purpose – to challenge, give direct feedback, for example, "Please remain silent while X is giving evidence"
4. Cathartic: purpose – to acknowledge and normalise tension, for example, "Question may be unpleasant, but you have to answer it as best you can"
5. Catalytic: purpose – to encourage analysis, for example, "Where does this line of argument take us?"
6. Supportive: purpose – to express empathy "I know you have left your patients waiting to be with us today, Doctor."

Manage tension

- Give yourself a break if you need one, and the timing permits it
- Give litigants a break if emotion is getting in their way, or offer a break or ask if they feel able to go on.
- Mutualise comments on emotion in order to neutralise them, for example, "There are moments everyone feels ..."
- Work on your own comfort with conflict and emotion: both are to be expected, especially in the court setting
- Saving face is valued by all, and does not diminish your standing.
- Talk with your peers: exchange insights and ideas.

Notes

* Edited version of an address presented to the National Judicial College of Australia Communication in the Courtroom Conference, 10 November 2007, and the Local Court of NSW Annual Conference, 2 July 2008.

Joanna Kalowski is a judicial educator who served eight years as a Member of the Administrative Appeals Tribunal and three on the National Native Title Tribunal. She has observed judicial officers across Australia in many courts, and runs workshops here and in Europe and Asia in communication, dispute resolution and crosscultural aspects of both.

1   G Lester, B Wilson, L Griffin, PE Mullen, 'Unusually Persistent Litigants', (2004) 184 *British Journal of Psychiatry* 352; "The Vexatious Litigant", (2005) 17 *Judicial Officers' Bulletin* 17.

CHAPTER 4

Mediating High Conflict Couples

By mediator Henry Brown[1]

Introduction

There used to be, and may still be, a misconception that mediation is really only appropriate for "reasonable" people – that all those who choose this process have an underlying wish to resolve their issues amicably and sensibly in a spirit of compromise. The truth, however, is that while reasonable people can and do benefit significantly by mediating rather than relying wholly on the traditional legal system, it is by no means uncommon for those who use mediation to exhibit all the stresses, emotions, challenges and elements of behaviour seen in the adversarial legal system.

Indeed, family mediators will be familiar with working with parties who are angry, hurt, disappointed, confused, anxious, resentful or feeling any of the myriad of emotions that people may go through in the course of separation and divorce. This is part of their training and experience. It follows, therefore, that mediators should be well able to assist couples who might present challenges to their lawyers in the traditional legal system.

One special challenge for mediators – and for the lawyers who represent them and others who work professionally with them – is the high conflict couple. This is because high conflict people tend to fall into a category of their own and cannot be effectively dealt with in the same way as other couples, even those who are emotional and difficult. Mediators who try to use the same strategies with high conflict couples as they ordinarily do may find that they do not work and in fact can often be counter-productive. A special approach and some specific strategies are needed; but first, it is necessary to identify what is meant by "high conflict" and how this manifests itself.

So what do we mean by 'high conflict'?

When referring to *high conflict* people, we do not merely mean couples who have difficulty in reaching agreement, who argue and remonstrate, or who are emotional, upset and angry. These, after all, are common features of many relationship breakdowns. We refer rather to something more than this, to a rigid 'world view' that doesn't readily allow for any other perceptions, to a stuckness that doesn't seem to shift, to a tendency to see the situation in terms of blame rather than joint responsibility, to a sense of wanting to punish the other party, and to other manifestations that take this category of conflict to a higher level.

Where there is a significant combination of the following manifestations and/or where the manifestations are intensely experienced it is likely that one is dealing with a high conflict situation:

1 *High levels of disagreement and conflict:* The couple have difficulty in avoiding continuing disagreement and conflict, often serious, intensive and emotional.

2 *Uncertainty about ending the relationship:* Although they may both seem to accept that the relationship is over, there may be some underlying uncertainty by either of them about this.

3 *High levels of blaming:* Either or both may blame the other for the relationship breakdown or for the problems that exist between them, with little or no understanding that there may be elements of joint responsibility or about the circular nature of a breakdown pattern.

4 *Poor communications:* Although they may perhaps talk and communicate extensively with one another, their communications are ineffective: they just don't hear one another.

5 *Polarised positions:* They tend to react to one another by taking opposite, polarised positions, with virtually no shades of grey and little room for compromise or problem-solving.

6 *Agreed terms hard to reach:* Negotiations are ineffectual, leaving issues unresolved and agreement frustratingly out of reach.

7 *Difficulty in implementing agreements:* Where arrangements are made, even short-term e.g. contact, they tend to break down or are ambiguous or difficult to follow.

8 *Children drawn in:* The children (perhaps unwittingly) are drawn into taking sides between the parents, maybe with physical, emotional or behavioural problems.

9 *Holding on to past structures and expectations:* Sometimes there is a tendency by either to recall better times or to try to recreate old family scenarios, e.g. setting up family meals.

10 *Punitive:* The behaviour of either may feel (and be) punitive to the other, even if this is not intended, or it is experienced by either or both as punitive.

11 *Partisan expectations:* Either or both may feel that lawyers, counsellors, mediators or family neutrals should support their view more strongly than the other's position.

12 *Vindication:* The views of third parties are sought and used – sometimes quite inappropriately – to support a particular position or 'world view'.

13 *Seeking reasons for changed behaviour:* The changed behaviour of either may be attributed to illness (physical, emotional or mental), stress or mid-life or other crisis.

14 *New process, new forum:* Each process (e.g. mediation, counselling or the court) feels like a new forum to retell the story rather than a place to seek resolution.

15 *Anxiety about the future:* There is likely to be anxiety (personal or financial) by either or both about managing without the other (whether or not actually expressed).

16 *Recovery delayed/non-existent:* It feels as though the patterns between the couple are set to continue until either or both are financially and/or emotionally exhausted.

It should be emphasised that the mere existence of some of these characteristics in a couple does not necessarily indicate high conflict. On the contrary, it is natural to expect them to some extent in most cases. It is their extent and high level that indicate high conflict.

High conflict couples are estimated to comprise no more than about 5-10% of couples, perhaps one in 20. For such couples, no proposal can form a basis for moving forward, no financial arrangement is fair enough, no arrangements for children are satisfactory enough and no interim agreement immune from falling apart and resulting in a new round of blame and dispute. With these couples, blame for the breakdown is commonly a central theme. The idea that they may in some way have contributed to the breakdown or that there might have been some mutuality of responsibility is simply not acceptable.

Children of high conflict couples are commonly drawn into their parents' dispute and may be implicitly required to takes sides, though the parents may protest that they are not influencing their children in doing so.

For the mediator, a sensible and fair outcome may seem to be the desired objective, but for the party this seems elusive and sometimes even undesirable. Small wonder that high conflict couples can often leave the mediator frustrated and emotionally exhausted.

Professor Richard Mathis, in an insightful article 'Couples from Hell: Undifferentiated Spouses in Divorce Mediation'[2] reviews the literature concerning such couples and adds his own views. There is a consensus among writers and practitioners that a common feature of such couples is that they are "enmeshed" with one another: they cannot function effectively together yet they cannot let one another go. Another term used in the literature is "undifferentiated" couples: we may view them as "emotionally inseparable".

Hugh McIsaac, with enormous experience in the Los Angeles family courts, reviewed such couples in the context of child custody disputes.[3] Having worked with more than 35,000 custody disputes, he identified a pattern in which "enmeshed" parents were "involved in an ongoing emotional morass" and seemed unable to work through the divorce process. While such couples can sometimes reach agreement, McIsaac considers that in most cases "they need a firm, fair, and final decision by some independent trier of fact". He identifies a clue that suggests that one is working with such a family: as soon as a solution is in sight it disappears "just like a mirage in the desert".

An additional difficulty with high conflict couples is that initially they may appear reasonable, rational and willing to work in the mediation process. Many high conflict individuals are effective, high functioning people who have achieved professional or business success. This apparent cooperation and "reasonableness" can make it even more challenging for a mediator and other professionals working with them, as they disguise a fundamental underlying problem of an inability to adjust to any view other than their own. As individuals, these people can generally function effectively, but as couples they are inclined to fight chronically "until one or both are financially or emotionally exhausted". This description aptly sums up the experience of such couples.[4]

What is the reason for this high conflict

Firstly, high conflict should be distinguished from mere impasse or difficulty in reaching agreement: there may be a number of reasons for impasse that do not take the situation into one of 'high conflict' as such. For example, parties may have genuinely different views as to their legal entitlement, fairness or values, without all the characteristics of high conflict, or there may be situations of real concern about the future that are not met by the proposals being put forward: there may be personal and financial imperatives to hold firm for a better outcome. The fact that parties cannot agree is not in itself high conflict.

High conflict with the characteristics outlined in the preceding section may be attributable to a number of inter-related causes, all of which point in the same direction: the personality of either or both parties. Some people – a relatively small percentage of the population – have 'high conflict personalities' and are prone to find themselves in disputes, the most significant and profound of which is likely to be when involved in relationship breakdown.

It seems likely that these high conflict personalities arise from any of the following causes:

- Disorganised attachment
- Personality disorder
- Maladaptive traits falling short of personality disorder.

Each of these will be briefly considered.

Disorganised attachment
Psychoanalyst John Bowlby formulated a concept that the infant is in effect programmed to seek closeness to a parent or carer who provides comfort and protection.[5] His thesis was that humans need to form close affectional bonds and that the carer, by offering that closeness, allows the infant the secure base from which to develop. If the carer can provide empathetic and well-attuned bonds for the infant, that infant is likely to develop greater emotional security as a child and adult. If however there is no carer or the carer cannot attune effectively to the infant, then the infant is likely to have later insecurity problems manifesting in different ways – known as insecure attachment and in the most extreme case, disorganised attachment. This is the essence of attachment theory.

Another relevant factor is the way in which people "try to understand each other's mental states: their thoughts and feelings, beliefs and desires in order to make sense of and, even more important, to anticipate each other's actions".[6] This *reflective function* (or *mentalisation*) is what enables people to understand their own and others' behaviour with reference to their mental states and feelings. There is a circular nature in relation to reflective function and secure attachment in that "a reflective caregiver increases the likelihood of the child's secure attachment which, in turn, facilitates the development of mentalisation".[7] This mirroring enables the child to develop a proper understanding of his or her own mental states and feelings and those of others.

People continue to form new attachments throughout their lives, many of which may have implications similar to those experienced as children. "The secure or insecure attachments made to parents in childhood often prefigure the attachments which we make in adult life."[8] "It seems reasonable to surmise that the bond we observe to persist in unhappy marriages is an adult development of childhood attachment."[9]

For most people, levels of attachment may vary between secure and insecure but will be substantially functional. Even where attachment is insecure, a couple may co-exist and function satisfactorily. However, for a small minority of people, the attachment system breaks down and becomes disorganised, dysfunctional and counter-productive. In such cases, trust, a critical component of secure attachment, may exist alongside its polarised opposite, not just mistrust, but paranoia. Both these attributes may co-exist simultaneously in the same person, with whatever confusion and paradox this may entail.

A person with disorganised attachment and a failure of the reflective function or mentalisation as mentioned above is likely to be unable to understand their own or their partner's mental states, feelings or behaviour without significant distortions, and is likely to fall into the high conflict category.

Personality disorder

It seems that personality disorders may also have a central role in high conflict cases and that practitioners should have at least a basic understanding of them in order to devise and implement strategies that are likely to be effective in dealing with the conflict. However, this is an area of brain function that is rather unspecific, unlike other brain disorders that may be attributable to observable physical signs of damage or chemical imbalances. It has been described as lying in "murky ground."[10] The UK Mental Health Foundation describes personality disorder as "a controversial diagnosis, covering a wide range of different attitudes and behaviours and affecting an estimated 10% of the general population" and says that the term is generally used "to describe behaviours that do not fit into any other obvious diagnostic category ...".[11]

There are various different types of personality disorders but they all share certain features:

- There may have been conduct disorders in childhood or adolescence.
- There is a rigid, long-standing, narrow and inflexible pattern of behaviour and 'world view' that

affects the way they think and perceive the world (falling outside the person's cultural norms) and how they relate to other people.

- This pattern causes distress to them and/or to others.
- It affects the person's coping mechanisms.

Many countries use the Diagnostic and Statistical Manual of Mental Disorders (DSM) published by the American Psychiatric Association, which provides standard criteria for the classification of disorders including personality disorders. A broadly corresponding system is used in the International Classification of Diseases (ICD) produced by the World Health Organization, and adopted by many European countries. The personality disorder category is divided into a number of specific types including for example Borderline, Histrionic, Narcissistic and Antisocial or Dissocial.[12]

Bill Eddy has been influential in linking personality disorder to high conflict, noting the overlap of characteristics in both. He believes that in the last decade the courts "have become the prime playing field for undiagnosed and untreated personality disorders."[13]

Maladaptive traits falling short of personality disorder

This refers to people who demonstrate various of the characteristics of personality disorder, but who fall short of a 'full-blown' disorder. This brings into focus the point that we all have our own characteristic way of thinking, feeling and relating to others, and there is a spectrum that varies between fully functional and adaptive at the one end and wholly disordered at the other. Clearly, some people fall within a shade of grey, and are not really functional or adaptive but yet are not disordered. This is the group that may be regarded as maladaptive.[14]

There is an inter-relationship between these three sources of high conflict. It seems that levels of insecurity in childhood may be one of the precursors of personality disorders in adulthood. Various writers have linked these factors, including for example Professor Peter Fonagy who has expressed the view that the capacity for mentalisation may be undermined by childhood maltreatment, with a distortion of the normal development of a reflective function, resulting in a borderline personality disorder.[15]

Cautions about 'diagnosing' causes of high conflict

These views as to the causes of high conflict are intended for mediators' general guidance and as a tool to help understand the reasoning for adopting various high conflict strategies. They are not intended to serve as a formal diagnosis. Indeed, it would be quite wrong for any mediator to try to do so: even if mediators were qualified mental health professionals – and most are not – the task of diagnosis is a highly specialised one with the benefit of intensive background enquiry and it would be entirely inappropriate for a mediator to undertake it.

Furthermore, the causes of personality disorders are still not fully known or understood. It is generally assumed that there are a number of possible causes including for example attachment problems in early childhood; maltreatment; trauma; neurological problems involving for example brain damage; hypersensitivity to stress; and genetic factors.[16] And as indicated in footnote 14, there is a blurring between normal personality functioning and personality disorders: where does the line get drawn between normalcy and disorder?

Any insights that might be gained from a better understanding of high conflict and personality disorder should rather be used by way of what the late John Haynes described as "working hypothesis": simply to have it in mind as a possible clue to an effective way of moving forward in the mediation. He also said "don't marry your working hypothesis": it is merely a tool that provides guidance and is to be abandoned if it seems that it may not be appropriate.

In any event, it is not the function of the mediator to discuss parties' personality traits or especially possible disorders with them. That would be presumptuous, inappropriate and insensitive. And almost certainly it would be badly received: one of the features of these traits is an inability to see other perspectives in any meaningful way. Eddy takes the view that feedback to high conflict parties is generally pointless, no matter how well-intentioned, and may be counterproductive in simply making the person more defensive, and may possibly even result in it being seen as a threat that requires some form of counter-attack.[17]

Perhaps mediators, lawyers and other non-mental-health professionals might devise terminology other than 'personality disorder' when dealing in the context of high conflict. Given that an inflexible world view is one of the cornerstones of the condition, perhaps something like 'rigid mindset personality' would be a better description.

Strategies for mediating high conflict couples

A few general points need to be made before considering some specific strategies:

- General principles of good mediation practice are important to maintain in any situation. However, with high conflict parties, some of the usual strategies may not be effective and ways of working may be needed that are to some extent counter-intuitive.
- Empathy is critical. It is possible to develop genuine empathy by understanding the parties even if one does not necessarily find them likeable or even if their behaviour and approach feel offensive to one's sense of justice and propriety. That does not mean abandoning personal values, but rather developing an understanding of and identification with both parties that enables a mutually respectful working relationship to exist.
- "Sometimes parties' co-opt their lawyers into their 'rigid mindset' approach. Their lawyer must be their champion and believe in their cause and values. Some lawyers may have that propensity in any event, others may not realise how they are being drawn into escalating the conflict. Mediators may need to apply similar strategies

with the lawyers as they do with the parties: they can sensitively support the lawyers in adopting a more positive and constructive role in moving towards a resolution of the issues.

There cannot be any strategies that are effective in every situation, and mediators will obviously have to adopt, adapt and apply the following to the needs of each individual situation as appropriate:

1. *Identifying high conflict situations*
There may be early indications of high conflict, especially for a mediator aware of the indicators set out above; but signs may only emerge as the matter gets under way. High conflict strategies cannot be introduced before identifying the nature of the matter. However, the general principles of good practice will invariably be sufficient to meet most needs until more specific indications become apparent. At that stage, applicable strategies can be introduced, using individual judgment to assess which are likely to be most useful.

2. *Establishing and maintaining professional boundaries*
High conflict parties place a huge strain on a mediator's need to maintain professional boundaries. The high conflict party holds out the permanent invitation to the mediator to enter his or her world view and to support him or her personally. The slope from there to becoming the party's 'rescuer' and emotional prop is a potentially slippery one.

From an attachment perspective, the risk of having poor boundaries is that the party views the mediator as a new attachment 'carer', with high hopes for his or her needs to be met, but with virtually no prospect of this being achieved.

Peter Fonagy, in a DVD interview, has suggested a way in which to maintain professional boundaries with a high conflict party. This is to be explicit as to the scope of one's professional functions. This might be along the lines of: "I can help you deal with these matters by doing 1, 2, 3 and 4. However, I cannot help you with 5 and 6 which are outside the scope of my functions." If later the party starts encroaching on aspects outside the mediator's scope, the mediator can gently remind the party of these limitations. This may obviously need elaboration and is not intended to be used verbatim, but it indicates the way in which boundaries can and should be maintained.

3. *Having and maintaining clear rules and records*
The need for a clear Agreement to Mediate is vital. In addition, the mediator needs to have and maintain clear rules as to how he or she will function. It is similarly important to be clear about practicalities such as the arrangements for meetings and costs: if the mediator is being paid on a time basis, the parties should be kept informed as to how these are escalating and perhaps interim bills should be rendered, unless some other cost basis is being used.

If interim matters are agreed, for example about interim contact with children, it can be useful for the mediator to make a short note in agreed form setting out what has been agreed and to copy this for each party. People under stress, and especially those in high conflict, do not necessarily remember things very well. In any event, it is sound policy to retain a record in case it should be necessary to refer to these at any later time.

It should be emphasised that the need for clear professional boundaries, rules and records does not mean that the mediator should be excessively formal. There is a balance to be struck between boundaried professionalism on the one hand and maintaining empathy and a friendly and sensitive tone on the other: these are not mutually inconsistent.

4. Dealing with blame and recrimination

As observed above, high conflict parties will commonly hold the other party responsible for the breakdown of the marriage. This goes hand in hand with recrimination and reproach. If only the other had been more reasonable or less selfish or had behaved differently, the problems in the relationship could have been overcome. The other party only has him/herself to blame for the consequences.

Mediators must obviously be particularly vigilant about saying anything that might be supportive of such a view or being perceived by either as doing so. The mantra runs along the lines of: "I can see both your perspectives, and I will do what I can to help you both." The mediator needs to indicate sensitively that reasons for relationship breakdown can be complex: there may also be other perspectives.

The mediator may try to help parties move past blame and recrimination, though this is more easily said than done. For example, the mediator might draw attention to the fact that mutual blaming has become a pattern of the parties' interaction, permeates discussions, colours every action and response, and inhibits any resolution. The mediator might

encourage parties to step back from doing so, perhaps even by adopting an agreed rule that the mediator will note when this is happening and the parties will then desist.

5. Establishing directiveness and proactivity

High conflict couples are inclined to be reactive rather than proactive in seeking ways forward. The pattern tends to be one of taking opposite positions, so that if one says "white" the other says "black", and few proposals from either side will meet with joint approval. This means that the mediator needs to be proactive in proposing mutually acceptable ways of dealing with matters in a way that neither party is likely to be.

Mediators are generally taught that they should not be directive. However, when working with high conflict, enmeshed couples, there is a view that mediators need to be far more robustly directive. Professor Richard Mathis, in a seminal article, goes so far as to say that in such cases, mediators need to be "active, even authoritarian, if needed, during the initial stages."[18]

Parties may resist the mediator's directive and proactive role; but if the mediator's approach is deft, sensitive and mutually supportive, also clear, reasonable and firm, the parties may well be guided by it. Directiveness and proactivity should not be confused with heavy-handedness, which is to be avoided.

6. Maintaining a child focus

A common manifestation of high conflict is that where there are children, they are almost invariably drawn into the couple's battle. There is no reason to think that couples in high conflict choose to be worse parents than others. They love their children, even if their love is coloured by their world view. The certainty of their belief that the other party is culpable in the breakdown and the intensity of their feelings may distort their appreciation of the adverse effects of their conduct on the children. Would they allow their children to go through the hurt and pain (whether overt or hidden) that their hostility so often causes if they really understood what effect it had?

As mentioned above, a high conflict person's 'mentalisation' or 'reflective function' – their ability to understand their own and others' behaviour with reference to their mental states and feelings – is compromised, resulting in a gap between the actions of the parents and the needs of the children that the parents are either unable to perceive or to address.

There is considerable authority that conflict between parents has an adverse effect on children and their well-being. It is important for mediators to help parents reduce conflict, to support their parenting, and to facilitate contact between children and non-resident parents.

Against this background, there are a number of child-focused strategies that may be helpful:

- *Increasing awareness of children's needs:* As indicated above, parents may not appreciate the effect of their actions on the children. They may believe that "the children are taking it well" or may feel "sorry the children are unhappy but it's not my fault". Mediators can support the parties and their children by providing information about children's needs and reactions and about resources for parents in addressing these.

- *Helping children to manage and accept change:* Parents need to help children accept change. This may be hard where the parents are themselves struggling to do so and especially if they are blaming one another. The mediator can help focus parties on the child's need to manage enormous change, in the knowledge that whatever hostility may exist in the couple relationship, there is a shared responsibility for effective and sensitive parenting.

- *Providing good role models:* Both parents may need to be reminded that their children's sound development and ability to form sound partnering relationships depend on good parental role models. Criticism and 'bad-mouthing' of the other parent can damage the child more than it damages the other parent.

- *Avoiding placing inappropriate responsibility on a child:* A child may feel responsible for the crisis in his or her parents' lives; may have to carry a secret so as not to upset mummy or daddy; may be used as a 'go-between' where parents do not communicate directly; or may inappropriately have to become the mature adult to protect both parents from their mutual antagonism. There may be direct or indirect pressure to choose between parents: from either or both parents, or from 'official' enquiries by judges, welfare officers or court officials. It is unfair to burden the child in this way. Mediators need to be able to identify situations where children are being placed in such positions of personal responsibility, to discuss this with the parties and help them back to a model of good parenting.

- *Avoiding allowing children to have excessive power:* A child may exercise power in various ways, such as playing parents off against one another, behaving in disruptive ways, or trading on parents' guilt to gain some benefit. This is neither healthy for the child, nor conducive to good parenting. Parents need to be able to communicate with one another to avoid being manipulated or triangulated by their child, and to provide mutual support in the child's interests as well as their own.

- *Helping the children to have harmonious transitions:* It is at the cross-over point, when children go from one parent to the other, that one of the greatest flashpoints exists for overt parental conflict. Classic research on children and divorce, 'Surviving the Breakup' (Wallerstein et al, 1980), found that "perhaps the most distressing of all the barriers interfering with smooth visiting were the parental conflicts which either preceded or brought each visit to a close as the majority of children felt cheated and betrayed by the prelude of hostilities between parents. They came to expect it but they respected their parents less for it."[19] One wonders whether parents would continue to behave in this way if they understood that their children felt this way.

- *Understanding children's reactions and allowing them to express themselves:* Every child is likely to react individually to the breakdown of his or her parents' relationship. They may be angry with either or both parents, they may be anxious about the future or they may feel shock, distress, shame (that their parents are divorcing), guilt or denial. Not all children will express their feelings directly. Younger children may regress in their behaviour, including for example bedwetting. Older children may become uncooperative, provocative and rebellious. Or a child may appear to accept the breakdown with equanimity but may be avoiding the issues and trying not to upset the parents by being upset himself or herself. Despite what appear to be positive indications, this is not a healthy response and needs to be addressed just as much as directly unhappy reactions.

The mediator can help parents to handle these situations with thoughtful, honest and age-appropriate communication, allowing children to express their feelings, reassuring them that both parents will continue to love them and care for them (though not living together) and taking control of necessary decisions so that children do not feel that they are adrift.

7. Taking small steps

In view of the difficulty in reaching agreement on anything at all when working with high conflict couples, it is sensible to take small steps and achieve limited incremental improvements rather than aiming for an immediate global resolution. That is not to say that global resolution is not possible, as indeed it might be, but rather that it is easier to build up to it than trying to achieve it in one fell swoop.

In practical terms, this may for example mean that when arranging contact, if there is difficulty in trying to establish a long-term programme, it might be sensible to fix one or two visits at a time, with very specific provisions about timing and how to manage unexpected contingencies. Gradually, as these take place and problems are ironed out, it may be easier to move towards a more established routine.

'Small steps' may also translate into a tolerance for change, insofar as progress towards overall resolution is concerned. Either party may propose a change to something already resolved and apparently now put aside. This is not an uncommon element for high conflict parties: it may well be necessary for the mediator to help the parties negotiate and renegotiate (with small steps as suggested above) until a comprehensive deal is available.

8. *Considering counselling or psychotherapy*

Where appropriate, the mediator may suggest to the couple that they enter into some form of couple's or family therapy to help them deal with the issues that they face. This can be done parallel with the mediation, or there can be an agreed adjournment while this to be done. If the parties are both committed to separation, the motivation for the counselling or therapy would be to help them do so in as reasonable a way as possible, especially if there are children for whom continued joint parenting will be necessary. If either party is holding on to the possibility of some form of reconciliation – and this is not unknown with the ambivalence that sometimes surrounds high conflict couples – the counselling could be to explore whether to separate and divorce and if so, to help deal with the emotional aspects of this; or if they elect to stay together, to help agree on a basis for doing so.

It may be that one or other party would benefit from individual counselling or therapy. The mediator may perhaps consider it appropriate to suggest this privately, in a discreet and sensitive way. People sometimes tend to react badly to the suggestion that they need therapy, and it wouldn't be appropriate to refer to personality disorder when discussing this, so the mediator may gently suggest the possibility of "professional support".

9. *Taking time out*

A 'cooling off period' is a well-established concept in many fields, such as credit agreements or doorstep sales, to allow a person time to reflect and change their minds about a proposed course of action. It can also be a useful strategy in dealing with high conflict, to allow a person time to re-evaluate the situation and the best way of dealing with it, rather than proceeding with what may be a knee-jerk and emotional action, especially where the parties have been working in a highly charged atmosphere. Unless there is a genuine urgency, taking time out can sometimes be a constructive policy, allowing time for reflection.

This may be a particularly helpful strategy where one person is highly emotional and unable to engage effectively in discussion. If the mediator can't help the party to move into a rational and productive mode, for example by gently engaging in conversation that allows him or her to 'change gear' or by having a short pause, for example to make a cup of tea, then a longer break may be very useful. This may be for a few minutes, or for a bit longer, or in more extreme cases, perhaps by adjourning the meeting to another time.

10. Aiming to achieve mutual autonomy
For each individual, at a time of profound and often painful transition, the future may feel uncertain and worrying, perhaps overwhelmingly so. The aim of trying to resolve matters and work out sensible and viable arrangements with the minimum of conflict is to move towards a time when both will feel secure and autonomous, and can give one another support with parenting where appropriate. The mediator can help the parties to maintain this vision and aspiration, and hopefully to achieve it – not with reassurances which may feel glib, but with a combination of empathetic support and practical solutions.

There is not always a happy ending

Understanding the issues affecting high conflict couples and having some relevant strategies will hopefully provide the mediator with a reasonable prospect of achieving a positive outcome. However, it is in the nature of high conflict that a significant proportion of cases will not be settled by agreement but will need to be decided by the court. It is perfect-ly right and proper that parties who are unable to reach agreement should be able to have a judge decide for them, and this should not be regarded as a failure but rather as an appropriate way of dealing with such matters.

Mediators need to keep this perspective in mind and should not 'beat themselves up' if a high conflict couple fail to resolve their issues in mediation. They should also anticipate the possibility that either or both of the couple will be critical of them. Here again, it is in the nature of disorganised attachment that what may start out as optimism and trust turns to paranoia and criticism. In such event it may not be particularly helpful to try to justify in detail what was done and why. This may merely open up further contentious exchanges. The most appropriate response might rather be to react in a courteous professional manner, briefly responding to any criticism, but not in such a way as to invite a contentious reply. The risk of criticism in working with high conflict disputes may be regarded as an occupational hazard.

In summary, working with high conflict involves having a better understanding of the dynamic, having some strategies to facilitate this special category of dispute, and not being unduly self-critical if the mediation does not result in an agreed outcome.

References

1. This chapter is largely based on the book and DVD programme co-written by the author with psychotherapists Neil Dawson and Brenda McHugh, 'Managing difficult divorce relationships: A multimedia training programme for family lawyers' published by the family lawyers' organisation Resolution [2006]. The author acknowledges his co-authors and the programme's consultant, Professor Peter Fonagy; also the work of William A Eddy and the US High Conflict Institute.

2. *Mediation Quarterly* Vol. 16 No. 1 (Fall 1998).

3. 'Toward a Classification of Child Custody Disputes: An Application of Family Systems Theory'; *Mediation Quarterly* 14/15 (Winter 1986/Spring 1987).

4. Isaacs, M.B., Montalvo, B., and Abelsohn, D. 'The Difficult Divorce: Therapy for Children and Families', Basic Books 1986. Quoted in Mathis (1998) at p.40.

5. Bowlby's 'Attachment and Loss' trilogy, published by Hogarth and the Institute of Psychoanalysis, comprised 'Attachment' (1969), 'Separation: Anxiety and Anger' (1973) and 'Loss: Sadness and Depression' (1980).

6. Peter Fonagy, 'Paper to the Developmental and Psychoanalytic Discussion Group, American Psychoanalytic Association, May 1999'.

7. Ibid Fonagy 1999.

8. Robert S Weiss, 'Separation and other problems that threaten relationships' *BMJ* 1998 Mar 28; 316 (7136): 1011-3.

9. Robert S Weiss, 'The emotional impact of marital separation' – *Journal of Social Issues*, 32, 135.

10. Barry J Gibb, 'The Rough Guide to the Brain' published by Rough Guides/Penguin (2007) at 130.

11. See their website at http://www.mentalhealth.org.uk/information/mental-health-a-z/personality-disorders/

12. For DSM-IV-TR (4th edition), the reference to these personality disorders is Code 301 at .7, .50, .81 and .83. For ICD, the reference is at ICD-10 'Chapter V: Mental and behavioural disorders: F60-69'. For a non-technical outline, see the Mental Health Foundation website (note 11 above) or the Royal College of Psychiatrists at http://www.rcpsych.ac.uk/mentalhealthinfoforall/problems/personalitydisorders/pd.aspx

13. See his important work, 'High conflict people in legal disputes' (2005) published by HCI Press, a subsidiary of the High Conflict Institute: http://www.highconflictinstitute.com/

14. Professor Thomas A Widiger questions whether personality disorders should more accurately be diagnosed as maladaptive variants of common personality traits. He points out that "researchers have been unable to identify a qualitative distinction between normal personality functioning and personality disorder" and suggests that all symptoms of personality disorders "can be understood as maladaptive variants of personality traits evident within the normal population." See his article in *World Psychiatry: the official journal of the World Psychiatric Association*, 2003 October; 2(3): 131-135 at http://www.ncbi.nlm.nih.gov/pmc/articles/PMC1525106/#B9

15. Peter Fonagy, 'Attachment, the development of the self, and its pathology in personality disorders'. See http://www.psychomedia.it/pm/modther/probpsiter/fonagy-2.htm

16. See for example http://www.mentalhealth.org.uk/information/mental-health-a-z/personality-disorders/

17. 'Handling High Conflict Personalities in Family Mediation' (2005) Summer ACR Resolution 15-16.

18. Mathis, RD, 'Couples from Hell: Undifferentiated Spouses in Divorce Mediation', (1998) 16(1) *Mediation Quarterly*.

19. Wallerstein, Judith S and Berlin Kelly, Joan, 'Surviving the Breakup: How children and parents cope with divorce', 1980, Grant McIntyre at p 141.

CHAPTER 5

Family Mediation and Children

By mediator Lisa Parkinson

The development of family mediation in England and Wales

Family mediation developed in England and Wales from the late 1970s onwards to offer a process of consensual decision-making in private law family matters, as an alternative to adversarial litigation and adjudication. Initially confined to issues concerning children, family mediation is available at many centres across the country to help family members reach agreed decisions, mainly with regard to a child's residence and contact with the non-residential parent, that take account of the needs and feelings of the child concerned. The Children Act 1989 created a legal framework in which joint parental responsibility continues to be held by both parents after they divorce (unless there are exceptional circumstances). The Children Act encourages parents to agree arrangements for their children, an approach that is entirely in harmony with the principles of mediation. Family mediators facilitate communication and co-operation between parents who may find themselves unable to communicate in a constructive way,

or who may have stopped speaking altogether. Separated parents may be in dispute over arrangements for their children because of their anger with each other and absorption in their own feelings and problems. Family mediation provides a forum in which parents consider their children's feelings and needs, as well as their own. In general, children do not take part directly. Parents are helped to focus on their children as individuals and to work out mutually acceptable arrangements and also to agree what they think needs to be explained to their children, in order to reassure them and help them adjust to major changes in their lives. From 1987 onwards, family mediation in England and Wales became available on all issues including financial and property matters, as these issues are often intertwined with arrangements for children.

Domestic abuse and mediation

A report by the National Audit Office concluded: *"Mediation is generally cheaper, quicker and less acrimo-*

nious than court proceedings, and research shows it secures better outcomes, particularly for children." (Review, 2007). However, mediation is not a universal panacea and it is not always suitable. The British Crime Survey 1992 found that the two most significant factors associated with risks of domestic abuse were if the women were separated or divorced and if they had children. Research studies have shown that women are at greatest risk when they attempt to leave an abusive relationship and/or seek outside help, particularly where there are children. Violence continues and sometimes escalates after separation. There are strongly held views that mediation is not suitable in cases involving violence or intimidation and that a consensual decision-making process is not possible between victim and abuser. These are major concerns that need special attention. The frequency with which violence erupts between couples behind the closed doors of their home is often not recognised. Reported violence is the tip of the iceberg. A three-year study in Bristol found that 40% of recently divorced couples reported that there had been physical violence in their marriage (Borkowski et al., 1983), while researchers in the United States have found that at least half the custody and access disputes referred to family court mediation services involved some violence (Thoennes et al., 1995). Contact between parents when collecting or returning children may be a flashpoint when further violence occurs. It is also extremely important to be aware that children are likely to have suffered physical abuse themselves in as many as 40–60% of domestic violence cases (Hester and Radford, 1992). In 90% of domestic violence cases, children were in the same room or the next room when the violence took place. The impact on a child of witnessing and/or suffering violence and fearing further violence is deeply traumatising and may be damaging to the child's development in the long term.

When the use of mediation grew in the United States during the 1980s, there was opposition from women's rights groups and feminists. The strongest objections were to mandatory mediation, where women who had experienced physical violence were ordered to take part in mediation with the abusive partner. Opponents of mediation objected that physical safety could not be ensured and that face-to-face meetings would increase risks of further violence occurring. The greatest risk could be immediately after a mediation meeting, if anger flared up again after leaving the meeting. There was heated controversy on these issues in the United States, involving many different organisations and professions. Legislation was enacted in at least sixteen American states exempting women who had been victims of violence from mandatory mediation. Women's groups tend to be strongly opposed to mediation whenever domestic abuse is an issue. Yet some women in certain circumstances want an opportunity to talk to their partner or former partner in a safe forum, with the help of one or more impartial and competent mediators. Particular safeguards may be needed. Careful screening for domestic violence and child protection issues is a pre-condition for family mediation in England and Wales.

Assessing suitability for family mediation

Before mediation takes place, each party is invited to attend an initial information and assessment meeting separately or together, as preferred. State-recognised family mediators in England and Wales are required to assess the suitability of mediation in the circumstances of each case. Mediators are trained to screen for domestic abuse and/or child protection issues and to recognise when another form of assistance or court process is needed, rather than mediation. Each participant should be seen separately at some point, even if they choose to come together, because an effective check cannot be done in the presence of a violent or potentially violent partner. There are at least five different categories of domestic abuse that have indications or contra-indications for mediation. Mediators need to be able to recognise and distinguish between these categories in making risk assessments. Research in different jurisdictions has shown that mediation may be helpful in some circumstances where some degree of violence has occurred, whereas in others, it could heighten dangers for adults and for children (Johnston and Campbell, 1993). Mediators need to be aware that being subjected to continual psychological and verbal abuse can be even more destructive of morale than physical violence. Participants in mediation should not be exposed to further risk or forced to negotiate if either party feels bullied or intimidated.

When the suitability of mediation is being considered, there may be warning lights that flash amber, without showing the clear and steady red that rules out mediation altogether. When there are amber lights, mediators may offer shuttle mediation, moving between participants in different rooms until safety is established and there is confidence to meet together. Such arrangements should be used sparingly, as family mediation seeks to help separated parents to communicate directly, rather than through intermediaries. Male-female co-mediation is very useful in high conflict and other special circumstances. The initial information and assessment meeting can allay fears and encourage trust in the safety of the mediation process and in the competence of the mediator(s). Mediation also needs to be suitable for different ethnic groups and cross-cultural couples. Ethnic minority groups need to be assured that mediators are able to address the needs of different traditions and cultures.

The shift towards seeing the child as the subject of rights

In the past, children were regarded as property, rather than as individuals in their own right. In different cultures and different periods in history, children have been regarded as the property of the father or as the property of the mother. In some cultures, this is still the case. As societies came to recognise responsibilities towards children, the child came to be seen as the object of parental love and care and, when necessary, state protection. Under divorce laws in many jurisdictions, the divorce court's paramount concern is the welfare of the child and the court has power to make orders concerning the child's residence, contact with the non-residential parent and other matters. The child is generally a passive bystander in these proceedings. However, there is a shift towards recognising that children have rights, as well as needs. In England and Wales and also in Scotland, the wishes and feelings of the child are factors that the court needs to take into account in making decisions concerning the child. If we think of children as subjects of rights and not only as recipients of care and protection, we are likely to approach decisions concerning children in a different way. We are more likely to consider whether and how children themselves should be consulted, without giving them responsibility for decisions. The child's right to have his or her wishes and feelings taken into account is upheld in Article 12 of the United Nations Convention on the Rights of the Child, adopted by the U.N. General Assembly in 1989. This Article states that in any matter or procedure affecting the child, the views of the child are to be given due weight, in accordance with the child's age and maturity.

Although children have the right to be consulted about matters that concern them, it seems that children are rarely consulted in practice. A study carried out at the Centre for Family Research at the University of Cambridge (Morrow, 1998) found that most children wanted to have a say in matters affecting them. Even young children could understand and talk about the notion of having rights and being listened to. Some children wanted to be heard and involved in decision making, whereas others wanted to be consulted but were anxious not to be given responsibility for choices or decisions. On the other hand, children who have had particularly bad experiences may demand the right to decide, because they know their needs and continuing risks. The majority of children who have talked to researchers about these questions feel that children should have opportunities to talk about their feelings and be consulted (Cockett and Tripp, 1994; Smart and Neale, 2000). An English Appeal Court judge has observed *"a growing understanding of the importance of listening to the children involved in children's cases. It is the child, more than anyone else, who will have to live with what the court decides. Those who do listen to children understand that they often have a point of view that is quite distinct from that of the person looking after them."* (Hale, 2007).

Many parents believe they understand their children's wishes and feelings. Mitchell (1985) found that some parents who claimed to know their child's views attributed their own views to the child, without realising that the child might have different views. If the child's view will influence the court's decision, children may be put under pressure or manipulated to say what a parent wants them to say. A further difficulty is that professionals do not necessarily agree on whether or how to seek children's views. There is a wide spectrum of opinion. Family mediators generally believe that parents should be empowered in mediation to reach their own decisions. Some mediators consider that involving children directly would undermine the parents' authority and the mediator's impartiality. In contrast, some family mediation centres have a positive policy of consulting with children and encouraging parents to be more aware of their children's views and feelings, on the grounds that parenting ability may be diminished in the stress of separation and divorce. Child-inclusive mediation offers benefits to children and parents, provided that there is careful preliminary planning about whether to involve the child and appropriate ways of doing so. There must be joint parental agreement, clarity about the family mediator's role and confidentiality, and informed consent from the child. Mediators need skills and experience in communicating with children. Family mediators in England and Wales are required to have additional training before they may undertake child-inclusive mediation.

Children's reactions to parental separation and divorce

Most children are upset when their parents separate. For children as well as for parents, the time of greatest stress and uncertainty is usually around the time of parental separation, rather than the divorce itself. Communication between parents often breaks down during separation and children may be left in the dark. If they do not know what is happening, they are confused and scared. Younger children often imagine that the separation is their fault. In the Exeter Family Study (Cockett and Tripp, 1994), children who had experienced separation and divorce were more likely than children in intact families to have health problems (especially psychosomatic disorders), to need extra help at school, to lack friends and to suffer from low self-esteem. However, the long-term consequences of separation and divorce for children are not inevitably harmful (Rodgers and Prior, 1994; Mooney et al. 2009). When parents co-operate following separation, children can adjust well. Longitudinal research shows that good quality parent-child relationships and flexible arrangements can reduce many of the potentially negative effects of separation on children's well being (Emery, 2004). What matters most for children is how their parents handle the separation and how they explain important changes to their children. Prolonged conflict between parents and the amount of physical disruption the children experience are significant factors. Parents who took part in the Exeter study admitted that they had known little about the process of divorce and how to organise post-divorce parenting. Many were aware of their reduced ability to communicate with each other and make sensible decisions during the early stages of separation when they were under particular stress. Many studies (e.g. Wallerstein and Kelly, 1980; Emery, 2004) have shown that when separated parents are able to agree arrangements and co-operate in parenting their children, children's adjustment to divorce is greatly eased.

Children's transitions through parental separation and divorce are therefore affected by the level of conflict or co-operation between parents, prior to and following separation, and by the support children receive in maintaining relationships with both parents and with other key people in their lives. If a loved parent suddenly disappears, a child is likely to suffer overwhelming grief and sadness, together with anger, confusion, a sense of rejection and self-blame. Some children do not recover from the total loss of a parent and these children may suffer from depression long after the divorce itself. A study involving 467 children aged 5-16 living in diverse family situations found that 25% of the children of separated parents said *no one* had talked to them about the separation (Dunn and Deater Deckard, 2001). Children do not always react in ways that correspond to their chronological age. Knowledge and understanding of child and adolescent development are important in helping parents to understand their children's reactions. It is also important to understand the child's individual personality, family history and family circumstances. In considering reactions at different developmental stages, chronological age is only a rough guide. Emotional and psychological maturity does not correlate closely with chronological age, and adults often underestimate children's capacity to understand feelings and relationships. Parents who think a child is too young to understand what is happening may be seeking to protect themselves, rather than the child. When children are struggling and not getting enough support, they often show their distress in behaviour, rather than words. The way in which they show their feelings may cause further conflict if each parent interprets the child's behaviour in a different way and blame each other for causing the problems. The following summary lists common reactions from children found by researchers in California (Wallerstein and Kelly, 1980), who undertook a longitudinal study with sixty families going through divorce. 131 children in the study group were seen over a five-year period. This study group was not representative of divorcing families generally and not all children show the reactions described by these researchers, but other researchers have found similar reactions (Emery, 1994). A great deal depends on how parents manage parental and child-parent relationships.

Pre-school children age 2-5 years

- Confusion, anxiety and fear: children are very confused and unsure about the changes in their family life, because the parents themselves are often unsure how to explain what is happening to children of this age.
- Strong reconciliation fantasies: children cling to hopes that their parents will get back together again and make up fantasies to comfort themselves.
- Increased aggression: the children's anger often stems from their feelings of loss and rejection. Their sense of loss when one parent disappears from their lives, often unaccountably, may lead to aggressive behaviour towards siblings, parents and in school. The remaining parent may be so preoccupied that the child receives less attention from this parent as well, increasing their sense of loss and rejection.
- Guilt feelings: children often imagine that they are to blame for their parents not getting on together. They may assume that their own naughtiness was the reason for a parent leaving them.
- Regression: children may demonstrate their anxiety and insecurity by lapses in toilet training, reverting to bed-wetting, showing increased clinging behaviour, increased fears – of the dark, for example – or developing feeding problems. Parents who are already strained may find these behaviour problems very hard to understand and tolerate.

Primary school age 5-7 years

- Pervasive sadness and grieving: this may be related to the level of turmoil in the home, but many children are intensely sad even when parents are not sad
- Yearning for an absent parent: similar to grieving for a dead parent but with greater feelings of rejection
- Feelings of abandonment and fear: there are often fears of being forgotten and of losing the remaining parent as well
- Anger: children often direct anger at whichever parent they believe responsible for the breakdown
- Conflicts of loyalty: the child feels caught between the parents and does not know how to be loyal to both
- Worry about parents' inability to cope: the more the child experiences parents having problems coping with the separation, the more the child becomes fearful that a parent they rely on is no longer going to be able to care for them
- Reconciliation fantasies.

Middle school age 8-12 years

- Children at this stage are more aware of the causes and consequences of divorce and more likely to take sides in parental conflicts
- Profound feelings of loss, rejection, helplessness and loneliness
- Feelings of shame, moral indignation and outrage at their parents' behaviour
- Extreme anger, temper tantrums, demanding behaviour

- Fears, phobias and denial
- Increased psychosomatic complaints: headaches, stomach aches, sleep disorders
- Making judgements: identifying one parent as the good parent and the other parent as the bad parent; rejecting the 'bad parent'
- Allying with one parent – not necessarily with the one to whom they feel closest
- Reduced self-esteem: the child may have difficulty concentrating at school and under-perform at school
- Acting out: some children, especially boys, are more likely to act out their distress and may become involved in delinquent behaviour.

Adolescents age 13-18 years

- Loss of childhood: older children may be burdened by increased responsibility for younger siblings and by the demands of an emotionally dependent parent
- Pressure to make choices – some parents expect older children to make their own decisions about visiting the other parent or which parent they want to live with
- Conflict between wanting to see an absent parent and wanting to keep up with peer group activities
- Worry about money: resentful that they may receive less than their friends, pressure on parents to compensate for the divorce by giving them more materially
- Heightened awareness and embarrassment about their parents' sexual behaviour and parents' involvement with new partners
- Jealousy of a parent's new partner

- Fears about forming long-term relationships and putting trust in people
- Depression: withdrawal, refusal to communicate
- Delinquency: stealing, drug-taking.

Young adults age 18 upwards

Young adults may be financially independent and less affected by their parents' break-up than younger children. However, students in higher education need a home to come back to and may be dependent on financial support from their parents. Equally importantly, older children often worry a great deal about their parents and are likely to be involved emotionally in their parents' troubles. Some parents depend heavily on older children – as well as on younger ones – for emotional support and practical help. Parenting roles may be reversed. An adolescent or even a young child may take on responsibility for looking after a parent who is unwell or unable to function properly. Taking care of an emotionally dependent parent is a great burden for children and adolescents. It can be very difficult for sensitive and conscientious children to free themselves from this burden and get on with their own lives.

Children's needs during separation and divorce

- Help to understand what is happening, with appropriate explanations according to their age and understanding and reassurance that they will continue to be loved and cared for
- Keeping their attachments and relationships with both parents and other important people in their lives
- Reassurance that they are in no way responsible for the break-up
- Emotional permission from each parent to go on loving the other parent
- Unless there are contra-indications involving risks or actual harm to the child, having regular and reliable contact with the parent who leaves home, including overnight stays and holidays. Many research studies have shown the importance for children to continue to have two caring parents who are able to co-operate with each other where the children are concerned (Wallerstein and Kelly, 1980; Emery, 2004).
- When their familiar world is changing, children benefit from extra attention and nurturing, especially at bed-time
- If possible, children need to stay in familiar surroundings. Although a move is often inevitable and sometimes welcomed, most children are attached to their home as well as to their parents. The disruption of moving home and changing schools adds to their confusion and stress and compounds the loss they experience.
- Children are helped if their own daily routine can be maintained as far as possible – both at school and at home
- Economic support, avoiding if possible a sudden sharp drop in living standards
- Parents who can make careful decisions and arrangements without involving the children too much or using the children for emotional support
- Knowing that each parent can manage, even if they no longer live together
- Parents who can still play and have fun with them.

Does 'joint custody' or 'shared care' mean that children spend equal time with each parent?

Some parents argue that parents should have equal rights in all respects, including the amount of time the children spend with each parent. Such arrangements can work well, but children have needs and rights of their own and there are risks that parents' concerns for equality result in children being shuttled to and fro like parcels. Research on the longer-term impact of family mediation found that reaching agreements in mediation is a vital component in maintaining co-operative relationships between divorcing parents (Emery, 2004). Family mediators help parents to consider possible arrangements and the benefits or difficulties for the child concerned. Children have a keen sense of fairness and they try hard to be fair to both parents. They may be very distressed if they think arrangements are unfair for one parent. Some will sacrifice their own needs in order to be loyal to both parents. When children move frequently between two homes, they may benefit a great deal from close continuing contact with both parents. However, such arrangements work better for some children than for others. Arrangements that work well at one stage may need to be varied as children grow up. Some children want to spend more time with one parent at a particular stage of their development, but fear hurting the other parent by saying so. Circular questions are particularly helpful in mediation in asking parents to put themselves in the child's place, without the mediator expressing opinions or giving advice. Parents often assume that their children's needs and feelings coincide with their own. Asking them how they think the child would respond to a particular question helps them to reflect.

Steinman (1981) found that frequent moves between two homes require:

- good co-operation and communication between parents who are clear about parenting tasks and day-to-day responsibilities
- willingness by parents to be flexible, within a clear structure
- physical proximity – reducing journey times to and fro
- the child not feeling burdened by responsibility to maintain total fairness
- good management of practicalities – having duplicates of some things in each home to avoid the child carrying everything to and fro
- encouragement for the child to take part in peer group activities – this is increasingly important as the child gets older
- willingness to listen to the child and recognise when an arrangement is no longer working well for the child.

For many parents, shared care is not possible because of housing costs and the time and cost of frequent commuting between two households. When parents live a long way apart, shared parenting may involve children spending longer periods away from their familiar environment and friends. The child's age, temperament and resilience need to be considered carefully, if the child is to manage frequent moves between different environments.

Including children in mediation indirectly

Some parents see issues over children as their main reason for coming to mediation, whereas others may be primarily concerned to settle financial issues. Parents are understandably preoccupied with their own problems and if there is no apparent disagreement over children, mediators should be careful about raising questions that parents have not asked to discuss. In the UK, family mediators have no responsibility to investigate children's welfare and they cannot ensure the child's well being. The aim is to help parents to work out decisions and arrangements that take account of each child's needs and feelings and to facilitate communication between parents and children.

When parents disagree over their children, mediators' knowledge about children's needs in separation and divorce is a resource that can be offered to parents. Offering a resource to assist parents' decision making is different from directive advice handed down by an expert. Parents' morale and self-confidence are often at low ebb. It is important to offer comments and questions thoughtfully, without any hint of criticism or imposing the mediator's own values. Parents may say that "the children are fine – there's no problem" because they are reluctant to admit even to themselves that their children are suffering as a result of the break-up. It is painful for parents to recognise that they have hurt their children. Mediators need to ask about children carefully and sensitively, without appearing to cast doubt on the parents' assertion that all is well. Focused questions are useful in clarifying how current arrangements are working. It may emerge that the arrangements are not working very well and that parents are willing to discuss some changes

Asking parents to give a brief picture of each child

When parents disagree about their children, they tend to bring conflicting versions of events in order to justify their own point of view. A helpful beginning is to invite each parent to give a brief picture of each child, so that the child is more than just a name in the discussion. Parents are usually proud of their children and like talking about them. It is helpful to ask for a 'picture' of each child before addressing difficult issues. Describing each child's personality and interests helps parents to focus on each child as an individual. It also serves a number of other purposes:

- sharing information about children. Often the parent who is involved in the day-to-day care of the children knows more than the other. Asking the residential parent to describe a child's personality and interests can be a means of updating the non-residential parent.
- there are often large areas of agreement even between parents who are in dispute over contact arrangements. Areas of agreement can be emphasised and some parents are surprised to find how far they are in agreement.
- easing communication in a non-threatening, non-adversarial way, allowing both parents to talk about matters that are often uncontroversial.
- establishing some balance and ground-rules by demonstrating that the mediator will ask each parent and give each of them time to respond.

- when conflict is high, focused questions about children help to contain and manage conflict.

The boundaries of the family mediator's role

In Sweden, qualified social workers trained in family law undertake 'co-operation talks' with separated parents concerning child custody and access, to help them to reach agreements and co-operate over their children. Under a law introduced in 1991, the municipalities in Sweden must provide co-operation talks for any parents who request it or who are referred for such talks by the court. These co-operation talks are free and confidential. Following a modification of the law in 1998, an agreement concerning custody and access reached by parents through family mediation has the same juridical status as a court decision, provided that the agreement has been approved by the social worker (familjerätts-socionom) in charge of the case as being in the best interest of the child. This gives the social worker a dual responsibility to safeguard the welfare of the child while also assisting parents to reach agreements.

Social workers in England and Wales who work for Cafcass (Children and Family Court Advisory and Support Service) have a similar role in undertaking conciliation with parents involved in court proceedings over residence of and/or contact with their children. *Conciliation* and *mediation* need to be distinguished as intrinsically different processes. In England and Wales, *conciliation* takes place under the court's direction and is provided by Cafcass social workers. It is activated by the court at the commencement of court proceedings, usually at first appointment. The outcome of conciliation is reportable to the court. *Mediation* is a confidential and independent process offering opportunities for parents to reach their own agreements while also providing a resource for court referral in suitable cases. The court may make referrals to mediation and has power to order attendance at a mediation information meeting as a 'contact activity' but under English law, the court cannot order mediation itself.

Mediation is recognised as a confidential process in the European Directive on Mediation issued by the Council of the European Union on 28 February 2008. This Directive has particular reference to international cross-border family mediation and is due to be implemented by Member States by 2011. In England and Wales, individuals may refer themselves or be referred to mediation by their legal advisors prior to court application, as well as following court proceedings if an order or agreement breaks down or needs to be changed. Meetings are held in the premises of private and independent family mediation services. Under current law, legal advisors must refer clients seeking legal aid for family matters (not only children issues) to an information and assessment meeting with a qualified and State-recognised family mediator. Mediation is arranged if both parties are willing and mediation is found to be suitable in the circumstances. Compulsory referral to mediation information and assessment meetings is likely to be introduced in 2011 in most family law cases prior to court proceedings, extending the requirement to consider mediation to private clients as well as to those eligible for legal aid. Initial information meetings serve a number of functions that can assist people in a number of ways, even where mediation does not take place. The voluntary engagement of both parties in the mediation process is seen as very important.

The following table may help to clarify the roles of family mediators and conciliators in England and Wales.

Mediation	Conciliation
Mainly prior to court application, most clients referred by legal advisors/representatives, courts increasingly encouraged to refer.	Court referral to conciliation is made following court application on children issues.
Essentially voluntary but attendance at information and assessment meeting with recognised mediator compulsory for legal aid applicants prior to court application. Court may make referral to mediation at any stage of proceedings, including appellate level, but cannot order parties to mediate. The court can order attendance at a mediation information meeting (but not mediation itself) as a contact activity (Children and Adoption Act 2006).	Parties in private law disputes over children are expected to take part in conciliation on direction of the judge. Conciliation is thus imbued with the court's authority.
Private and independent, mainly out of court. Courts may also refer parties to a mediator who may be available in court on the day. Mediation may continue out of court if both parties willing.	Conciliation often takes place at court in court hearing.
Participants are charged fees if ineligible for legal aid.	Free of charge.
All issues – children, family home, finance etc. Not only separation and divorce – grandparent contact and other proceedings over children.	Children issues only.
Independent, qualified mediators do not report to court.	Cafcass social workers are officers of the court.
Impartial and non-directive: parties encouraged to co-operate and to take account of children's needs, parties remain in control of their own decisions, with legal advice from their own solicitors.	Not neutral – welfare of child is paramount and conciliator may be directive in seeking settlement on residence and/or contact.
Confidential and legally privileged, but both parties may give joint consent for mediation summary to be made available to the Court to facilitate consent order.	Conciliation by Cafcass is not privileged, outcome reportable to the court.
Facilitates dialogue, often several sessions, seeks individualised and flexible arrangements for children.	Usually a one-off meeting, one hour on average. Tends to produce standardised agreements.
Wide spectrum from co-operative to high conflict.	Difficult disputes over children.
May change attitudes and perceptions and have longer-term effects in improving relationships.	Unlikely to change attitudes or relationships.
Agreements reached in mediation by the parties themselves (with court orders made with consent where needed) more likely to last over time.	Research (Trinder et al., 2002) shows conciliated agreements are more liable to break down, but some parents renegotiate contact arrangements.

A family mediator in England and Wales is not the child's legal representative or advocate for the child's welfare, nor a counsellor or therapist for the child. If family mediators see children, they should be careful not to make interpretations of a child's feelings and wishes, such as a child psychologist or therapist might make. The mediator's role is a simpler and more limited one – to offer children and adolescents an opportunity to express their views, needs and feelings and to facilitate communication between children and parents. Parents need to listen to their children as well as explain things to them. When there are difficulties, family mediators can offer additional suggestions, resources and options.

Including children directly in mediation

When separated parents are in dispute over their children's needs, children can be helped to talk with a skilled and impartial third party, without the further trauma of involvement in court proceedings. Child-focused and child-inclusive family mediation help parents to consider the needs and feelings of their children. As well as agreeing residence and visiting arrangements that take account of the child's needs, parents are helped to consider what their children need to hear and how to respond to their children's wishes and feelings. Many children do not take part in mediation directly because they are too young or because parents prefer to talk to them at home. When one parent is in favour of seeking a child's views and the other parent is against the idea, or even where both parents are strongly in favour, possible problems in involving children directly need to be considered, as well as possible benefits. It is important to clarify objectives and confidentiality, before any decision is taken.

Reasons that may be given for not involving children in mediation
- children are not responsible for their parents' conflict and should not be drawn into it
- involving children increases their distress and confusion
- children will be upset if they become more aware of parental conflict
- children should not be involved in adult negotiations
- power imbalances between parents and children lie outside the boundaries of mediation
- empowering a child risks dis-empowering one or both parents
- parents' decision-making authority is undermined if the mediator acts as an expert
- the mediator's role may be confused with the role of counsellor or child advocate
- involving children may create expectations that things will be made better for them
- children may feel under pressure to express their views and feelings
- children may fear being asked to make a choice
- children may not be reliable judges of their own long-term interests
- the mediator may become triangulated between parents and child
- the mediator could be left holding secrets or confidences from a child that the child does not want shared with parents: this would be an untenable position for the mediator

- the child's conflicts of loyalty may be heightened
- parents may be unable to manage their distress in front of the children
- parents may pressurise and brief the child on what to say to the mediator
- feedback to parents afterwards may result in them being angry with the child
- young children who see their parents talking in a friendly way may think their parents are going to get back together again – feeding hopes of reconciliation.

Benefits of involving children in family mediation
- the majority of the children studied have reported benefits (Garwood, 1989; Saposnek, 1991; McIntosh, 2000)
- explanations and reassurance can be given to children
- children can adjust more easily if they understand their parents' decisions more clearly
- involving children shows them that their views and feelings matter and that they are treated with respect
- listening to children is a way of showing care
- may help both parents to listen to their children
- parents may explain their decisions and arrangements to their children in a family meeting (some parents need the mediator's support to do this)
- dispel misunderstandings: for example, that a child does not want to see a parent when the child actually wants to do so
- give children opportunities to ask questions, comment and contribute their ideas

- enable children to express a worry or concern, such as where the family's pets will live
- ease communication and reducing tensions in parent-child relationships
- give children an opportunity to talk about their feelings and concerns, without being anxious about how parents will react
- help children to work out the messages they may want to give to their parents (or other people involved) and to feel able to give these messages
- enable a child to receive a message from a parent who cannot give it directly, for some reason
- with the child's agreement, give feedback to parents to help them understand the child's concerns and feelings, so that these can be taken into account in the parents' decisions.

Mediators should encourage parents to explore the options and sources of help available. When parents think that a child should be involved in some way, there is important planning to do with the parents before any meeting is arranged with the child or children directly.

Exploring possible ways of involving children
Some parents may prefer a relative, family friend, counsellor, educational psychologist or other person close to the child to talk with the child. If this person is expected to report back to the parents what the child has said, this will raise problems for the child, because children see confidentiality as a key issue. Mediators can explore with parents whether there are family member/s, friends or professionals who can talk with children individually or with siblings

together, in a way that would be acceptable and helpful to each child. Exploring these possibilities with parents is a way of considering options and there are often many considerations to work through.

Some parents decide that they would like to include the children in a family meeting with the mediator present, to help them explain things to the children with the mediator's help. Depending on the age of the child or adolescent and particular circumstances, other parents may ask the mediator to see a child alone. Parents may think it would be particularly helpful for an adolescent to be consulted and given a chance to talk alone with an impartial third person who knows both parents but who is not emotionally involved. Some adolescents welcome having a space to talk through their feelings and decisions, especially when they are old enough to take decisions themselves. Occasionally there are direct requests from children who ask to meet the mediator, because they know that the mediator has detailed knowledge of their family situation, whereas a school counsellor may not have this detailed knowledge and is often not in contact with both parents. Many children are anxious not to be labelled as having problems and needing counselling. Even young children are able to understand that mediation is not the same as counselling or therapy and that the mediator is not a social worker or investigator.

If there are suggestions that the mediator might meet with a child without the parents being present, there are questions to consider such as: should siblings be seen together or separately? Is the mediator expected to report back to the parents, or to anyone else? A model developed in Australia involves a specially trained child counsellor who meets with the child and then gives feedback to the parents and the mediator together (McIntosh, 2000). There are resource implications to consider in developing these models, but the main considerations should be the needs and preferences of the parents and child concerned as well as careful consideration of potential benefits for the child.

Research has been undertaken on different ways of including children in mediation. In some family mediation centres, children may be invited to meet with the mediator without the parents being present, albeit with their full agreement. 24 out of 28 children interviewed in a follow-up study in Edinburgh (Garwood, 1989) said they had definitely benefited from seeing the mediator. The other four said everything was all right for them anyway, so it had not made much difference. Research in Australia compared child-focused mediation, in which children did not take part directly, with child-inclusive mediation in which children met with a child counsellor (McIntosh, 2008). In both groups in the year following mediation, the researchers found lasting reductions in levels of conflict and improved management of disputes, as reported by the parents and the children. The child-inclusive group showed more significant improvements in parental and child-parent relationships, particularly between fathers and children, and more noticeable benefits in children's developmental recovery from high-conflict separation.[1] These services are of course time-consuming and costly and high-quality professional training is very important.

Research in Britain and Australia shows that children are more competent to take part in family decision making than adults generally believe. We need to take time and trouble to listen to what children tell us and to understand how they feel. The challenges of consulting with children and young people concerning changes in their family life are considerable for all concerned. Adults need sensitivity and awareness, non-judgmental attitudes and a good sense of humour. With these qualities and good professional training, professionals are likely to find conversations with children illuminating and life-enhancing, despite the sadness and anger felt by many children when they lose the security of living with both parents in an intact family. Children understand far more than adults generally imagine and insights and practical suggestions from children can often help adults to resolve problems in ways that will work as well as possible for the family as a whole.[2]

Notes

1. McIntosh J. et al. (2008), 'Child-Focused and Child-Inclusive Divorce Mediation' *Family Courts Review*, Association of Family and Conciliation Courts, Vol. 46, No.1.
2. Much of this chapter can be found in Lisa Parkinson's book, "Family Mediation" (Sweet & Maxwell, 1997) and/or in the 2nd edition (Jordan Publishing, in press).

References

Borkowski M., Murch M., and Walker V., 'Marital Violence', Tavistock, (1983).

Cockett M. and Tripp J., 'The Exeter Family Study: Family Breakdown and its impact on children', University of Exeter Press, (1994).

Dunn J. and Deater-Deckard K., 'Children's Views of their Changing Families', Joseph Rowntree Research Findings 931, (September 2001).

Emery R. 'The Truth about Children and Divorce', Viking, (2004).

Garwood F., 'Children in Conciliation', Scottish Association of Family Conciliation Services, (1989).

Hale, Baroness of Richmond, in 'Re D (A Child)', AC 619 FLR, (2007).

Hester M. and Radford L., 'Domestic Violence and Child Contact in England and Denmark', Polity Press, (1996).

Hunt J., 'Parental Perspectives on the Family Justice System in England and Wales: a review of research', (2009).

Johnston J. and Campbell L., 'A clinical typology of interparental violence in disputed custody divorces', *American Journal of Orthopsychiatry*, 63 (2), pp. 190-199, (1993).

McIntosh J. et al., 'Child-Focused and Child-Inclusive Divorce Mediation' *Family Courts Review*, Association of Family and Conciliation Courts, Vol. 46, No.1, (2008).

Mitchell A., 'Children in the Middle', Tavistock Publications, London, (1985).

Mooney, A. et al., 'Impact of Family Breakdown on Children's Well being: Evidence Review', London, DCSF, (2009).

Morrow, V., 'Children's Perspectives on Families', Rowntree Research Findings 798, York, (July 1998).

National Audit Office, 'Survey of Family Mediation', (March 2007).

Parkinson L., 'Separation, Divorce and Families', BASW/Macmillan, (1987).
'Family Mediation', Sweet & Maxwell, (1997).
'Child-Inclusive Family Mediation', *Family Law*, (June 2006).

Rodgers, B. and Pryor, J., 'Divorce and separation: the outcomes for children', Joseph Rowntree Foundation, (1994).

Saposnek D., 'The Value of Children in Mediation – a cross-cultural perspective', *Mediation Quarterly*, (1991), vol. 8. no 4.

Smart C., Neale B., 'It's My Life Too – Children's Perspectives on Post-Divorce Parenting', *Family Law*, (2000).

Smart C., Neale B. and Wade A., 'The Changing Experience of Childhood: Families and Divorce', Polity Press, (2001).

Steinman S., 'The Experience of Children in a Joint Custody Arrangement', *American Journal of Orthopsychiatry*, (1981), Vol. 51.

Trinder L. et al., 'Making contact: How parents and children negotiate and experience contact after divorce', Joseph Rowntree Foundation Research Findings 092, (October 2002).

Trinder, L. et al., 'Making Contact happen or making contact work? The process and outcomes of in-court conciliation', DCA Research Series 3/06, (2006).

Thoennes N., Salem P., Pearson J., 'Mediation and domestic violence: current policies and practices', Family and *Conciliation Courts Review*, Vol. 33 (1), (1995).

Wallerstein J. and Kelly J., 'Surviving the Break-up – how children and parents cope with divorce', Grant McIntyre, (1980).

CHAPTER 6

Family Violence and Family Mediation in Australia

By mediator Dale Bagshaw, PhD[1]

In this chapter, the author provides an overview of recent family violence research in Australia in the family law field, and implications for family mediators. She argues that family mediators need to be aware of the gendered and complex nature and effects of domestic or family violence, which is prevalent in most, if not all, cultures in the world, in particular when mediating disputes during and after separation and divorce. Family violence occurs at all levels of society and is often hard to detect as the control aspects are often hidden, subtle and complex, and victims are too intimidated, fearful or ashamed to disclose the abuse. Family mediators must therefore be educated and trained to recognise and screen for violence and abuse in family relationships, not only prior to mediation but also during the process. If mediators decide to mediate where there is family violence, they must ensure that they have the appropriate expertise and put safeguards in place to ensure that the participants are safe and that mediated outcomes are fair and just for all involved.

Introduction

Domestic violence is prevalent in most, if not all countries and cultures in the world[1] so it is important for mediators of all cultural persuasions to be mindful of the tensions between the promotion of peaceful resolutions to conflict through mediation and the importance of making sure that the mediation process and outcomes are socially just and address the human rights of all involved, in particular the rights and safety of those who are relatively powerless, such as women and children.

In this chapter, I briefly examine the prevalence, definitions and nature of domestic or family violence in Australia and the implications for family mediators who are mediating disputes during and after separation and divorce. I argue that family mediators need to be aware of the gendered and complex nature of family violence and must be educated and trained to screen for violence and abuse in family relationships, not only prior to mediation but also during the process, to ensure that the participants are safe and that mediated outcomes are fair and just for all involved and/or that appropriate referrals are made.

Domestic violence occurs at all levels of all societies and is very hard to detect as generally the victims are too intimidated, fearful or ashamed to report the abuse. In 1996 and 2005 national personal safety surveys were conducted in Australia: one in four Australian women reported experiencing domestic violence and ex-partners were the group identified as the most common perpetrators of violence against women. In the 2005 survey, approximately one in three of the women surveyed said they had experienced physical violence in their lifetime, and almost one in five had experienced sexual violence. In a twelve month period, 31% of these women who said they were physically assaulted were assaulted by a current or previous partner (compared to 4.4% of men) and in 49% of these cases children were present.[2]

Women and children are most at risk during separation and divorce, when family mediators are likely to be asked to intervene. Family mediators need special knowledge and skills, therefore, to recognise and respond to different forms and levels of violence and to know when and how to refer, and when and under what conditions they should proceed with mediation. Mediators also need to be aware of their own professional and cultural conditioning, personal values and tendencies to stereotype, which may prevent them from picking up signals that violence is occurring and lead them to respond inappropriately.

Definitions and nature of violence against women

The World Health Organisation's World Report (2008)[3] of a multi-country study of 'Violence against women by intimate partners', noted that in all of the countries in their study, "one of the most common forms of violence against women is that performed by a husband or male partner." They also noted that "this type of violence is frequently invisible since it happens behind closed doors, and effectively, when legal systems and cultural norms do not treat it as a crime, but rather as a 'private' family matter, or a normal part of life." The violence they identified in their study included 'physical and sexual violence, emotional abuse and controlling behaviours by current partners or ex-partners', which had serious consequences for women's health worldwide.

There are many definitions of domestic or family violence in use. The following definition captures the gendered nature of violence and outlines the broad range of behaviours that many studies have found commonly occur in domestic violence situations. It was framed by the 'Partnerships Against Domestic Violence Statement of Principles' agreed by the Australian Heads of Government at the 1997 National Domestic Violence Summit:[4]

> Domestic violence is an abuse of power perpetrated mainly (but not only) by men against women both in relationship and after separation. It occurs when one partner attempts physically or psychologically to dominate and control the other. Domestic violence takes a number of forms. The most commonly acknowledged forms are physical and sexual violence, threats and

intimidation, emotional and social abuse and economic deprivation.

Generally the most persistent and controlling forms of violence (described by Johnson as 'intimate terrorism') are perpetrated by men toward women and give rise to fear and intimidation.[5] Gender-neutral laws and definitions tend not to recognise the coercive pattern of men's physical violence, intimidation and control of their female partners, whose descriptions of living in fear are rarely replicated by men.[6] It must be acknowledged that a much smaller percentage of men are also abused by women, but the nature and effect of the abuse tend be different.

One research study of domestic violence that I co-led in South Australia (2000)[7] confirmed the findings of many other researchers in this field, previously and since that time. The victims (who were mostly women) reported that they found it extremely difficult to leave abusive situations and found family violence hard to report for many reasons. Many thought that 'domestic' or 'family violence' was only physical even though they were experiencing other extremely controlling and belittling forms of behaviour. Others did not want to shame their family or had been brainwashed into feeling responsible for the violence and blamed themselves. Some feared losing contact with their children or thought that they and/or their children would be harmed if they reported it. Some feared that they would not be believed. Others still loved their partner (when they were not being abusive) and hoped they would change. Given that violent episodes tend to occur in cycles, many victims described how the perpetrator could be very loving and remorseful between violent episodes, but most reported that over time the frequency and levels of violence and control increased. Victims were often isolated from family and friends by the perpetrator, did not have enough funds to leave or to employ a lawyer, and did not know where to go for assistance. When women did leave they were often rendered homeless. Younger and older women, women with disabilities, from indigenous or culturally and linguistically diverse backgrounds and from rural areas were doubly disadvantaged.[8]

In Australia, family violence is significant in the population of families that attend for dispute resolution and other support services during separation and divorce and is even more likely to be present in the client population that proceeds to trial in the family court system.[9] 'Intimate partner homicide' reports indicate that abused women are most at risk when separating from their partners – at the extreme end of domestic violence, murder is the ultimate attempt to exert power and control.[10] It is imperative, therefore, that the safety of women and children be given priority in all dispute resolution processes during and after separation and that all allegations of violence and abuse are treated seriously.

Recent research has shown that in spite of many studies of family violence and its prevalence in Australia,[11] the needs of these families and their children are currently not being attended to in any significant way in the Australian family law system, in particular where children who are at risk of abuse fall between the national family law system and the State child welfare systems.[12] A previous Australian

Government's initiative, 'Partnerships Against Domestic Violence', funded numerous research and evaluation of practice initiatives to address the problem, including two earlier studies undertaken by myself with colleagues.[13]

In 2009, the Australian Attorney-General's Department funded an unprecedented number of studies of the current family law system, three of which specifically examined family violence in the context of the changes made to Australia's Family Law Act (Cth), 1975 with the introduction of the Family Law (Shared Parental Responsibility) Amendment Act (Cth), 2006.[14] Many of the recommendations from these reports (including recommendations from our Family Law and Family Violence study described in the next section) have been incorporated into a new Family Law Amendment (Family Violence) Bill (Cth), 2010, which is currently before the Australian Parliament.

Since the family law changes in July 2006, separating couples have been required by law to see a family dispute resolution practitioner (mediator) before a judge will hear their case, but are exempt if they can provide evidence of family violence. The definition of family violence has also been amended in the Family Law Act and the word 'reasonably' added:

> Family violence means conduct. Whether actual or threatened, by a person towards, or towards the property of, a member of the person's family that causes that or any other member of the person's family to reasonably fear for, or reasonably to be apprehensive about, his or her personal well being or safety.[15]

This change has brought criticism as the word 'reasonably' is not defined and if allegations of violence cannot be substantiated sanctions can be imposed.

As previously explained, central to family violence is the inappropriate exercise of power and control, leading to fear and intimidation.[16] It is difficult, if not impossible, to make an objective assessment about a subjective emotion such as fear in order to say whether or not it is 'reasonable'.[17] There are also no definitions or guidelines as to what constitutes 'reasonable grounds' to believe there has been family violence or child abuse and it is not clear what evidence is required to substantiate such grounds.[18] Even where evidence can be provided, many adult victims choose to proceed with mediation, as the alternative is too costly. It is therefore important to focus on ways in which family mediators can effectively identify and respond to family violence to achieve safe and fair outcomes for those victims, who are usually women and children.[19]

The so called 'friendly parenting' provision contained in sec 60CC(3)(c) of the Family Law Act means that in essence when making a parenting order one of the factors the court is required to take into account is "the willingness and ability of each of the child's parents to facilitate and encourage a close and continuing relationship between the child and the other parent". Problematically, recent research has found that this section has discouraged parents from disclosing violence to the court for fear that if the allegations are unproven they will be viewed as an 'unfriendly parent' and the very children whom they are trying to protect will be exposed to the perpetrator for longer periods of time.[20]

A summary of the findings of the 'Family Violence and Family Law in Australia' study (2010)[21]

In 2009, I co-led one of four research projects which were commissioned by the Australian Attorney-General to investigate the effects of the 2006 changes to the Family Law Act (Cth), 1995. Our brief was to investigate adults' and children's experiences of family violence and the impact of that violence on their experiences and perspectives of family law services they had used post-1995 and post-2006, including family dispute resolution services (mediation). We conducted a national online survey for adults who had separated post-1995 and post-2006 (931 responses), a separate national online survey for children (105 responses), and two phone-in surveys for adults (105 responses) and children (12 responses), one in Queensland and one in South Australia. Family violence was an issue for most of the respondents (89.7% of women and 63% of men surveyed) and 65% of the women surveyed said they had ended their relationship because of family violence, involving researchers from the University of South Australia, Monash University and James Cook University.

In the qualitative responses in our study, women consistently said that fear of losing the primary care of their children was a major factor influencing decision making; for the men it was fear of losing contact with their children. One fifth of women who accessed services post-2006 said they felt 'forced' to agree or were 'bullied' into agreeing to equal time parenting arrangements. Most respondents (68.7% of women and 52.2% of men) were critical of their inability to achieve suitable and safe arrangements for themselves and their children after separation.

In the qualitative responses to the survey and the phone-ins, a large proportion of respondents, in particular women, who had accessed services from 2006 onwards, indicated that concerns for their safety and the safety of their children were not heard or considered when parenting decisions were made. A larger proportion of women than men stated that their children were 'not safe' when with the other parent. In 256 qualitative responses from mothers there were many repeated and overlapping statements about men's abusive behaviours toward their children and some of these were extreme. They described acts of psychological, emotional, verbal, sexual and physical abuse and neglect to which child victims were exposed as a result of inappropriate parenting arrangements and described many negative consequences for their children. At the extreme end, some women stated that their ex-partner had 'assaulted', 'hit' or 'thrown' the children across a room, had accessed 'guns' in front of the children, 'exposed' them to domestic violence, or 'threatened' to 'throw' their child down three flights of stairs, with a small number alleging that their children had been sexually abused by their father. In contrast, there was very little repetition or overlap in the 59 responses from fathers, partly because there were fewer and less detailed responses and the men tended to focus more on the mother's emotional and psychological abuse and abuse from a mother's male partner.

In contrast to the women's responses, very few of the men in the study (who were not partners or ex-partners of the female respondents) who said that their ex-partner was violent reported having been hurt by the other parent or that they had been fearful of the other parent. These findings replicated those of another large Australian Institute for Family Studies (AIFS) study where it was noted that mothers who held safety concerns were more likely than fathers to report that their relationship was a fearful one.[22]

In 2000, Bagshaw and Chung[23] argued that quantitative data alone cannot measure or show the more complex, non-physical aspects involved or the subtle nature of the abuse of power and control in family violence, which was evidenced in our 2010 study. An analysis of the quantitative data did not show the complex nature of family violence and the contextual differences in experiences of violence for males and females. However, the qualitative responses to questions in the survey and phone-ins regarding men's and women's experiences of violence showed that overwhelmingly the women and children were far more likely than the men to be the victims of severe abuse, intimidation and threats, giving rise to fear and intimidation.

The men and women surveyed constructed family violence differently – they reported different definitions, experiences and effects of violence and different responses to it and to their violent partners. This is consistent with the findings of other studies.[24] In qualitative responses women commonly reported violence toward them by men as unprovoked, more often physical (including destruction of property) and sexual. It was described in many different ways as an extreme form of social, emotional, psychological and financial control. Women more commonly reported serious violence by men (fathers, stepfathers and male relatives) towards their children. Women reported life threatening acts but men did not. One in three women reported extreme physical or sexual harm. Only one in seven men did.

One quarter of the women and just over one quarter of the men surveyed said that mental health problems and/or misuse of alcohol or other drugs and/or criminal activity were a factor in their concerns for the safety of their children following separation, factors which were also reported in the AIFS study. It is important to note that mental illness can be a cause, context for, or consequence of separation and can be caused by and/or exacerbate family violence and therefore all screening and assessment processes in family law matters should take this into account.[25]

Respondents were asked about the degrees of harm suffered as a result of the violence against them and their children. Women surveyed were more likely than men to report experiencing *considerable or extreme harm* from physical abuse (29% of women; 15% of men), sexual abuse (31% of women; 21% of men); emotional abuse (87% of women; 74% of men), and social abuse (72% of the men and 73% of the women) but more men reported experiencing financial harm (60% of men, 58% of the women).

Both women (54%) and men (46%) nominated implementing parenting arrangements, and making decisions about children (47% men, 55% women) as the contexts where violence against them was frequently or mostly occurring. In no context did a majority of men agree that violence was frequently or mostly occurring. Men's responses were mainly distributed to the 'never' or 'occasionally' end of the spectrum, whilst women's responses were skewed to the 'frequently' and 'mostly' end of the spectrum.

Being a victim of violence and being too afraid to tell anyone was a problem for around two in five of the women surveyed and one in three of the men. The post-2006 data showed that men's and women's experience of violence from their ex-partner, and being too afraid to tell anyone, affected around two in five men and women.

A minority of respondents whose ex-partner had used violence were advised by their lawyer not to raise it. Men (30%) were twice as likely to say they had been advised not to disclose their ex's violence than were women (16%). In the post-2006 cohort, 34% of men and 18% of women said they had been advised not to disclose their ex-partner's violence.

Only 60% of the respondents who attended Family Relationship Centres (FRCs) said they disclosed their experiences of family violence and only 10.5% of those who reported violence to a Family Dispute Resolution (FDR) Service were given an exemption from using the service. In this context, women were more likely than men not to disclose violence and twice as likely to report that family dispute resolution proceeded if family violence was disclosed.

Women (34%) were more likely than men (19%) to feel that the *allegations* of violence by their ex-partner were believed and taken seriously, but around half of both the men and women felt their allegations were not taken seriously. In the post-2006 data, 19.5% of men felt believed and taken seriously but

the proportion of women who felt this way dropped to 28%. This may indicate that the 2006 changes, which introduced penalties for false statements, fostered beliefs that allegations of violence were likely to be viewed as false if evidence could not be provided.

Men (24%) were more likely than women (15%) to feel their *denials* of family violence were believed. Men (41%) were also more likely than women (30%) to feel their denials of violence were not taken seriously. However, in the post-2006 cohort, 27% of the men felt their denials of family violence were taken seriously compared to 15% of the women.

Of 628 adult survey respondents (76 men and 295 women) to a question about children witnessing family violence, 58.9% said they had engaged in abusive behaviours with their ex-partner and their children had both *seen and heard* the violence. In addition, 11.9% said their children had *seen* the abuse and 15.9% said their children had *heard* the abuse. Only 13.1% said they had *neither seen nor heard* the violence. Fathers and mothers provided graphic accounts of how their children had been harmed emotionally, psychologically, socially, educationally and physically and some, sexually.

Prior research indicates a close connection between domestic violence and the abuse of children and pets.[26] Of the 65 children who answered a survey question, 52.3% (34) said they *saw or heard* their parents argue prior to separation. Significantly, 30% (18) reported that they were usually hurt or frightened following their parents' arguments. One child wrote: "you won't let me give you more answers so I did lots of things you put but mum killed my dog and my bird and I am not allowed to use a phone and no one can help me." Another child reported being held by her father while he was hitting her mother.

Children reported feelings of hopelessness and powerlessness – 39% of children surveyed said they did not feel safe when with their father after separation and 10% said they did not feel safe when with their mother. While 67.8% (40 of 59) of children reported that they felt frightened or scared when their parents fought post-separation, 52.5% (31) also felt helpless because they could not stop the fights and 28.8% (17) also thought that the arguments and fights were their fault. Other research suggests that parental arguments and fights can affect children's emotional health, especially their feelings of self-worth, agency and efficacy, and can lead to adjustment difficulties in later life.[27] All children said that they wanted to be consulted when parenting decisions were made and most felt that their voices had been marginalised in the family law system, in spite of the introduction of child-inclusive mediation in Australia.

Family mediation and family violence

As family mediation has grown in popularity in Australia, feminists have been concerned that the rights of the participants could be compromised in mediation, in particular those of women and children in situations where there are structural imbalances or abuses of power[28] In mediation there is the potential for women to be coerced into negotiating with their abusive partners or ex-partners in the privacy of the mediation room, in particular with a mediator who (in spite of screening) is not aware of the violence, or who has patriarchal attitudes, thereby placing the women's safety in jeopardy and making it difficult, if not impossible, for them to negotiate fair outcomes for themselves. The mediation field in Australia, along with family law policy-makers and legislators, have therefore paid close attention to this issue.

Three earlier reports were influential in ensuring that the issue of family violence was drawn to the attention of family mediation policy makers and practitioners when family mediation was first introduced in family law proceedings in Australia: Hilary Astor's 'Position Paper on Mediation' for the National Committee on Violence Against Women,[29] the Australian Bureau of Statistics' 'Women's Safety Australia'[30] and Keys Young's 1996 'Research Evaluation of Family Mediation Practice and the Issue of Violence'.[31] The Keys Young research indicated that abused women generally experienced less pre-mediation anxiety, a more positive experience of the mediation process and a higher level of satisfaction with agreements where they:

- had been subject to emotional abuse or one-off physical threats or threats only;
- had been separated from their ex-partners for a considerable time;
- had received personal counselling (as opposed to *relationship* counselling);
- reported that they no longer felt intimidated by their ex-partner; and

- felt confident in their legal advice and knew what they could reasonably expect from settlement;

and where *mediators*

- asked specific questions about violence and abuse, including non-physical types;
- offered women specific guidance in considering the possible impact of violence and abuse on the mediation process;
- offered women separate time with the mediator before, during and after sessions;
- worked as a gender-balanced, co-mediation team;
- demonstrated that they understood the women's concerns both within and outside the mediation session by implementing specific strategies to deal with these concerns;
- demonstrated they could control abusive behaviour within the session; and assisted women to deal with any harassment and intimidation which occurred outside the actual mediation sessions itself.[32]

Two Australian family mediators – Susan Gribben[33] and Andrew Bickerdike[34] – have pointed out that, in reality, family dispute resolution (FDR) services in Australia have always provided mediation to clients affected by family violence, and over the years community-based organisations have improved their capacity to provide specialist services to these clients. With the recent introduction of 65 new Family Relationship Centres (FRCs) across Australia offering free dispute resolution services, many more people are coming for family mediation.[35] These FRCs, along with other government-funded community-based organisations, are compelled to use a comprehensive screening and assessment framework before proceeding with mediation. The Family Court of Australia and the Family Magistrates Court also have family law violence strategies and there are now many written guidelines for screening procedures available to family mediators so they can detect family violence before selecting mediation as an approach.[36] Of significance for mediators is that the victims interviewed in our South Australian family violence study in 2000[37] said that they needed to be asked *specifically* and *directly* about violence and abuse in their relationship. Women also talked frequently about the need for non-physical forms of family violence to be more widely understood by professionals and the community.

Feminist research and practice tend to be based on the theoretical premise that women are oppressed and need to be protected. However, Kelly stresses the importance of understanding how women categorise their own experience.[38] Women experiencing family violence may not see themselves as oppressed and may choose to proceed with mediation. Denying women individual agency and choice can further add to their oppression. Where they have left the abusive relationship, and the perpetrator has accepted responsibility for the violence, mediation may offer some women a welcome opportunity to negotiate for themselves, significantly increasing their self-esteem and sense of empowerment. Thus, some mediators in Australia may proceed with mediation where violence has been identified if the victim makes an informed choice to do so and if the conditions identified by the Keys Young research are in place and the safety of all parties is assured. However, where the perpetrator is not accepting responsibility for the violent behaviour, or where the woman is fearful and her ability to negotiate a fair outcome for herself is likely to be compromised, litigation may be the preferred option. Much more research is needed to be sure that mediation leads to satisfactory outcomes in the short and long term in these cases.[39]

Mediation can be difficult, if not impossible, where there has been a history of family violence and, if not handled carefully, can lead to unfair and unjust outcomes for the victim(s). If the victim makes an informed choice to participate in mediation where violence has been acknowledged, desirably the mediation should only proceed if the perpetrator has admitted responsibility for the violence, the victim is aware of his/her legal rights and entitlements and is linked to sources of support, strict guidelines and rules are in place and enforced by two highly experienced, trained mediators (male and female), the mediators use 'shuttle' mediation or offer separate interviews, and an advocate or support person is available for the victim during the process.[40]

Conclusions

Given the prevalence and relative invisibility of family violence in most countries in the world, and given its prevalence in family law disputes, all professionals working in family law systems should receive regular education, training and supervision in order to be able to effectively screen for violence and recognise, understand and respond appropriately to its complex and private nature. If family mediation is selected as an approach where there has been a history of family violence, then the mediators have a responsibility to ensure that the victims of abuse are protected, supported and safe and, at the very least, are not worse off as a result of the mediator's attitudes or the process and outcomes of mediation. It is also essential that family mediators know when, where and how to refer victims and perpetrators for assistance and that appropriate services are available for the women, children and men involved.

Unless family mediators are trained to recognise and understand the subtle, gendered and private nature of family violence and its effects on victims, who are more often than not women and children, the oppressive, intimidating, controlling and harmful behaviours of the perpetrator will continue to silence and marginalise the victims. The private nature of mediation could place a victim at risk of ongoing and escalating violence or abuse, in particular where the perpetrator does not admit responsibility for the violence and seek help.[41] It is important, therefore that mediators exercise caution before proceeding with mediation in these cases.

The development and introduction of family mediation standards by the Attorney-General's Department for family dispute resolution practitioners (mediators) working in the family law system in Australia has contributed to ensuring that appropriate education and screening occurs for family violence in all family law cases and that mediation is not chosen as a dispute resolution process in cases where there is family violence, unless the mediators are knowledgeable and experienced and know how to put safeguards in place to ensure that the victims are protected and the mediated outcomes are equitable and just. However, this chapter has summarised the findings of recent research that has indicated that a significant number of cases of family violence are still not being detected by family mediators in the system and appropriate responses are not always being made, in particular since the 2006 changes to the Family Law Act. In addition, children report that their voices are still not being heard, in spite of the introduction of child-inclusive mediation practices. Given the serious consequences for victims of family violence more attention needs to be paid to ensuring that priority is given to their safety.

Notes

1. Davies, M., ed., 'Women and Violence: Realities and Responses World Wide'. Second ed. 1997, Zed Books Ltd: London and New York.
2. Australian Bureau of Statistics, 'Personal Safety Survey' *2005*. 2006, Commonwealth of Australia: Canberra.
3. World Health Organisation, 'Violence against women by intimate partners'. 2008 [cited 2008 19/02]; Available from: http://www.who.int/gender/violence/who _multicountry_study/summary_report/chapter2/en/ index.html
4. Bagshaw, D., et al., 'Reshaping Responses to Domestic Violence'. 2000, Partnerships Against Domestic Violence and Department of Human Services: Canberra.
5. Johnson, M., 'Patriarchal Terrorism and Common Couple Violence: Two Forms of Violence Against Women'. *Journal of Marriage and the Family*, 1995. 57(May): p. 283-294.
6. Bagshaw, D. and D. Chung, 'Gender Politics in Research: Male and Female Violence in Intimate Relationships'. Women Against Violence, 2000(8): p. 4-23 – Mulroney, J. and C. Chan, 'Men as Victims of Domestic Violence'. Australian Domestic and Family Violence Clearinghouse Topic Paper, 2005.
7. Bagshaw, D., et al., 'Reshaping Responses to Domestic Violence'. 2000, Partnerships Against Domestic Violence and Department of Human Services: Canberra – Bagshaw, D., 'Contested Truths: Family Mediation, Diversity and Violence Against Women, in Handbook of Conflict Management', W.J. Pammer and J. Killian, Editors. 2003, Marcel Dekker, Inc: New York. p. 49-84.
8. Bagshaw, D., et al., 'Reshaping Responses to Domestic Violence'. 2000, Partnerships Against Domestic Violence and Department of Human Services: Canberra – Salthouse, S. and C. Frohmader, 'Real trouble in the home: the domestic violence reality for women with disabilities'. DVIRC Quarterly, 2005/2005(4) – Victorian Indigenous Family Violence Task Force, 'Victorian Indigenous Family Violence Task Force Final Report'. 2003, VLRC: Melbourne.
9. Kaye, M., J. Stubbs, and J. Tolmie, 'Negotiating Child Residence and Contact Arrangements Against a Background of Domestic Violence'. 2003, Family Law and Social Policy Research Unit, Griffith University: Brisbane – Moloney, L., et al., 'Allegations of family violence and child abuse in family law children's proceedings: A pre-reform exploratory study'. (Research Report No. 15). 2007, Australian Institute of Family Studies: Melbourne.
10. Mouzos, J., 'Femicide: An Overview of Major Findings'. 1999, Canberra: Australian Institute of Criminology. 1-6 – Mouzos, J. and T. Shackelford, 'Partner Killing by Men in Cohabiting and Marital Relationships. A Com-

parative, Cross-National Analysis of Data From Australia and the United States', *Journal of Interpersonal Violence*, 2005. 20(10): p. 1310-1324.

11. The *Australian Domestic and Family Violence Clearing House*, for example, has commissioned a number of studies and papers which are available on their website.

12. Brown, T. and R. Alexander, 'Child Abuse and Family Law. Understanding the issues facing human service and legal professionals'. 2007, Crows Nest: Allen & Unwin – Bagshaw, D., et al., 'Family Violence and Family Law in Australia. The Experiences and Views of Children and Adults from Families who Separated Post-1995 and Post-2006'. Volumes 1 and 2. 2010, Australian Attorney-General's Department: Canberra.

13. Bagshaw, D., et al., 'Reshaping Responses to Domestic Violence'. 2000, Partnerships Against Domestic Violence and Department of Human Services: Canberra – Bagshaw, D. and D. Chung, 'Men, women and domestic violence'. 2000, Office of the Status of Women, Commonwealth of Australia: Canberra.

14. Bagshaw, D., et al., 'Family Violence and Family Law in Australia. The Experiences and Views of Children and Adults from Families who Separated Post-1995 and Post-2006. Volumes 1 and 2'. 2010, Australian Attorney-General's Department: Canberra – Chisholm, R., *Family Courts Violence Review*. 2009, Australian Government Attorney-General's Department: Canberra – Family Law Council, 'Improving responses to family violence in the family law system: An advice on the intersection of family violence and family law issues'. 2010, Australian Government Attorney-General's Department: Canberra.

15. Australian Government. 'Family Law Act'. 1975 [cited 2008 May 3]; Available from: http://www.austlii.com/au/legis/cth/consol_act/fla1975114/index.html.

16. Bagshaw, D. and D. Chung, 'The needs of children who witness domestic violence: a South Australian Study'. Children Australia, 2001. 26(3): p. 9-17, 22. Laing, L., 'Children, young people and domestic violence, in

Australian Domestic and Family Violence Clearinghouse. Issues Paper 2'. 2000, University of New South Wales: Sydney.

17. Kirkwood, D., 'Behind Closed Doors, Family Dispute Resolution and Family Violence. Discussion Paper'. 2007, Domestic Violence and Incest Resource Centre: Collingwood, Melbourne.

18. Brown, T. and R. Alexander, 'Child Abuse and Family Law. Understanding the issues facing human service and legal professionals'. 2007, Crows Nest: Allen & Unwin.

19. Bagshaw, D., 'Contested Truths: Family Mediation, Diversity and Violence Against Women, in Handbook of Conflict Management', W.J. Pammer and J. Killian, Editors. 2003, Marcel Dekker, Inc: New York. p. 49-84 – Kirkwood, D., 'Behind Closed Doors, Family Dispute Resolution and Family Violence. Discussion Paper'. 2007, Domestic Violence and Incest Resource Centre: Collingwood, Melbourne.

20. Bagshaw, D., et al., 'Family Violence and Family Law in Australia. The Experiences and Views of Children and Adults from Families who Separated Post-1995 and Post-2006. Volumes 1 and 2'. 2010, Australian Attorney-General's Department: Canberra – Chisholm, R., 'The meanings of 'meaningful' within the Family Law Act Amendments of 2006: A legal perspective'. *Journal of Family Studies*, 2009. 15(1): p. 60-66 – Family Law Council, 'Improving responses to family violence in the family law system: An advice on the intersection of family violence and family law issues'. 2009, Australian Government Attorney-General's Department: Canberra.

21. Bagshaw, D., et al., 'Family Violence and Family Law in Australia. The Experiences and Views of Children and Adults from Families who Separated Post-1995 and Post-2006. Volumes 1 and 2'. 2010, Australian Attorney-General's Department: Canberra.

22. Kaspiew, R., et al., 'Evaluation of the 2006 family law reforms'. 2009, AIFS: Canberra.

23. Bagshaw, D. and D. Chung, 'Gender Politics in Research: Male and Female Violence in Intimate Relationships'. Women Against Violence, 2000(8): p. 4-23.

24. (Bagshaw and Chung 2000a; Mulroney and Chan 2005; James, Seddon and Brown 2002)

25. (McInnes, 2008).

26. Laing, L., 'Children, young people and domestic violence, in Australian Domestic and Family Violence Clearinghouse. Issues Paper 2'. 2000, University of New South Wales: Sydney.

27. Carpenter, G.L. and A.M. Stacks, 'Developmental effects of exposure to intimate partner violence in early childhood: A review of the literature'. Children and Youth Services Review, 2009. 31: p. 831-839. Postmus, J.L. and D.H. Merritt, 'When child abuse overlaps with domestic violence: the factors that influence child protection workers' beliefs'. Children and Youth Services Review, 2010. 32: p. 309-317.

28. Bagshaw, D., 'Contested Truths: Family Mediation, Diversity and Violence Against Women, in Handbook of Conflict Management', W.J. Pammer and J. Killian, Editors. 2003, Marcel Dekker, Inc: New York. p. 49-84 – Kirkwood, D., 'Behind Closed Doors, Family Dispute Resolution and Family Violence. Discussion Paper'. 2007, Domestic Violence and Incest Resource Centre: Collingwood, Melbourne – Astor, H. and C. Chinkin, 'Dispute Resolution in Australia'. 1992, Sydney: Butterworths – Astor, H. and C. Chinkin, 'Dispute Resolution in Australia'. Second ed. 2002, Chatswood: Butterworths Australia – Bagshaw, D. 'Gender Issues in Mediation. in (FIRM) Annual National Conference'. 1990. Derbyshire, England: Forum for Initiatives in Reparation and Mediation – Bagshaw, D., 'Mediating Family Disputes in Statutory Settings'. Australian Social Work, 1995. 48(4): p. 3-12 – Bagshaw, D., 'Mediation of Family Law Disputes in Australia'. *Australian Dispute Resolution Journal*, 1997. 8(3): p. 182-189 – Mack, K., 'Alternative Dispute Resolution and Access to Justice for Women'. *Adelaide Law Review*, 1995. 123 – Bailey, A. and A. Bickerdike, 'Family Violence and Family Mediation'. *DVIRC Quarterly*, 2005(1).

29. Astor, H., 'Position Paper on Mediation'. 1991, Canberra: National Committee on Violence Against Women, Office of the Status of Women, Commonwealth Government of Australia.

30. Australian Bureau of Statistics, 'Women's Safety Australia'. 1996, Canberra: Commonwealth of Australia.

31. Keys Young, 'Research Evaluation of Family Mediation Practice and the Issue of Violence'. 1996, Legal Aid and Family Services, Attorney-General's Department, Commonwealth of Australia: Canberra. The Keys Young study found that the incidence of violence was high in the relationships presenting to mediation agencies, with almost three-quarters of the women reporting they had experienced some type of violence or abuse. Client views of the process, and/or outcomes of the mediation were generally positive, with men expressing higher levels of satisfaction than women. Women who had experienced substantial abuse sometimes found that mediation represented a positive, empowering experience that could assist them in reaching a fair and reasonable agreement. A significant minority, however, reported not being asked by the agency about violence and abuse Keys Young reported that a number of women disclosed domestic abuse for the first time in their study, but their needs for information and referral were not necessarily met by the mediators involved. The degree of harassment, intimidation and threats of physical violence reported by women as occurring before, during and after mediation suggested that mediators needed to be more aware of ways that men use mediation to continue the abuse and intimidation of their ex-partners. In a small number of cases, mediators may have misjudged the appropriateness of a case for mediation, especially where there were issues related to children's primary residence or spending time with a parent. As an outcome of the

study ongoing domestic violence education and training has since been compulsory for all family dispute resolution practitioners accredited by the Australian Attorney-General's Department.

32. Ibid.

33. Gribben, S., 'Mediation of Family Disputes'. Australian Journal of Family Law, 1990. 5(2): p. 126-136.

34. Bickerdike, A., 'Implications for family dispute resolution practice: Response from Relationships Australia (Victoria) to the Allegations of Family Violence and Child Abuse in Family Law Children's Proceedings report'. Family Matters. Australian Institute for Family Studies., 2007(77): p. 20-25.

35. Ibid.

36. Kirkwood, D., 'Behind Closed Doors, Family Dispute Resolution and Family Violence. Discussion Paper'. 2007, Domestic Violence and Incest Resource Centre: Collingwood, Melbourne.

37. Bagshaw, D., et al., 'Reshaping Responses to Domestic Violence'. 2000, Partnerships Against Domestic Violence and Department of Human Services: Canberra.

38. Kelly, L., S. Burton, and L. Regan, 'Beyond Victim or Survivor: Sexual Violence, Identity and Feminist Theory and Practice, in Sexualising the Social: Power and the Organization of Sexuality', L. Adkins and V. Merchant, Editors. 1996, Macmillan Press Ltd: Houndmills, Basingstoke and London. p. 77-101.

39. Bagshaw, D., 'Contested Truths: Family Mediation, Diversity and Violence Against Women, in Handbook of Conflict Management', W.J. Pammer and J. Killian, Editors. 2003, Marcel Dekker, Inc: New York. p. 49-84.

40. Ibid.

41. Bagshaw, D., et al., 'Reshaping Responses to Domestic Violence'. 2000, Partnerships Against Domestic Violence and Department of Human Services: Canberra.

CHAPTER 7

Mediation as a Process for Healing

Mediating the effects of sexual and physical abuse within religious institutions and the lessons that can be applied to mediating disrupted relationships

By mediator Greg Rooney

Can mediation be recognised in its own right as a valid and effective process to help people who have suffered a deep emotional trauma move forward with their lives? Can it be used as an agent for healing in situations involving people who have suffered deep emotional hurt through the actions of others?

It is rare for any dispute to come before a mediator without a significant emotional element in play. High levels of emotion are not just restricted to family law disputes; they can also be observed in most areas of conflict, including commercial and organisational disputes. Parties who have lost money or feel betrayed in commercial disputes can be overwhelmed by the emotions of loss, despair and rage. While it is often said that mediation is carried out in the shadow of the law (Mnookin & Kornhauser, 1979), it can also be argued that it is in carried out in the shadows of the parties' emotions.

It is quite natural for people, at the focal point of their conflict, to feel strong emotions, emotions which usually dissipate once the core issue has been resolved. However, many people live with deep emotional trauma caused by events that are not related to the issue in dispute. Mediators might feel that a sudden outburst of emotion is caused by the issue under discussion, when in fact it might be symptomatic of a much deeper emotional malaise.

The issue for mediators and the mediation field is how to distinguish between emotions generated by the heat of the moment alone and emotions born out of a deep psychological trauma. At what point in the continuum of emotional disturbance and trauma does mediation, as a method of resolving practical issues, cease to be appropriate? Should mediation be denied simply because one or both parties is suffering from a pre-existing deep emotional trauma that has been reignited by a dispute?

Family and relationship breakdowns are a common cause of conflict in the community. Their prevalence exposes a significant section of the population to the traumas of separation. Many people in long-term relationships can, over time, become emotionally enmeshed. Not only is the ending of a relationship a traumatic event in itself, it can trigger a resurgence in any latent emotional wounds and traumas. These latent traumas can be the result of many factors, including the effects of the disrupted relationships of the parents of those experiencing such traumas.

It is ironic that, at the time when separating parties are required to decide extremely important practical issues such as where the children will live or how to divide the property, they are emotionally at their most vulnerable. Mediation can play a valuable role as an alternative to adversarial litigation, in helping people resolve these important practical issues.

This paper will examine the issues of dealing with heightened emotions in the mediation session, identifying deep psychological traumas, and assisting those who experience them to resolve disputes by way of mediation. It will do so in the context of claims of child sexual abuse by clergy in religious institutions. It will focus on the process of delivering an apology and offering assistance to the victims which will help them move forward with their lives (there is no involvement by the perpetrator of the abuse in these meetings). It will seek to consider transferable skills and approaches that can be applied to mediating family law disputes where one or both parties has a significant long-term emotional trauma.

In many respects, religious communities are like families. There is a hierarchy and a collective group mentality bonded by deep spiritual beliefs. The sexual abuse of young children within that community can have a devastating emotional impact, not just on the victim but on the group as a whole. Many victims of child sexual abuse complain that, not only are they emotionally damaged, they have also lost their connection to their religious community.

This abuse can have long-term effects on the young person's ability to form and maintain relationships, and often eventually results in quite traumatising relationship breakdowns. Many such breakdowns are caused by the hidden effects of childhood sexual abuse. Much of this can be hidden, because many people do not disclose even to their partners that they have suffered this form of abuse, leaving its presence to go unnoticed – even with very effective pre-mediation conferences.

This paper's particular focus will be on mediating the apology and the provision of retrospective reparation by the church for abuse by the clergy. The examination will be from the perspective of the practising mediator, and will not focus on restorative justice procedures between the victims of sexual abuse and the perpetrator.

This topic will be looked at from three different but interconnecting perspectives. Firstly, it will explore some techniques and approaches that can be used by the mediator to prepare parties for the mediation, especially identifying and focusing on the role which heightened emotions play in the process. Secondly, it will consider the mediator's relationship with his or her own emotions, memories and desires, as well as the urge to understand and help, and examine how these influence the dynamics of the mediation session. Thirdly, it will explore the process architecture of a number of differing dispute resolution systems that have been put in place by religious organisations and complainant groups to pursue or manage claims of sexual abuse.

Techniques and approaches to manage the mediation session in a highly charged emotional context

Mediating between parties who have suffered deep emotional trauma can present many difficulties and risks for the mediator. The onus is squarely on the mediator to assess the parties' suitability for mediation fully, prior to undertaking the session. The primary duty of the mediator is to do no harm. Mediating between victims of sexual abuse and religious institutions falls into this category.

These mediations have added difficulties, partly because the abuse took place when the complainant was a child and extremely vulnerable. There appears to be a common pattern to the way perpetrators groomed their victims. They generally targeted young boys and girls just prior to puberty or in early puberty; they focused on young children whose parents had a close connection with the church, thereby allowing them access to the children in the parental home. Their preference was to target the more spiritually inclined children, who were generally more trusting of religious figures. They kept well away from the more robust and streetwise children; the more spiritually inclined child is likely to be easily threatened and embarrassed into not making a complaint.

More often than not, the young victims were able to suppress these traumatic events for a number of years by simply getting on with their lives. Often the emotions would lie dormant until middle age, when long-term memories of traumatic events would begin to resurface. In the last few years, victims have also faced constant publicity of sexual abuse cases in the media. All of this has contributed to the re-emergence of the symptoms associated with the deep emotional trauma, and the shattering of their sexual identity by the original abuse. The issue for the mediator is how to manage these emotions sufficiently to allow a constructive meeting between the complainant and the religious leader to take place safely.

In some respects, mediating with people who have suffered sexual abuse is somewhat easier, in the sense that it can be readily assumed that the complainant has suffered a deep emotional trauma by the event. Therefore, the mediator is 'on notice', and can take the appropriate precautions, where in family law cases the presence of a deep emotional trauma can be masked.

The importance of a pre-mediation meeting with both the complainant and the church representatives cannot be underestimated. The aim is for the mediator to make a reasoned determination as to whether the complainant is emotionally capable of receiving some benefit from the mediated meeting, and to avoid re-traumatising the complainant.

The following are some techniques that can be used to assess the capacity of the victim to take part in the mediation. They attempt to identify how far the complainant is along the continuum of readiness to move forward with life. This is the key issue. However, it has two distinct parts to it. Firstly, have victims reached the point where they are ready to revisit the abuse through meeting the current head of the religious organisation? And secondly, are they ready to move beyond the actual meeting with the current head of the religious organisation in question – and, if so, what might that 'movement beyond' look like? In being asked to focus beyond the mediation, victims' capacity to disengage from the past is being tested.

There are two questions that can be helpful at this point. The first is to ask complainants to assume that the forthcoming mediation meeting turns out to be a success. They are then asked whether they are able to visualise sometime in the future when things might be better than they are at present, and, if so, what that would look like. The purpose of this question is to ascertain whether complainants have the capacity to look to the future. Some complainants say that they cannot see a future, and that they can only consider the prospect of suicide. In such situations, complainants are certainly not ready for a face-to-face meeting. Others, while struggling with the question, are able to turn their minds towards a future point. This is a good indication that they are sufficiently robust to at least consider the possibility that they can move forward with their lives.

There is some similarity between the purposeful framing of this question and the objects of solution focused therapy (de Shazer, 1985). However, in cases such as those discussed here, framing is used more as an assessment tool to determine how the victim might cope with exploring the future. Over the years, I have trialled a number of forms of this question; however, in a heuristic sense, I have found that form of words to elicit the best response. (The question was adapted from a course in Dispute System Design with CDR Associates in Boulder, Colorado, 1994.) When designing a dispute resolution system for an organisation, it was suggested that the question be posed – "if the system were to work well, what would it look like?"

Another technique for assessing the emotional capacity of the complainant is to suggest, in the pre-mediation meeting, the following: "although you are a mature person and can think like a mature person, it is the x-year-old boy or girl (where x is the age at which the sexual abuse occurred) that will be meeting the religious representative". I have found that victims' responses to this question can indicate how far they have emotionally progressed. The purpose is not to get an answer from them, but to plant the thought in their minds, opening them up to a different way of thinking about themselves in relation to the forthcoming meeting. In fact, any answer they give at the time is not important. The most powerful questions a mediator can ask are ones that do not need to be answered.

I have found it helpful, at an appropriate time in the mediation session, to ask complainants how the x-year-old boy or girl is feeling at that moment. It often allows them to reflect openly on their progress. It also helps the religious leader to understand that, while the person sitting opposite them appears calm and rational, there is a fragile and emotional person within.

The apology

There has been much written on how to make an effective apology (Schneider, 2000; Deutschmann, 2003). The most effective apology is one that is not prepared in advance. It is one that evolves out of a process of listening, and allows an emotional connection to form in the here and now of the session. If this can be achieved, then the words that follow often do not automatically need to contain the actual word 'sorry'. The power comes from the emotional connection and energy that flows from the interaction between the giver and the receiver. It is the sharing of this emotional experience that gives the apology its healing force.

To help achieve this, it is important to prepare both the complainant and the religious leader for the mediation encounter. Many senior religious figures are of an advanced age, and have spent many of their later years in administrative positions. They can tend to take a somewhat academic or intellectual view, from reading the history of the abuse and the medical reports. A way of breaking down this intellectualism is to ask religious leaders not to prepare any formal apology in advance of the mediation. They are asked to sit quietly while complainants give their thoughts and feelings about how they feel at that particular moment.

Complainants too are requested not to prepare for the mediation. They are advised that the opening question to them at the beginning of the mediation session will be: "what thoughts come to you about all of this, as you sit here today?" This is a deliberately open question. Most complainants at first struggle when trying to collect their thoughts and express their feelings. This allows church leaders time to find a connection with claimants before being asked to speak. At this point, the mediator tries to hold the space and to encourage the complainant to continue. When the mediator feels that the complainant has expressed him- or herself sufficiently, the mediator will turn to the religious leader and ask them to reflect on what has been said. It is often interesting to watch senior religious figures also struggle with their words, a struggle which forms the basis of a personal connection between the two. This emotional response from church leaders, if they allow themselves to properly engage with complainants, can often demonstrate a more profound sense of sorrow and regret than any formalised set of words.

Mediators' relationship with their own emotions, memories, desires and understanding

Parties in mediation who are suffering a deep emotional trauma require very sensitive handling by a mediator. It is not sufficient to have good pre-mediation structures in place and a good pre-mediation conference. The other essential ingredient is the mediator him- or herself. To undertake this form of work, mediators have to be really clear about their own emotional status, so that it does not exacerbate the parties' own emotional state. The mediator's presence in the room has as much impact as that of the parties.

A mediator is not an empty vessel. Mediators bring all their own life experiences and their own particular traumas into the room. We should not assume that we sit in the session passively observing the proceedings while occasionally drawing from our toolbox of skills to make interventions here or there. A mediator's emotions, desires and beliefs and worldview all have an impact on how s/he behaves in the session. It is important that we recognise this, and accept that mediators have these impulses, which influence their behaviour. This awareness allows mediators deliberately to let go of any of these attachments, so as to be totally present in the here and now of the session. It is important that mediators are able to create a safe space for the parties, without letting their own emotions and beliefs impinge.

So, how does a mediator suspend or detach from his or her emotional responses and desires, so as to remain totally attuned to both parties' reactions and emotional status?

Wilfred Bion (1967) looked at this issue from the perspective of an analyst. He suggested that, to be fully present in the here and now of the session, the analyst had to detach from his/her memories, desires and the need to understand what was happening at a particular point in time. The problem, he said, was not having memories, desires and an interest in understanding what was happening; we all have these urges. He suggests that it is not about forgetting them; what is required is a deliberate act of letting go of an attachment to such urges within the session. The problem with having memories, desires and a need to understand is that they occupy a space

in the mind of the therapist that should be left empty for something new to enter.

Bion drew on Freud's elegant and insightful passage on the techniques of analytic practice, where he suggested the state of mind that physicians who wish to practice analysis should develop:

"It consists simply in not directing one's notice to anything in particular and in maintaining the same 'evenly-suspended attention' (as I have called it) in the face of all that one hears. In this way we spare ourselves a strain on our attention which could not in any case be kept up for several hours daily, and we avoid a danger which is inseparable from the exercise of deliberate attention. For as soon as one deliberately concentrates his attention to a certain degree, he begins to select from the material before him; one point will be fixed in his mind with particular clearness and some other will be correspondingly discarded, and in the making of this selection he will be following his expectations or inclinations. This however, is precisely what must not be done. In making the selection; if he follows his expectations he is in danger of never finding anything but what he already knows; and if he follows his inclinations he will certainly falsify what he may perceive. It must not be forgotten that the things one hears are for the most part things whose meaning is only recognised later on." (Freud, 1912, p. 432).

What Freud is suggesting is that therapists allow themselves the space to experience the new, and do not try to understand it until after the experience has been completed. Bion has suggested that if we over-invest in our need to understand what is happening, or become attached to our memories and our desires, it can prevent us from sharing the parties' experience. He postulated that people only grow or evolve through "experiencing an experience" (Grotstein, 1981). Freud recommends that we should be open to allowing ourselves to be surprised (Havens, 1989). He suggests that it is important that we can fully experience what happens in the session before allowing our thoughts to crystallise. Both Freud and Bion, in effect, recommend de-cluttering our brains, so that there is space for the new to enter. It is by allowing this empty space to be filled with what is actually happening in the here and now of the session that triggers the mediator's intuition response. This response can aid the mediator in deciding what to do next in this session (Rooney, 2007).

Theorists such as Zariski (2010) suggest that theory, rather than intuition, should inform the mediator's view of any situation. However, in mediations involving people with deep emotional stress and high levels of conflict, it is important for the mediator to be fully present to monitor proceedings at each moment. The mediator must be ready to respond instantly. The pre-mediation conference is the opportunity to question and test the complainant in preparation for the mediation session; theory can help us make sense of what happened in that session. However, once the mediation session starts, it is the mediator's prime role to hold the space and respond when required. Our response has to be instantaneous and relevant to what is occurring at each particular point in time. While mediation theory might frame a lot of what we do, it can unwittingly distract us if we stop to ponder the theoretical implications of what is happening before us. Theory is best if it used as a reflective tool. It can be used to frame an explanation of something that has occurred.

Our memories and desires can seem so natural to us that we can assume that anyone who does not see the world as we do must be somehow wrong in their thinking. We can make the assumption that our worldview and our observations are valid and correct. This is referred to as naïve realism (Ross and Ward, 1996; Zariski, 2010).

Naïve realism is based on the premise that some people believe that they see the world clearly, and that those who do not share their view see the world through biased eyes due to incorrect beliefs. It is therefore important to be aware of one's own sense of realism, and that it might be divergent from others'. Again, it is not problematic to have differing perceptions of reality; what is problematic is if we become attached to our own worldviews.

If mediators begin to focus on their own emotions and desires, or start assuming that the parties see the world as they see it, they then create obstacles which prevent themselves being fully present in the here and now of the session.

Other factors can also influence how we behave in the mediation session. People in the helping professions (such as therapists and mediators) can be drawn to these professions by the natural desire to help people. While this desire is admirable, it can have the unintended consequence of distorting our behaviour as professionals. Salzberger-Wittenberg (1970) addresses some of these issues in her advice to social workers. She warns against this desire to help, and suggests that it must be tempered by what is realistic and beneficial to the patient. She submits that this need to want to help can lead to social workers seeking approval from the patient, in being reassured that they are providing something of value. The focus thereby moves away from the patient's needs to those of the social worker. This can blur the professional distance that social workers, mediators and other professionals need to maintain when dealing with patients or clients, especially those who have suffered a deep emotional trauma. It can lead to a more directive or parental stance, resulting in a more interventionist style.

The mediation of an apology in sexual abuse claims is enhanced by the ability of complainants to express their thoughts and feelings freely, and the openness of church leaders to receive them. The mediator's role is to create a safe place and to hold that space, allowing such an interchange to occur. The ability to be in the moment and to observe both the claimant and the church leader clearly is extremely important. This helps determine when to turn to the church leader and ask for his/her thoughts on what the complainant has said. It is this interchange between the complainant and the church leader that forms the basis of the apology.

Process architecture

Preparation is always extremely important for the success of a mediation, especially for parties and disputes with the potential for a highly-charged emotional exchange. All issues leading up to the mediation need to be considered and designed so as to support not only the parties but also the mediator.

A mediation does not typically take place in isolation; there is always a process leading up to the first mediation session, which in turn gives the mediation a context. This context is a construct of the drivers that led the parties to choose mediation, the dominant mediation model that is agreed upon, the jurisdiction within which the mediation takes place and which any agreement will be subject to, and other factors including the choice of venue, the presence or otherwise of legal representation and support personnel. The mediation takes place in the shadow of these factors, all of which influence what happens in the face-to-face session.

This influence has a subtle but significant effect on the parties and the mediator within the mediation session. It is similar to the influence that the architecture of a building has on its inhabitants. The shape, design and ambience of a building and the effects of light and shade have an impact on those who inhabit the building. In much the same way, the architecture and shape of the context or process within which the mediation takes place has a direct impact on the behaviour of the parties and the mediator.

It is therefore important fully to consider the design of the process architecture that is built around the mediation session, particularly where the parties have suffered deep emotional trauma. The underlying process architecture is more than just carrying out an effective pre-mediation meeting.

The process architecture of the 'Towards Healing' process

The sexual abuse of young children by religious clergy can result in significant psychological damage and emotional trauma, which can impact on children for the rest of their lives. Any attempt to mediate between victims and current church authorities has to proceed with caution. An example of a process architecture that is supportive of both the parties and the mediator is one set up by the Catholic Bishops of Australia in 1996 to resolve complaints of sexual abuse made against the church. This process has been called 'Towards Healing', and has been refined and developed over the past 16 years (Parkinson, 2002; Rooney & Ross, 2007).

The essential feature of the architectural design of this process is that it is voluntary, and open to anyone who wishes to make a complaint of sexual abuse and who is willing to enter the program. Its primary focus is to deliver a pastoral response to complainants without them needing to prove legal liability.

Other features include the creation of a Professional Standards office in each state of Australia to manage all complaints of sexual and physical abuse. Although this is a church body, it is designed to be one step removed from the clergy about whom the complaints are made. The director of each Professional Standards office is required to advise complainants of their rights to make a formal complaint to the police or to take civil action against the church. The director is also required to assist complainants in contacting the police, and to act with concern with respect to their well-being in cases where they choose to pursue civil claims against the church.

If a complainant chooses either to go to the police or to commence legal action, then the process is suspended until such action is completed. The Towards Healing process is specifically designed for people who do not want to or are not able to mount a successful legal case for compensation. It does not depend on the complainant proving that the church is legally liable for the abuse. All that is required is, firstly, that there is evidence that the complainant was actually present at the time of the alleged abuse, and that on the balance of probabilities the alleged abuse occurred. Even in situations where, for historical reasons, the complaint cannot be verified because of the passage of time, there is still provision for a pastoral response from the church.

The Towards Healing process is a good example of a process architecture that has a direct impact on a face-to-face mediation session. The most important part of the design is that the complainant has personal contact with the director of the Professional Standards Office throughout the investigatory part of the process. The complainant is given personal assistance in progressing the complaint, and can be provided with immediate counselling at the expense of the church if in emotional distress.

In many cases, complaints can be quickly accepted in a short space of time, especially where the accused has a well-documented history of abuse. There can sometimes be delays in the assessment process, due to lack of records and other factors. At all times, the director of professional standards maintains personal contact with the complainant. There is a requirement on the director to limit the number of times complainants have to relate their story.

For the mediator, this process can be of great value. By the time the complaint is ready for mediation, the director has built up an understanding of the complainant's needs and fears. The mediator is then able to build on that work. In difficult and highly emotional cases, much of the groundwork in preparing the complainant for the session can be undertaken, including the provision of significant amounts of therapy, prior to the face-to-face session.

The other advantage is that the Director of Professional Standards can work with bishops and heads of religious organisations who will be present at the face-to-face meeting. The director can help church representatives to prepare for the mediation session by getting them into the right frame of mind for the meeting.

For victims of sexual abuse, it is important that not only do they get an apology but they also get something that is a real and tangible representation of acknowledgement – usually money, or some direct in-kind assistance. In a family law separation, both parties also require something that is a real and tangible representation of their contribution to the relationship. The true value of someone's contribution to a relationship over many years or the loss caused by being sexually abused as a child is incalculable. Therefore any attempt to perform such a calculation can trigger a significant emotional response.

The Towards Healing process attempts to address this issue by using the word 'reparation' rather than 'compensation'. This is an attempt to acknowledge that no amount of money can repair the damage caused by this form of abuse. It seeks to differentiate itself from a court process that is simply designed to measure a loss. The prime aim of Towards Healing, as its name implies, is to help victims move forward with their lives. The Towards Healing process defines reparation as:

> "A monetary sum or some form of in-kind assistance that is directed to the provision of practical means of support in order to promote healing for the victim. It is provided by the church authority as a means of recognising the harm suffered by a victim of a criminal offence or civil wrong, and as a tangible expression of the church authority's regret that such abuse occurred. Reparation may be offered independently of whether the church authority is legally liable."

Paragraph 41 of the Towards Healing principles and procedures document outlines the outcomes that relate to the victim. This section provides:

> " 41.1 in the event that the church authority is satisfied of the truth of the complaint, whether through admission of the offender, a finding of a court, a penal process under canon law, an assessment under these procedures or otherwise, the church authority shall respond to the needs of the victim in such ways as are demanded by justice and compassion. Responses may include the provision of an apology on behalf of the church, the provision of counselling services or the payment of counselling costs.

> 41.1.1 financial assistance or reparation may also be paid to victims of a criminal offence or civil wrong, even though the church is not legally liable.

41.2 a bishop or leader must seek the advice of the consultative panel in determining how to respond to the complaint.

41.2 and the church authority may seek such further information as it considers necessary to understand the needs of the victim, including a report from a suitably qualified and independent professional concerning the impact of the abuse on the victim. Such a report will be at the church authority's expense.

41.3 the facilitation shall be the normal means of addressing the needs of the victim."

These protocols are built around the facilitative or mediation process, with a pastoral approach as its key driver.

There are a number of other approaches aimed at resolving sexual abuse claims against religious institutions. Firstly, there is the traditional legal approach, where complainants instruct lawyers to represent them in claims for damages against the church. In many of these cases, lawyers are happy to advise their clients to work through the Towards Healing process because it offers a without prejudice opportunity to resolve the matter quickly, as well as allowing clients to have face-to-face meetings with religious leaders as a way of obtaining some personal and emotional closure. If complainants are not satisfied with the outcome of the Towards Healing process, they can still commence a civil action for damages against the church.

However, there are many lawyers who understand their duty to act in the best interests of their clients to exclude opportunities to obtain a personal apology from a religious leader. This group tends to

see the lawyer's duty as limited to maximising the compensatory dollar return to their client. They often see the face-to-face apology as an attempt by the church to mitigate its own losses by providing some form of on-the-spot healing, and take the attitude that, the longer their client is able to remain in a distressed state through the negotiation period, the better their dollar return. They therefore resist any attempt at a face-to-face apology.

The process architecture of this approach remains adversarial and accusatory, and often includes the use of the media as a means of putting negotiation pressure on the church's representatives. The negotiations hinge only on the strength or otherwise of the complainant's legal case. The claims are often drawn out over a longer period of time, with significantly higher legal costs. This process architecture has a marked effect on the mediation session, with some lawyers keeping the client well away from the church leader and, in some cases, away from the mediator.

Some lawyers request access to the Towards Healing process as a vehicle for negotiation, but do not want a face-to-face meeting nor any pastoral element other than monetary compensation. This issue was dealt with in a recent review of the Towards Healing program by Professor Patrick Parkinson from the University of Sydney (unpublished). In his review in 2010, Professor Parkinson made the following comments with respect to the two approaches for dealing with victims of abuse:

"The first is the legal approach-both to complaints and accused. The strengths of this approach are the emphasis on due process including proving claims to a requisite standard, assessing compensation fairly in accordance with the objective gravity of the harm caused, and treating like cases alike.

The second is the pastoral approach of giving a compassionate response, seeking to promote healing for the victim, and to the extent that it is possible, bringing about some level of reconciliation between the victim and the church, while also being fair to the accused persons. This also has great strengths. It does not aim to offer a quality legal approach to the resolution of civil claims for compensation, but rather to engage in restoration and healing, acknowledging within that the importance in many cases of making reparation is a tangible expression of sorrow and also as a means, but not the only means, of promoting healing for the victim. The pastoral approach also needs to address properly the requirements of due process for the accused."

There is a deliberate separation between the Towards Healing process and formal legal claims for compensation. If the complainant does not participate directly in the process, then by definition, it is not a Towards Healing case. However, even within the Towards Healing protocols there have evolved two different variations with respect to the process architecture for negotiating the amount of reparation.

The traditional approach is to provide the opportunity to deal with an apology and a resolution of the reparations issue at the one mediated meeting. This process proceeds along lines of a welcome and introduction by the mediator, the opportunity for the complainant to express his/her current thoughts and feelings about what has happened and where s/he would like to get to in the future, and a personal response from the church leader. There is then a break, followed by a negotiation to consider a fair and reasonable sum of money to represent a reparation. The parties' lawyers are usually in attendance, and take part in both the apology stage and the negotiation for the payment of reparation. These meetings usually take between three to four hours; in situations where final agreement on the reparation has not been completed, offers are usually left on the table for a number of weeks for parties to reconsider their positions.

An alternative approach favoured by some directors of professional standards is to have the negotiations with respect to the amount of reparations resolved by arm's-length negotiation before having the face-to-face pastoral meeting. If and when that agreement is reached, the face-to-face meeting is scheduled for the formal apology. The stated reason for this approach is that it avoids a situation where a complainant feels let down after the apology, particularly when the amount of reparation does not meet what s/he considers to be an adequate response.

While these two approaches both fall within the context of the Towards Healing protocols, they have a different effect on the dynamics of the mediation, as well as on the parties and the mediator themselves.

Separating the apology from the calculation of reparation

An example of a successful mediation program in which the apology was separated from the payment of reparation was the Goodwood Orphanage Program, developed by the Catholic Archdiocese of Adelaide and the Sisters of Mercy. The Goodwood Orphanage was set up in Adelaide in the early 1900s by the Sisters of Mercy. During the 1950s and 1960s, the orphanage had a culture (or process architecture) of discipline, regimentation, corporal punishment and deprivation. This paralleled the post-war culture that existed in Australia at the time. Two teaching nuns were appointed to live with and educate 100 orphans, 24 hours a day and seven days a week. Many of these orphans were British child migrants sent to Australia after the Second World War.

Over the last two decades, there has been a growing number of complaints from those orphans about the physical and emotional abuse they suffered at the orphanage at that time. The complaints included harsh and excessive physical punishment, bedwetting programs that involved ritual humiliation of the children, poor food, lack of the provision of a proper education, forced unpaid labour and the general lack of Christian love and compassion.

The Archdioceses commissioned a study into what would have been considered a proper level of education and proper care practices for the time. Each complaint was measured against those standards, and when it fell below that general standard, a set amount of reparation was offered for each claim. The decision as to whether the care fell above or below that standard was referred to an independent lawyer for assessment. As with Towards Healing, the process architecture of the Goodwood program had at its heart a pastoral response. This was achieved by providing an additional amount of money for extra benefits, provided the complainant agreed to a face-to-face pastoral meeting. The aim was to encourage the orphans to engage in the pastoral part of the process. At first, a small number of people took up this option. However, as the word spread from those who had experienced the mediation process and received the personal apology, more chose this option.

Each claimant knew in advance that his/her claims had been accepted, and knew the amount of reparation which would be received. The meeting provided an opportunity for claimants to give their personal accounts of what had happened, and to allow the current Sisters of Mercy to express their personal regret and sorrow. These meetings often ended in an emotional release, involving tears and hugs. In addition, a number of orphans whose complaints were not able to be substantiated under the programs formula for assessment were offered and did accept a mediated apology without compensation.

In a sense, the program worked because the Goodwood protocols contained an element of uniformity that reflected the culture of the institution at the time. The protocols effectively paralleled this, by looking at the levels of abuse in a group sense that reflected the shared institutional suffering of the orphans.

However, claims of child sexual abuse by members of religious orders are unique to each victim. In some sense, they lack the uniformity of the institutional abuse that occurred in the orphanage situation. For example: some victims suffered horrendous sexual abuse over long periods of time, yet through their personal coping mechanisms were able to cope with life reasonably – notwithstanding retaining a deep emotional scar. Others, whose abuse could be described as occurring at the lower end of the scale, suffer hugely disrupted lives through the deep emotional scarring of the event. It is thus much harder to characterise victims into groupings without appearing overly callous.

Negotiating the reparation package separately from the apology tends to put a focus onto a comparative mathematical exercise. It can descend into an exercise of comparing levels of abuse. However, combining the apology and the monetary negotiation provides a greater visible link between the two. Often religious leaders will be so moved by the interaction surrounding the apology that they will draw deeper into their financial reserves to assist the complainant – more than they would otherwise have done in the standard commercial arm's-length type negotiation.

The writer has experienced a situation in which two cases of child sexual abuse by clergy were resolved on the same day. Although they involved clergy from two different Christian-based religions, the levels of abuse and the effects on both victims were very similar. The first was resolved under the Towards Healing protocols, with a personal apology given by the head of the religious organisation. The process took three months to set up from the first complaint. The reparation was 20% higher than what would have been the normal amount of reparation, mainly because the religious leader was so moved by the complainant's experience.

The second matter was the resolution of a class action of twenty claimants brought by a lawyer. They each received 20% less than the Towards Healing complainant. In addition, each of the claimants had to pay five times the legal costs to the lawyers than the legal costs paid by the Towards Healing claimant. The class action took two years of bitter negotiations, and resolved without any formal face-to-face apology. This is one example of where the non-adversarial Towards Healing approach delivered a larger monetary package to the claimant, in addition to all the benefits associated with receiving a personal apology.

The difficulty with negotiating the reparation package first is that it can leave the more pastoral aspects of the process and the apology as simply an afterthought. Combining the apology and the negotiation for reparation in the one mediation session is a more holistic approach. It allows for a much more dynamic interaction to occur between the parties, and establishes a direct link between the apology and the reparation which stand or fall together. This creates a lot more pressure on mediators; however, if it is handled well by the religious leader, it can open the door to a deeper level of experience and, in many cases, deliver a more profound apology.

The mediation of claims of sexual abuse has to proceed with caution. At all times, it has to be assumed that the victim has suffered some deep psychological impact that will have an effect on the process. All structures that are put in place to bring the victim and the church authority together have to have a process architecture that is supportive of both the victim, the church authority and the mediator.

Summary

The presence of deep emotional scarring and heightened emotions by a party in a mediation creates unique challenges, both in deciding whether to mediate and – if so – how to mediate. This is applicable whether the issue is the division of matrimonial property, access to children in a family law dispute, or the apology to the victims of child sexual abuse within religious institutions.

The decision whether to mediate must be made carefully. The process of deciding must include continual assessment and monitoring of the party or parties. It is also important to encourage active involvement by the parties in helping make the final decision whether to go ahead with the process.

In court-appointed mediations or mediation arising out of a government or private sponsored programs, it is important that there is sufficient flexibility in the process architecture of those programs to cater for people who suffer from deep emotional traumas. The Towards Healing process and the Goodwood Orphanage Program are two examples of a process architecture that is both supportive of the mediator's role and promoting the ownership of the process by the emotionally damaged party. Some family law jurisdictions, such as the Family Court of Australia, are making tentative moves in this direction by experimenting with less adversarial processes and court-annexed mediation, particularly in determining children's matters.

Once the decision has been made, and it has been accepted by all parties that the mediation should proceed, then the onus is on the mediator to manage the facilitation in such a way to maximise the chance of a resolution without re-traumatising any party. The key to achieving this rests with mediators' ability to detach from their own emotional state. This allows the parties uncluttered space to engage with each other. Mediators can benefit from having regular supervision, particularly with respect to recognising and then detaching from their memories and desires.

It is the mediator's ability to achieve a form of reverie that allows him/her to be fully aware and awake and attuned to the parties' individual and collective needs. This is the key for any professional who works with people who have suffered deep emotional traumas. It allows the mediator to form a connection with the parties in the here and now of each particular moment of the session. For the mediator, it allows a more heightened awareness, and thereby greater access to his/her intuitive thoughts. This connection helps the mediator to sense when and how to intervene.

Mediation has a place in resolving practical issues for people who are suffering an emotional trauma, whether as a result of being a survivor of sexual abuse, or through the trauma of a relationship breakdown. However, mediators need to be at one with their own emotions, and have the support of the institutions that are involved in this challenging area of work.

References

Bion, W.R. (1967), 'Notes on Memory and Desire'. In R. Langs (ed.) Classics in Psycho-Analytic Technique. New York: Jason Aronson, 1981.

De Shazer, S. (1985), 'Keys to Solution in Brief Therapy'. New York: Norton.

Deutschmann, M. (2003), 'Apologising in British English'. Umeå, Sweden; Institutionen för moderna språk, Umeå Universitet.

Freud, S. (1912), 'Recommendations to Physicians Practising Psycho-Analysis'. In R. Langs (ed.) Classics in Psycho-Analytic Technique. New York: Jason Aronson, 1981.

Grotstein, J.S. (1981), 'Do I Dare Disturb the Universe'. London: Karnac Books Ltd.

Havens, L. (1989), 'A Safe Place'. Cambridge: Harvard University Press.

Mnookin, R.H. & Kornhauser, L. (1979), 'Bargaining in the shadow of the law: The case of divorce' [Electronic version]. *Yale Law Review*, 88, 950-997.

'National Committee for Professional Standards, Towards Healing – Principles and Procedures in Response to Complaints of Abuse against Personnel of the Catholic Church in Australia (2010)' – para 41, ISBN 978-1-86420-336-3.

Parkinson, P., 'What does the Lord Require of Us? Child Sexual Abuse in the Churches'. *Journal of Religion & Abuse*, Volume 4(2) 2002: The Haworth Press.

Rooney, G. (2008), 'The Use of Intuition in Mediation. Conflict Resolution Quarterly', Volume 25, Issue 2, 239-253.

Rooney, G. Ross, M. (2007), 'Mediating Between Victims of Sexual Abuse and Religious Institutions'. 18 Australian Dispute Resolution Journal 10. Sydney: Thompson Law Book Company, 2007.

Ross, L. and A. Ward. (1996), 'Naïve realism in everyday life: implications for social conflict and misunderstanding'. In Values and Knowledge, edited by E.S. Reed, D. Turiel, and T. Brown. Nahwah, NJ: Lawrence Erlbaum Associates.

Salzberger-Wittenberg, I (1970), 'Psycho-analytic Insight and Relationships (A Kleinian Approach)'. Routledge and Kegan Paul, London, p. 4.

Schneider, C.D., 'What it Means to be Sorry. The Power of Apology in Mediation' *Mediation Quarterly* Volume, 17. Number 3, Spring 2000.

Zariski, A. 'A Theory Matrix for Mediators'. *Negotiation Journal* April 2010, 203-235.

CHAPTER 8

Neighbour War and Peace on Danish TV

By journalist Camilla Emborg

In the late summer of 2010 DR TV broadcasted three television programmes entitled "Neighbours at War".

The programmes' mission was to show how extremely deadlocked conflicts between neighbours can be resolved.

The method was mediation, or conflict resolution as it is commonly called.

And the results weren't lacking. The programmes were a success: both with regard to the individual neighbours' cases and the viewers figures.

This is the story behind them.

The central point is emotion and conflict

Conflict and emotions make good TV.

Every good TV journalist is always looking for the resistance, challenges and disagreements in a story because it is in this field of tension that those taking part in the programme become interesting to the rest of us.

This is right where people's feelings come into play.

When conflicts arise and challenge the participants in a programme, their super-egoes and their control automatically take a back seat and people suddenly express how they really feel, driven by impulses and emotions that are not feigned or deliberate. They just "feel" and react according to their instincts and the viewer is automatically caught up in the scene, because they too instinctively identify with what is happening. The viewers know the feelings and problems from their own world – they see themselves reflected in the emotional reactions.

Because, after all, feelings are universal and deeply rooted in each and every person – for good and for bad. And they are therefore the incontrovertible way to the viewer's heart.

Because we want to get gripped when we watch TV. We want to come so close to the participants that we feel as though we know them. We want to have goosebumps, we want our heartbeat to race and maybe feel a lump in our throat, and this requires that what we see is genuine and touches upon some of the fundamental challenges in life.

But feelings alone don't make good TV. More is required.

In other words, it is just as much about the process of bringing a person through an emotional conflict in such a way that (s)he comes out whole on the other side. And not just whole, but also smarter, happier and maybe even as a better person.

Conflicts and obstacles are, so to speak, indispensable and completely necessary for a work's dramaturgy to hang together because it is impossible to create a happy ending and turn the story's main characters into heroes if they haven't fought for their victory. If we haven't deeply doubted on the way that they could ever find the courage, strength and ability to get through the tough challenges.

What would Sleeping Beauty be without the hedge of thorns, the Lord of the Rings without the evil Sauron and Donald duck without mishaps? Dull, to say the least ...

So the key ingredients in a good story are emotion, resistance and a happy ending.

Conflict resolution as a public service

However, when the story is to be told on a public service broadcaster such as DR (The Danish Broadcasting Corporation), it also has to be something more.

Among other things, it has to enlighten and inform about subjects that are factual and socially relevant to the population – these requirements are stated precisely here:

"The public service corporation as a whole shall provide the Danish public with a wide range of programmes and services, comprising news coverage, general information, education, art and entertainment, via television, radio and Internet or the like. Quality, versatility and diversity must be aimed at in the range of programmes offered. In the programming, the consideration of freedom of information and expression must be a primary concern. In the provision of information, emphasis must be placed on objectivity and impartiality. The broadcasting corporation shall provide access to important information on society and debate. Furthermore, particular emphasis shall be placed on Danish language and Danish culture. The broadcasting corporation shall furthermore reflect the breadth in production of art and culture and provide a range of programmes that reflect the diversity of cultural interests in Danish society."

With these principal criteria in the back of our minds as well as the wish to work with personal development through conflict and opposition, there was very little disagreement around the table when, in the autumn of 2009, DR decided to make a lifestyle programme with the mission of seeking to resolve disputes between neighbours.

Earlier in the year, DR had shown a documentary about the subject where, among other participants, a pair of sisters on the island of Funen fought bitterly with their neighbour - an old man - about the height of a hedge, wood fires and physical nuisances. The programme described this conflict and others in detail, and everything was commented on by a behaviour expert who explained how things can escalate in this way.

Over a million people watched the programme! This fantastic viewing figure brought to DR's attention that this was a subject that really affected the population.

But the new programme about neighbour conflicts was to go a step further than the documentary programme.

We weren't just going to describe and comment – we were going to *intervene*!

We were going to help people *through* the conflicts and out on the other side where the minimum goal was a tolerable neighbourly relationship. We would have to see what was wrong but, not least, how people can move on when it all seems completely unfathomable, deadlocked and terrible, and they feel threatened, afraid and sad. We would show just how beneficial it is to intervene. To take up the fight and challenge one's feelings, even though it is difficult and it hurts, because you will get a better quality of life and greater insight and understanding on the other side of the conflict.

Because this was the real public service job – to be solution-orientated about an inflamed country-wide issue that is a growing and extremely costly problem for an unbelievable number of Danes. One in five actually. More and more neighbours are fighting, and very few are able to stop again. So there is a real need for guidelines about how to extricate oneself from these tiring neighbourly conflicts if you are unfortunately stuck in one. Even so as to become smarter and happier as a result.

So the first important job was to find out *how* we would help neighbours to solve their problems.

And, already here, it gets difficult.

Behind the conflict

First we direct our attention to the authorities to which people automatically resort in this kind of case.

The police, the local boundary committee, the courts.

Because if solutions to squabbles and strife are to be found, surely they are to be found in the public system where society helps people by taking a position on who has the right to what, why and how?

It quickly became clear that the answer is both yes and no.

"Yes" because these objective legally-rooted decisions put an end to the disagreement in relation to working out who has the law on their side.

But absolutely "no" because it actually rarely resolves the conflict. On the contrary. The bad atmosphere between the contending parties is often just made worse as a result of society's intervention and the real conflict seems to be far from resolved.

Actually, we quickly got wind of the fact that neighbourly disputes are often the result of something completely different from the actual hedge or track. Conflicts may well start off with a dispute about a "something or other" - a hedge, a track or smoke from a wood burning stove - but, with lightening speed, they are about much more than that. They become personal.

Bad feelings arise, that quickly become enmity and hatred, and frustrations are directed against the other party's personality, their way of reacting and their overall behaviour.

The feelings discussed earlier come into play and take all common sense out of commission, and when conflicts reach this stage they seem to just explode. And the probability for peace gets close to the chances of winning the Lottery ...

How on earth do we resolve it then?? Something which on the face of it looks unresolvable?? This was the big question we were faced with at the start of our research phase, and we were well aware that a lot was needed if we were to continue to dare to have as a premise that the programme was to improve people's relationship with their neighbours.

We instinctively agreed that it would have to be about communication. About being able to talk together, listen to one another and tackle the case constructively. But how? How were we to get people to talk together?

Our fine host, Jens Blauenfeldt, is good at talking to people, but it was obvious to us all that these cases were so explosive that it would be an absolutely hopeless act to send him into the field to resolve the conflicts. He needed help. But who should his helpers be?

Mediation is the method

We found the answer at the Centre for Conflict Resolution and with the lawyer and mediator Pia Deleuran, who introduced us to the idea of mediation. This is a new and, in Denmark, relatively uncommon method of resolving conflicts that is based on dialogue and encouraging understanding among the parties.

The method consists basically in helping the parties themselves and, not least, *together*, to find ways to resolve the conflict with the help of a completely neutral and impartial third party as a facilitator.

That is, a so-called mediator or qualified conflict resolution specialist helps the parties through a structured process. This is first and foremost to give the neighbours the opportunity to unload and express their frustrations as directly as possible to the other party. After this they will hopefully listen to the other party's experience of the conflict, after which they are given time and space for reflection. That finally ends in the parties bringing suggestions for resolving the conflict to the table that can result in a nice signed agreement on peace in the neighbourhood.

Almost too good to be true. Sweet music to the ears, fits like a glove – all of a sudden we dared to believe in the project again. Or did we? Because it *did actually almost sound* too good to be true. We had already spent some time casting cases for the programme and, to put it mildly, we were shocked about on *how* bad terms people were, so it seemed utopian that one or two conversations could be able to bring to an end conflicts that had lasted years and hardened to stone, like that with a snap. A certain amount of scepticism was lurking under the editorial surface but, on the other hand, we were so far from having other options for ways of resolving the conflicts, so we took the chance. We trusted our experts, who told us success stories from earlier mediations. And we got started.

Magic ...

Before the actual mediations, we had three case-stories that, in each their own way, had become completely deadlocked.

In two of the cases the parties didn't even want to be in the same room during the mediation because they couldn't stand the bare sight of one another. And in one of these, which was also the wood burning fire case from the documentary programme, the parties were throwing stones, and the air was thick with malicious abuse.

Everyone in production was convinced that we wouldn't get anywhere with these cases. It would simply be the ultimate uphill battle, if not decidedly impossible to budge either of the parties one jot. The trenches were truly dug in deep.

In this way we had to ourselves stories with all the resistance and emotional unrest we could wish for – even to the extent that there was fear of not achieving a happy ending. In any case, we did not need to do anything extra to create conflict or doubt about whether the parties would ever resolve things – the challenges were clear to see, and, at this point, this clouded any optimism in the production team.

In this way prepared for the risk that we might be telling the story of a semi-failure, we got to work.

And, well I never: we started out with a success!

A farming couple from Northern Jutland in open conflict with an acting couple, who had moved to the area, after two sessions in the mediation room, reached a signed resolution to the conflict. It dealt with concessions relating to taking into consideration each other's different occupations *and* about something as simple as remembering to greet one another. And talk with one another. Just think – they were signing an agreement that they would henceforth talk together!!! That this should be necessary seems silly, but it appears to be this kind of thing that is needed.

In the next mediation the parties started each in their own room and one said unambiguously: "Never, ever, ever will I be in the same room as someone like him (the neighbour)". Neither of the parties went into the mediation with the expectation that it was possible to find something that even resembled a solution, but bingo! After the two mediators having spent a day wandering back and forth between the two rooms and speaking with the parties, they all met together in the middle and shook hands on being better neighbours from now on. Reflections on the expenses the conflict had had for them, and especially the prospect of more of the same, brought resolution suggestions and the will to negotiate onto the table. And they wandered off together to the ferry to go home.

And finally – the case from Funen – the warring parties from the documentary programme. The worst and most escalated conflict of them all, with smashed windows, harassment, physical scuffles and constant unrest.

Despite the good results up to now, the odds had dropped for another successful mediation. It was very difficult to believe that the neighbours could make any progress. And definitely not achieve anything resembling a tolerable relationship as neighbours.

The neighbours were also very pessimistic themselves. They agreed to attempt mediation – albeit each in their own room – but there was absolutely no belief in achieving a good result. "Let's get it over with so I can go home," said one of the neighbours at the start of the mediation.

And then – believe me. A while into the mediation it became obvious that, for one of the parties, there was under the problems lurking an old conflict with a former neighbour who had made a nuisance in the neighbourhood with smoke from his wood burning stove. The mediators brought these circumstances onto the table, which opened the way for a whole new mutual understanding and, not least, the will to find solutions.

After a day's work, the parties shook hands and moved on from there as better neighbours. Two months later they cut the hedge together, greet one another and have a "normal" neighbourly relationship, as they say.

It was magic to say the least.

As passive observers it simply appears to be pure magic for someone to be able to move people *so* much in such a short time without doing more than helping them to talk to one another and understand one another.

Of course, we are aware that our experts, the mediators, have spent many years learning the tricks of the trade, but the process is so fascinating because it is often nearly indiscernible what they are doing.

But the changes in the warring parties were clear. As if an angel had come through the room.

And we got three fantastic episodes in the bag.

There was a lot to identify with in the form of strong emotional conflicts and almost impossible challenges for the participants. As well as a fascinating insight into a process that, against all odds and in quite a short time, is able to bring incensed parties to agreement so that they are stronger and smarter on the other side. A wonderful happy ending.

And then we can just hope that it can inspire other neighbours at war so that society can save blood, sweat and tears and many millions on close combat in the neighbourhood.

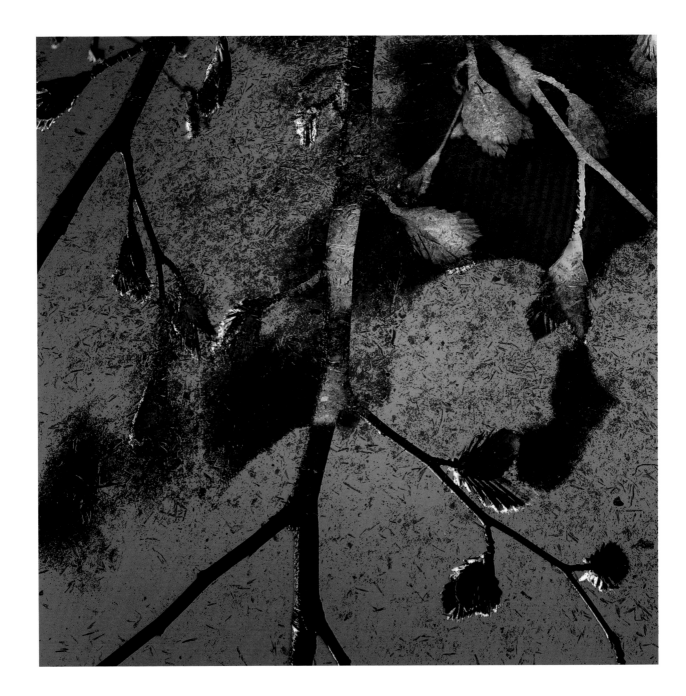

CHAPTER 9

Interview with Fay Weldon about Sex and Gender Issues in Conflict Situations

By journalist Sabrine Mønsted

In this chapter the British author Fay Weldon is interviewed by journalist and MSc Sociology Sabrine Mønsted. Fay Weldon gives us her opinion on gender/sex issues in conflict situations in close relations.

Gender in general

How do you see the relation between the genders today and the historical development of this relation?
We are after all an animal species. Girls are born girls and boys are born boys. Female and male brains are wired differently at birth. Brain surgeons can tell which is which just by looking. Blind instincts instruct us how to eat, mate, flee, kill, survive. We were bred to procreate: nature is indifferent to our happiness. But we have minds too, and here in the West we do what we can to impose order and control upon our primitive selves and thus achieve individual contentment and social justice. To this end women in particular try these days to minimise the difference between male and female. Men don't try

so hard, since the primitive order is not so hard on them as it is on women.

It can be done to a certain extent; men, for example, over the last couple of decades, have been very successfully socialised in the West to be good fathers. (One hopes the phalates in the plastic baby bottles of their infancy is not a contributory factor.) Women have got quite a long way in resisting the idea that it is their function to please and charm men.

In other cultures (e.g. Iran, Saudi Arabia) the understanding is that social justice and individual happiness is best achieved by emphasising the difference between men and women, not in minimising it. In such places the suicide rate amongst women is higher than it is in ours, where male suicide rates are double that of women.

Today we say that we are all individuals, so can you consider women as one group and men as another? And do we feel solidarity with our own gender?
We all still take our place on a scale that has extreme femaleness (yin) at one end and extreme maleness

(yang) at the other, dictated initially by the levels of oestrogen and testosterone that determined the wiring of our brain in the foetal stage. Recent neurological research suggests that more of both genders in the West cluster in the middle of the bell curve than they once did – especially as we get older, and we spend a greater percentage of our lives old than young – and that this may result from social conditioning. That is to say we are now less stuck in procreational mode. Nonetheless, this has not gone so far that we cannot perforce regard men and women as separate orders.

I think men feel more solidarity with other men than women feel solidarity with other women. Put a man in the army and he dies for his comrades; women show little sisterhood in their office careers as they seek promotion.

Does gender play a significant role in parents' relations to their children?
It depends. If both parents are, say, university professors, gender probably won't make all that much difference. Intellect will guide them. If the parents are less educated, instinct will probably guide them more.

What is the difference between being a mother and a father?
Well, the physiological and emotional differences are evident to the child. Just ask one!

I'd argue that mothers instinctively 'bond' with babies (of both genders) in a way, and on a level that father's just don't. 'Bonding' for women ends up as a life-time burden of maternal anxiety. Fathers feel protective to new-borns, but not compulsively anxious about them. The father often has to be reminded to pick up the child from child-care; the mother seldom so. It is not fair, but Nature did not build justice into the equation. The birth of the child, now that social sanctions against divorce have weakened, is often the end of the parental partnership, when the mother tries to bring about domestic justice, and puts the interest of the child above that of the father and he objects.

Legislation

The law in Denmark (and in several other Western countries) is working towards making the rules in relation to contact and visitation between children and parents gender-neutral. How do you see this trend and its consequences?
Should we not look at this from the child's point of view? Children like to have fathers and mothers living in the same house, and if the State is going to interfere at all perhaps it should encourage parents to remain together, as once it compelled them so to do. As it is, there is no perfect outcome for children when the parents split, only least-worse. Most couples can agree as to who loves the children most and is the better carer. They should be left to decide this for themselves. A minority cannot agree, and in these cases contact and visitation rights are probably better gender-neutral. Some fathers make better parents than mothers. Some parents of either gender hate the partner more than they love the child. Some are violent and cruel, go mad, take to drink and

drugs: these are the people the State should concern themselves with, and leave the rest alone.

In Denmark parents can be sentenced to a fifty-fifty arrangement in which the child shall stay half the time with one parent and the other half with the other parent. How do you view such an arrangement?

As completely disastrous, not to mention exhausting, for the children. This is Judgement of Solomon stuff. The State is recommending cutting the baby in half. One parent needs to make a sacrifice, for the sake of the child, or else risk losing the child's love and respect. Parents long for the company of their children after the split, but if the child tends to prefer the company of its electronic devices to a sit-down meal, can they be surprised – especially if there's a new sexual partner around. The child will certainly have a problem with packing suitcases for the rest of its life! Children of divorced parents are more readily socialised by their peers and their teachers. How can they have any concept of family loyalty? Easier to mock their parents on Facebook.

Do you see any consequences for the child to grow up this way?
The child belongs nowhere.

Do you see any consequences for the parents?
They only have half a child.

Do you see any consequences for our society?
Our social problems are doubled.

What do you consider the best solution for the state to manage and resolve children-related conflicts when parents split up? Should sex be reflected in the management of these conflicts? Is a law that forces the parents to cooperate a solution?
Back to the Judgement of Solomon. That conflict as to who owned the child (between two women, as it happened) was solved by a threat from the State. 'If you can't resolve this, the child dies.' Moderate this to 'if you can't decide this within three months, the child goes into care.' It might work. One or other of the parties might give in, as they did at Solomon's court.

No, I don't think the gender of the parents should be reflected in the judgement, but I think the age of the child should be. Mid- to late-teenage boys are better off with their fathers; teenage girls with their mothers. But charming small children are the ones parents usually get so passionate about: by the time children get to be spotty and gawky, conflicts are probably more easily resolved anyway.

You can't force parents to work together, but threats and/or bribes might help. Parents and lawyers could be charged for Court time spent, and rewarded for time saved by not going to court.

Remember any law must be applicable to our immigrant communities too.

The state authorities in Denmark require that a father should have contact with his child from the child is 3-4 months of age and often up to its 12th year, regardless if the primary care-giver protests, the child objects, major conflicts between the parents exist or if the father has not had contact with the child before. When the father has been granted contact with the child, police assistance may be requested by the court and fysical force may be applied to implement the courts decision. Ultimately, the mother may be imprisoned if she refuse to inform the court on the whereabouts of the child. How do you view this procedure?

I don't think sharing DNA with a child gives anyone automatic parental rights. If the child is the product of stranger-rape, or its grandfather is its father too, or, whatever, surely the father forfeits these rights. Mothers sometimes keep the child from the father spitefully or vengefully. Mothers are not necessarily nice people. But if I were a child I'd rather trust a jury of neighbours to decide my fate than a clutch of lawyers representing the State.

In Denmark there is a tendency asking children down to five years of age how they want to live after their parents have split up: However, their opinion does not form the basis of the court settlement. And the parents have a right to know what the child told the judge. How do you see the consequences for the children of such a procedure?

Of course, ask the child. But perhaps the parents should wait until the child is 21 before finding out what it told the judge.

Do you see any consequences for a child if the child's wishes are not complied with?

Of course. The child will blame all ills for the rest of his life on the Court decision. Bad enough if you don't send a child to the school of its choice, but the home of its choice? It will also blame the parents for failing to control the Court. Forget it.

How important is the child's opinion? How much should the children be consulted and how?

The child's opinion is all-important. He or she is the only one who should be consulted, shown the new homes on offer, the new sexual partners of the parents (if any), the new step-siblings, or the choice of an orphanage, and asked where he or she wants to go. What business is it of anyone else? If disputing parents wilfully deprive the child of its home they really have no right to a say in what happens next.

Children's interest

Is it possible to separate the relationship between the parents from the relationship between the parents and the child if a parent has been violent towards the other in presence the child?

Long-term emotional violence between the parents can be more damaging to the child than physical violence. The child can separate the relationship between himself and the parents, and the parents' relationship with one another, easily enough. If the child can forgive the violence, so can you the social worker. And try reversing the genders – if the woman was hitting the man how would you react?

If the father has been accused of violent or sexually abusive behaviour towards the mother or the child in Denmark, the court often decides that there should be supervised contact between the father and the child. One-two hours of contact a week is common, and if the child achieve any positive contact with the father un-

supervised contact will be granted. How do you see this practice?

It seems reasonable enough. In custody cases the court must be careful that the woman is not making false claims out of malice, or because she is told by her lawyers that it's to her advantage. Again, ask the child, ask the neighbours, what really goes on. The Court must emerge in the child's eyes as benign and wise, not some kind of ogre.

The responsibility of society

Is domestic violence generally gender-related in your opinion? If yes, should the state have a higher obligation to protect women against domestic violence?

Yes, domestic violence is generally gender-related, and often a substitute for satisfactory sex. Free Viagra would probably help. The State should certainly protect women against violence, but should ask itself to what extent it is legitimate to interfere with the citizen's private life. Why make domestic violence a special case? It's just violence. They could tax 'living together' so no one did it lightly, and make the having of children outside formal marriage more difficult still. If the State can stop suspect couples adopting children I suppose it could stop suspect couples from producing their own children. And it could ban drinking, as it seeks to ban smoking, when there are children in the home. But do we want Big Brother watching our every move in the home?

Should society ensure that fathers get a closer relationship with their children through social legislation? In Denmark we discuss maternity leave earmarked for men.

Yes, we all work too long and too hard at unimportant jobs: exhaustion makes all our family relationships fractious and fragile. If governments are really concerned about the welfare of children they could improve it at a stroke by cutting working hours to 35 a week. Any child will welcome 35 hours a week respite from parents, and parents from the child also.

The situation in England

How do you see the situation in England when it comes to society/the law dealing with conflicts in the family?

I think it's worse here because we have such a large and uneducated underclass, overworked social workers with arrogant views, currently under attack for removing children from their families without due cause. Our Family Courts, not without reason, are infamous for their secrecy, their tardiness and their unfairness to fathers. Women in search of sole custody are too often encouraged by their divorce lawyers tactically to claim sexual abuse on the part of the fathers. But the Courts are being reformed and journalists at last can be present at most cases. Our new Government is making changes. We look forward to better things!

Women and the labour market

You have argued that women cheated themselves in the 70's, in fact scored an own goal by entering the labour market so massively, and as a consequence they failed the children. Do you still see it that way? And do women still traduce themselves?

We didn't exactly traduce ourselves. We 70's feminists were young, middle class, educated and privileged, as are most revolutionaries, and naively assumed that what suited us would suit all women – that 'going out to work' was a better fate than staying home running a family. We vaguely assumed that earning would be a choice for women, but it became a necessity. We did not foresee that by flooding the labour market we would *de facto* diminish the value of the male wage to such an extent that two wages would be necessary to support the family unit. Pre-feminism, men flourished, children flourished, and women sacrificed their own lives in order that it should be so. Post-feminism, men flourish, women flourish, and children suffer as they are left to the State to raise, and become depressed and alienated from their parents. They would rather go on Facebook than a family outing.

We try to solve the problem of 'who will now look after the children?' by passing legislation that forces men to take on more of the emotional and physical burden of child-care than before, but it's an uphill task, and I suspect that even as we succeed, more and more partnerships and marriages collapse. The father just takes up with someone childless, or more domestically-inclined than the one he has left. (See my novel *She May Not Leave*.) I really hope I am wrong. The answer is certainly not women going back into the boredom of the home – even if they could afford to, which they can't – and depending once more on the capricious goodwill of men. A more fundamental restructuring of our wealthy societies so a 35-hour working week (including travel!) became the norm, would resolve a great many conflicts within the family.

Also, so might a return to some version of the old institutional orphanage system. It should remain at least a choice for the child, who might well see it as preferable to staying home: somewhere sane where he or she would have the company of other children, and adults be kept at a safe distance. The possibility that the child could use its own iniative and simply leave, might induce both parents to behave better. (Both would have visitation rights.) Doing away with orphanages was a mixed blessing, as was the doing away of our mental institutions as sanctuaries for the deranged.

CHAPTER 10

Negotiation Styles and Strategies: The Influence from Sex and Gender Dynamics

By lawyer Tina Bolbjerg Winther-Nielsen

During my final year of studying law at the University of Copenhagen I took a course in negotiation and dispute resolution. My interest for the subject was such that I chose to write my master thesis about negotiation. Many factors influence the process and ambience of a negotiation and, as a result, its outcome. How the parties are seated, how the lighting is, how the negotiators are dressed, how they talk and countless other factors play important roles. Many of these things are in the control of the negotiator, but factors such as age, colour and gender are not. As a young female, my gender will always be relevant in my negotiations. I was therefore interested in finding out what influence it has on the other party.

It soon became obvious that a large part of the answer to this question would lie in understanding female stereotypes. I, like most people, don't like the idea of being 'put into a box' by others. Unequivocally negative stereotypes, for example that 'women are bad drivers', particularly irritate me

because the tacit accusation seems so groundless. But when I chose to research and write about the effects of female stereotypes on the other party in a negotiation situation, I felt that I had to be honest with myself and question whether I also make generalisations about others based on factors such as their gender. The truth is that I would be more likely to expect a man to be logically minded and a woman to be emotional. I would also automatically link traits such as physical strength and maths skills with men, and on the other hand sensitivity and people skills with women. I was forced to face up to the fact that, despite believing that I disliked them, I was not unaccustomed of using stereotypes myself.

But I am by no means alone in this respect. The Bem Sex-Role Inventory (BSRI) is a tool that lists widely held stereotypes about males and females. According to the descriptors contained in the BSRI, women are 'other-orientated' while men are 'self-orientated'. According to J. T. Jost and A. C. Kay, it is a common opinion that the typical masculine and feminine traits (in other words, the gender stereotypes) are complimentary and that each gender possesses strengths and weaknesses that balance out the strengths and weaknesses of the other gender. It was quickly becoming obvious to me that gender stereotypes were not just an undesirable set of beliefs held by an unfortunate few: they were part of a much bigger and more complex phenomenon across society. On top of this, they serve a purpose. Stereotypes 'fill in the blanks' when we meet strangers. They make life easier for us by allowing us to apply knowledge we have acquired prevor to new situations.

But, widespread as gender stereotypes were now appearing to be, surely if someone stereotypes me then it's their problem, right? This turned out to be too simplistic an approach. Many gender stereotypes are descriptive but, by contrast, some can be prescriptive. The latter create expectations and rules governing the genders' behaviour. Women can be good drivers – it might be surprising to some, but there is no social rule that prescribes that women must be bad drivers. However being caring is a prescriptive female stereotype. The same is not a typical male stereotype. Women who are not caring may easily be described as 'ice queens' or 'bitches' whereas a man displaying the same behaviour would not be held to the same standard. He might 'just' not be a people person. It is never positive to not be caring but there is often a more severe consequence for women who are not caring than there is for men. Generally speaking the stereotypes of women being communal are prescriptive and if women are not behaving accordingly they risk a backlash.

Within the field of gender studies, reference is made to a 'social hierarchy', according to which women are traditionally seen as being subordinate to men. Research made by L. A. Rudman and P. Glick (2001) shows that for the social hierarchy to be maintained, society causes us to form stereotypes about various groups of people. The stereotypes characterise people according to their place in the hierarchy. For example, to maintain the power balance between the genders, men are attributed dominant and aggressive traits while women are attributed communal and submissive traits. 'Social punishment' is the tool that encourages people to conform to the prescriptive stereotypes and thereby keep the social hierarchy intact.

Social punishment is a sign of disapproval of the behaviour of another person and tends to discourage the person from behaving in that way. The social punishment can take many forms, such as social isolation, loss of influence, emotional withdrawal, others trying to modify the violating behaviour and a negative perception of the violator. Men and women both inflict a social punishment upon women who violate the prescriptive stereotypes, however research is not in agreement whether men tend to be faster to inflict the punishment. So the gender of the perceiver is no reliable guide as to whether one risks the infliction of a social punishment or not.

So disregard for the gender stereotypes could obviously have consequences, but would this be of importance in the context of a negotiation? According to L. Babcock and S. Laschever in their book *Women Don't Ask*, a woman is more influential when she is liked by the persons she is addressing. Men are equally influential whether they are liked by the people they are addressing or not. The infliction of social punishment equates to dislike. Not only is it 'uncomfortable', but, for the female negotiator, it has a direct impact on her ability to influence the other party. Negotiation is all about influencing people, so if violating stereotypes can lead to a loss of ability to influence the other party it is obvious that their role is more than just superficial. My research led me to believe that female negotiators should take gender stereotypes into account when deciding which negotiation strategies to use.

If I am preparing for a negotiation I have a choice of how to conduct it. When choosing my negotiation strategy I would consider the following factors: 1) The bargaining context and whether it hinders a joint-gain outcome? 2) The importance of my relationship with the other party – is this a one-shot-deal or do I want to continue to deal with the other party in the future? 3) The strategy of the other party. As a negotiator I need to be flexible enough to change strategy in order to respond to the other party's strategy. 4) My own personality – are there some strategies I feel more comfortable following and that suit me better than others? 5) The stage of the negotiation. In Western cultures negotiations usually start out more 'rough' but become less so towards the end, where solutions need to be found. 6) My bargaining power. What is my BATNA (Best Alternative To a Negotiated Agreement)? The better the alternative; the higher my bargaining power is.

If I have a strong bargaining position and do not value the relationship with the other party, I could be very competitive. I would use tactics such as extreme opening demands, threats, false concession patterns (if I were to concede at all) and anger to try to seek out the other party's bottom line. However, if I appreciate my relationship with the other party, I would plan a cooperative strategy, using a fair standard and a fair opening offer and sharing more information in an effort to find a fair solution. The aim of this strategy is not to push the other party close to or beyond his or her bottom line, as in the competitive strategy; it is based upon trust and goodwill between the negotiators and aims to find a just solution and preserve the good relationship. If I am convinced that we could expand the pool of what is negotiated and find a more creative solution, and if the other party is someone with whom I have been working for a long time and with whom I would like to keep a good relationship, then I would plan a problem solving strategy which would involve active listening, information-sharing and brainstorming.

Knowing what I now do about the possible impact that my gender can have on my interactions, I would also be inclined to take other factors into consideration. By choosing a competitive strategy, for example, my behaviour would be dominant and aggressive. This would increase the possibility of my incurring a social punishment and would also increase the pressure in an already pressurised negotiation environment. The other party is more likely to detach himself or herself from the negotiation in such a situation. The risk would be higher for me, as a women, in choosing this strategy that a premature deadlock would arise, than if a man were to act in the same way.

But gender stereotypes needn't always be of concern to the competetive female negotiator. Some negotiators with whom I have discussed competitive negotiation say that there is an element of surprise when women negotiate competitively because few people expect women to be comfortable in what is a stereotypically male role. In some situations it may be advantageous to disguise a competitive strategy in a cooperative style. Perhaps this will be easier for women since, according to C. B. Craver (2004), both male and female negotiators do not expect female negotiators to follow a competitive strategy.

If I were to follow a cooperative strategy I would not incur social punishment as the behaviour characterising this strategy corresponds well with the female stereotypes. However, the effectiveness of the cooperative strategy is limited when negotiating with a competitive negotiator. The competitive negotiator may use the information you share against you to find your bottom line. The problem solving strategy also fits very well with the female stereotypes but there exists the same risk of exploitation by a competitive negotiator. I may therefore be forced into negotiating competitively, despite having the will to be cooperative or to follow a problem solving strategy. We arrive again at a high probability for social punishment.

The strategies used by negotiators can change in the course of the negotiation. According to D. G. Gifford (1989), most negotiations in Western cultures start out in a competitive way but develop into cooperation or problem solving. Knowing what we do about the dangers of a competitive strategy for the female negotiator, there is an obvious risk for her in this type of negotiation. If I receive a negative reaction to my initial competitive approach, there is a higher likelihood for me as a female, than for a male in the same situation, that the other party will end the negotiation before reaching the cooperative or problem solving stages or that my ability to influence the other party will be reduced in these stages.

In addition to my pre-existing relationship with the other party and the behaviour involved in putting into practice the various strategies, an additional consideration that I, as a female negotiator, should take into account is the nature of the negotiation. According to research made by M. E. Wade in 2001, dominant or assertive behaviour on the part of a woman is met with a different reaction when she is negotiating on behalf of herself than when she is negotiating on behalf of others. In my opinion, the reason for this is that when women make requests for others they are not threatening the social hierarchy. On the contrary, acting in the interests of others corresponds with the female stereotype that women are communal. Therefore, it can be easier for women to negotiate as agents than on their own behalf, and women in these situations may have access to a wider range of strategies and tactics than when negotiating on their own behalf without the risk of social punishment.

Even having planned my negotiation taking into account my gender, gender stereotypes can still have an impact on its outcome. Gender-related 'attacks' is an expression used to describe effects of the gender stereotypes that are more directly detrimental to a female in a negotiation situation. They can take many forms: from doubting and undermining the female negotiator's competence and authority to reducing her to a 'plain' member of her sex and disregarding her individual traits and characteristics. D. M. Kolb and J. W. Williams wrote in *The Shadow Negotiator* that demeaning gender-related 'attacks' must be taken seriously immediately in order for the female negotiator not to be captured in the stereotypical 'woman group'. They did, however, also write that this can be difficult. The offending behaviour is often dressed as a joke, which makes it difficult for women to object to it without then being labelled as overly sensitive. The behaviour must be disrupted before it gets to linger between the negotiators. If it gets any momentum, the female negotiator is already disadvantaged, but if she disrupts too much, the attention stays on her reaction. A fine balance and feel for the situation are key.

There is a range of tactics that I can use to counter gender-related 'attacks'. Among them are diverting, correcting, interrupting and naming. Some aim to reframe the 'attack' constructively, avoiding letting them define me and without my relationship with the other party being damaged. However, where the 'attack' is of a more serious nature, more severe tactics must be used.

Diverting would be an appropriate response to behaviour from the other party that I felt was unprofessional and wished to put to an end, for example if undue attention was drawn to how I look. The focus of diverting this kind of behaviour is the content, and the diversion must show that how I look does not have an effect on how I negotiate or how intelligent I am. If the other party becomes personal and attacks my motives or abilities, I can shift the focus back to the problem, and in that way refute any implication that I am a part of the problem. There are different ways of diverting an 'attack'. I can, for example, respond to the 'attack' with a better idea of how to solve the problem, and in that way underline that I am not the problem. Diverting is also a useful way to postpone further action while one waits to see if the behaviour will continue. If it does continue, one or more of the further tactics may have to be used.

If the other party makes assumptions about me and jumps to conclusions based on those assumptions, they may come to view my motives in a negative light. This would undermine my position. Correction involves offering an alternative and positive explanation for the actions I take. This may involve countering stereotyped images, supplying a legitimate motive or shifting focus to the positive. Countering stereotyped images is especially important when the other party makes assumptions based upon the my gender. It is important to react to these biases by correcting the image the other party has of me, in order to be taken seriously. Not many negotiators will openly admit to believing in negative stereotypes about others, and it can be a very effective way for a female negotiator to separate herself from the stereotype by exposing the bias behind the negative stereotypes in order to undermine the argument the other party gives. Supplying a legitimate motive is characterised by shifting the power balance back from being, for example, unreasonable, greedy, or insensitive to being rational and having a reason for one's actions. Focus is shifted to the positive, when the negotiator aims to correct negative images to give what she sees as a more balanced representation of the situation.

If the other party is excluding me from the negotiation, interruption of the negotiation may be necessary to attempt to make myself more visible. The way the interruption is conducted depends on my role in the negotiation and my bargaining position. The interruption may be a dramatic or humorous remark that stops the action that excludes the me. The interruption can have the effect of surprising the other party or catching him off-guard. By interrupting the action, I also interrupt the momentum working against me. The interruption may also consist of standing up to get a cup of coffee from the other end of the room, taking a quick phone call or going to the office or car. This can be enough to break the momentum and give me time to think and gather myself.

The purpose of naming the other party's tactic is to let them know that I am aware of what is going on, and that the tactic is not going to work as intended. If I put a label on the other party's tactic to describe how it looks to me, I both give the other party a chance to change the behaviour and let him or her know that I know what is happening. The naming must be carefully balanced and directed towards the tactic and not the person. The label I give the tactic should fit the tactic and the other party's perception of the tactic. I have to be careful not to label too harshly because I could otherwise appear overly sensitive or inexperienced. Naming is often enough to make the other party stop the tactic and change the dynamics of the negotiation. Some negotiation tactics and behaviours can have unintended effects. By highlighting the consequences of the behaviour, I allow the other party to know how I am affected without necessarily calling into question his or her good faith.

Knowledge of all of the above tools could prove very useful to me during the negotiation to deal with some specific problems that I, as a female negotiator, may encounter.

It can be concluded that female negotiators do not have access to competitive tactics on the same terms as men do. In general the tactics used by a competitive negotiator do not correspond with the female stereotypes, and in most cases the female competitive negotiator will be acting very dominantly, so there is a great risk of social punishment, which the female competitive negotiator must take into account. In addition to social punishment, the female negotiator must be prepared for gender-related 'attacks' and know how they can be countered. The process of writing my thesis about how my gender affects others in a negotiation has taught me a lot about how women are stereotyped but, more importantly, it has taught me what I can do to prevent these stereotypes from disadvantaging me. I believe that this knowledge is important for all women.

Literature

Babcock, L. & Laschever, S., 'Women Don't Ask' (New York, 2007).

Craver, C.B.: 'The Impact of Gender on Bargaining Interactions', (2004), accessed at http://www.negotiatormagazine.com/article204_3.html on 31 May 2008.

Gifford, D.G., 'Legal Negotiation: Theory and Applications' (St. Paul, 1989).

Kolb, D.M. & Williams, J.W., 'The Shadow Negotiation' (New York, 2000).

Rudman, L.A. & Glick, P., 'Prescriptive Gender Stereotypes and Backlash Toward Agentic Women' (2001) 57 *Journal of Social Issues* 4:743-762.

Wade, M.E., 'Women and Salary Negotiation: The Costs of Self-Advocacy' (2001), 25 *Psychology of Women Quarterly* 65-76.

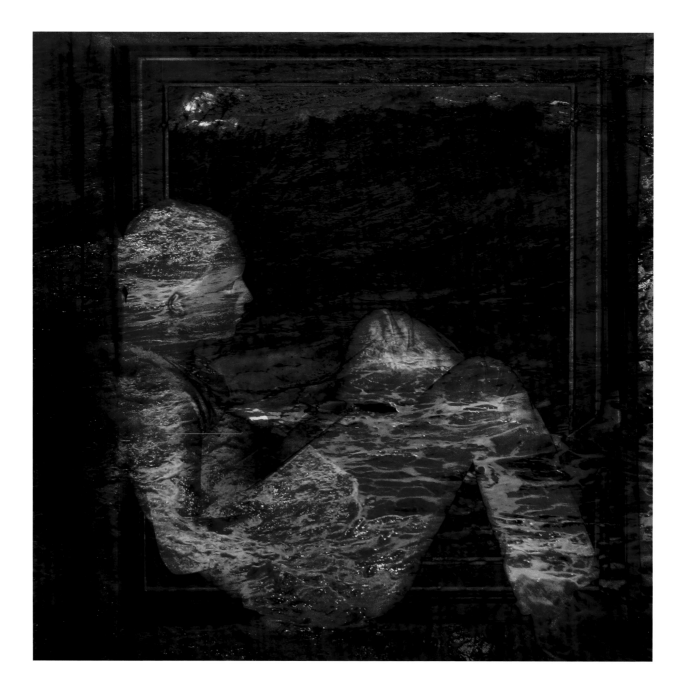

CHAPTER 11

Silencing the Self: Inner Dialogues and Outer Realities

By psychologist Dana Crowley Jack

And I think on my inside, private things I say to myself, I still really feel that I'm not – I wrote it down – that I'm not patient enough, I'm too selfish. I mean I haven't gotten that self-acceptance, I just haven't. With my husband, I would say we, I have to be able to say my feelings of anger or resentment, or wanting things different when they happen. And he has to be able to hear them without being too defensive, and say his feelings back so that we can have a mutual understanding of each other.

> (Carol, age 41, physician in practice 13 years,
> married with two children, ages 9 and 11.
> Diagnosed with unipolar major depression.)

How does one listen to themes that recur in depressed women's talk – of negative self-judgment, low self-esteem, and moral failure? Are they merely symptomatic distortions of depression? Or do these themes offer a new path to understanding the complexities of women's vulnerability to depression?

Women's rates of depression are two times higher than those of men in most Western industrialized countries (Nolen-Hoeksema, 1990). Among women in three major ethnic groups within the United States – Blacks, Whites, and Hispanics – the 2:1 sex ratio holds, even though the lifetime prevalence of depression is lower among Blacks than among Whites and Hispanics (Blazer, Kessler, McGonagle, & Swartz, 1994). Researchers have not found a satisfactory explanation for this gender difference (Coyne & Downey, 1991; McGrath, Keita, Strickland, & Russo, 1990; Nolen-Hoeksema, 1990), although they have identified social factors that make women vulnerable to depression. Circumstances associated with increased depression in women include the dual impact of poverty and young children; the psychological disadvantage of women's negative social status; the lack of a close, confiding relationship; and the difficulty of communicating with a partner who is hostile and critical and cannot be relied on in times of crisis (Coyne & Downey, 1991). Furthermore, exposure to stress is socially organized in gender-specific ways; women are more often victims of partner violence and poverty than are men, for example (Stoppard, 1989).

Nor only women in poverty are vulnerable to depression; professional women have a higher incidence of depression and suicide than do women in the general population (McGrath et al., 1990). Known stressors that affect this privileged group of women come from discriminatory institutional structures (Whitley, Gallery, Allison, & Revicki, 1989), including sexual harassment, and from family responsibilities historically arranged to accommodate men's careers (Gross, 1992; Myers, 1988; Sells & Sells, 1989).

To understand women's higher rates of depression, it is not enough to detail the social stressors that affect women more often than men. Individuals moderate stress differently. Not all women become depressed in a given environment, yet little is known about how social factors translate into the meaning women make of themselves in their world or about how these factors work interpersonally and psychodynamically to affect women's vulnerability to depression.

To learn more about how social factors become internalized and affect depression, researchers need to listen carefully to women's inner dialogues and negative self-assessments. In what follows, I offer a phenomenology of clinically depressed women's subjectivity, particularly focused on what their negative self-assessment reveals about underlying images of relatedness. Such images, and the dynamic of silencing the self, have been found to be reliably associated with depressive symptoms, as I describe later.

Silencing the self

My work on silencing the self theory began by listening to 12 clinically depressed women participating in a longitudinal study in an attempt to understand their experience in their own terms (Jack, 1987, 1991). In addition to the frameworks provided by relational theorists such as Bowlby (1980, 1988) and Mitchell (1988), who have documented the fundamentally social nature of the self, new theoretical frameworks for the psychology of women provided a standpoint from which I heard and interpreted women's inner worlds within specific social contexts. Feminist theorists point to specific female ego strengths, weaknesses, and fears that grow out of women's ego identity development (Chodorow, 1978; Gilligan, 1982; Miller, 1986). Relational feminists stress that as part of gender-identity processes and socialization, women's sense of self is organized around connection, mutuality, and relationships. Self-esteem is tied to the quality of attachments; feelings of guilt, shame, and depression are associated with the failure of intimate ties (Gilligan, 1982; Miller, 1986). The challenge of development is not to separate (or to loosen emotional bonds) from core relationships but to stay connected to one's own feelings, goals, and voice while developing and changing within relationships (Brown & Gilligan, 1992; Gilligan, 1982; Jack, 1991).

According to the relational viewpoint, depression is interpersonal for both genders; despair arises when the person feels hopeless about the possibility of intimate connection with others (Bowlby, 1980). However, beliefs about how to relate interpersonally are powerfully influenced by gender as well as by power differentials. To learn how a person's gendered beliefs about relatedness affected depression, I listened closely to the moral themes in depressed women's narratives.

Not surprisingly, depressed women constantly use moral language – words such as *selfish, bad*, and *worthless* – as they assess themselves and their role in causing problems in their relationships. Because both the fall in self-esteem and negative self-evaluation are considered basic symptoms of depression according to the *Diagnostic and Statistical Manual of Mental Disorders* (4th ed.; American Psychiatric Association, 1994), researchers often overlook the vital information they contain. Developmental and psychoanalytic theorists have consistently portrayed differences in the formation and functioning of women's and men's moral concerns. Regardless of theoretical perspective, observers find a female morality attuned to relationships and affection, and a male morality based on abstract principles expressed in laws and rules (Freud, 1925/1961; Gilligan, 1982; Kohlberg, 1981; Piaget, 1932).

I have found that standards used for self-evaluation are key in understanding gender differences in the prevalence and dynamics of depression. In a person's self-reproach, standards for the ideal self are used to judge the actual self. These standards alert researchers and clinicians about what a person believes she or he should be like and how she or he should interact in order to be loved, socially valued, and safe. They come from three major sources: the individual's family, the current social context, and the wider culture. Thus, self-evaluation provides a window through which to view the social standards a person accepts and uses to judge the self, how competing standards may come into conflict within the self, and how such standards are embedded in images of relatedness that direct interpersonal behaviors. Because standards of "goodness," including measures of social worth, vary by gender, ethnicity, and social context, inquiry into moral language allows a way to honor each person's individuality; in its fully contextualized richness, by observing what values she or he strives to attain.

Gender inequality also affects the standards women and men use to evaluate the self. Inequality affects the lives of all women through the culturally explicit or implicit message of women's inferiority to men (Fredrickson & Roberts, 1997; Westkott, 1986). However, the degree to which any woman internalizes this message varies by social class, ethnicity, and personal history, and it is powerfully influenced by the gender relations she sees modeled as she grows up. Particularly when the mother displays submissiveness in relation to dominating men, a girl can incorporate gender inequality into her images of relatedness. Inequality then becomes part of an understanding of how to interact with others, particularly in intimate relationships, and also becomes part of the standards used to direct behavior and evaluate the self.

Searching for the standards depressed women use to judge themselves negatively, I found a model of goodness that, although varying from woman to woman in specifics, contains norms of the "good wife" and "good mother." At the core of these roles lies the belief that selflessness is good, a standard that is unattainable and self-defeating in relationships. Such women believe that in order to be loved, they have to put the needs of others first. If a girl learns that others' needs always come first, the unspoken corollary is "my needs are less important than those of others and they will never be met, or they will be met reciprocally only if I care for others first." This childhood learning, passed on through the daughter's identification with her mother (and her mother's relational position), in tandem with a social structure in which women hold a lesser position, lays the basis for pervasively low self-esteem as well as for repressed anger over unmet needs. An internalized hierarchy of needs, with hers lower than those of the people she cares for, can then become part of a girl's feminine identity and understanding of feminine goodness.

When being "selfless" in relationship is linked in a woman's mind with "goodness" (morality), with femininity (out of identification with a mother who was "selfless" and subordinate in relationship), and with intimacy (providing safety from abandonment), she must deny whole parts of herself, including negative feelings and direct self-assertion. Yet for many such women, the measure of goodness and social worth also includes the image of "superwoman." Being a superwoman requires behaviors premised on self-reliance, aggressiveness, integrity, and self-esteem. Thus, "goodness" can include measuring up to two sets of norms that oppose each other. One requires selfless behavior; the other, "selffull" behavior. Later in this chapter, I provide examples of how these factors are reflected in depressed physicians' inner dialogues.

How are images of relatedness, including moral standards about how one should interact as a "good" woman or man, associated with depression? If one accepts the idea of relational theorists that making and maintaining relationships is the primary motivation throughout life (Bowlby, 1980; Mitchell, 1988), then analysis of images and beliefs about the self-in-relation becomes vital to research and treatment of depression. Silencing the self theory proposes that early experiences of growing up female (or male) provide a basis for forming certain images about relatedness: how to make and keep attachments and how to remain safe within them. These images are experienced as moral beliefs about how to be a good woman or man, or as what one must be like to be loved or socially valued. Depressed women's narratives are filled with examples of how such images led them to subordinate their own needs and voices to those of others and to believe that acting an their own behalf is selfish or will lead to isolation or retaliation.

Depressed women describe how certain images of relatedness – "oneness," "goodness," "self-sacrificing," "pleasing" – direct them to silence vital aspects of self out of fear that voicing them would threaten their relationships or their safety. Self-silencing contributes to a fall in self-esteem and feelings of a "loss of self." As depressed women use the metaphor *loss of self,* it serves as a verbal shorthand for a complex process that includes, most centrally, a loss of voice. *Voice* does not mean the literal act of speaking but refers to the ability to manifest and affirm in relationships aspects of self that feel central to one's identity. Speaking one's feelings and thoughts in relationship is part of creating, maintaining, and recreating one's relational identity. Thus, *voice* refers more to the *substance* of what is communicated or hidden in relationship than to speech acts themselves.

Self-silencing, therefore, refers to removing critical aspects of self from dialogue for specific relational purposes. How a person uses his or her voice is profoundly affected by the anticipated response from the social context. Women and men face different cultural and relational consequences for voicing their anger, oppositional feelings, or demands; women are often more at risk for negative economic, physical, or interpersonal consequences than are men (Christensen & Heavey, 1990; Dobash & Dobash, 1979; Jacobson & Gottman, 1998). For women and men, behavior that appears outwardly similar (such as self-silencing) may come from a different origin and carry a different intent regarding its desired effect on relationship. In distressed couples, for example, men are more likely to use "stonewalling" – withdrawal through silence or passive resistance – from the partner's "demand" behaviors for change, intimacy, or engagement (Babcock, Waltz, Jacobson, & Gottman, 1993; Gottman, 1994). These researchers have hypothesized that men's withdrawal behavior (which can look like self-silencing) may be an attempt to control women's emotional, engaging style and to maintain the status quo of power relations. In other words, when men self-silence, they may intend to create distance and to control interactions in relationship. Researchers must look behind self-silencing for its gendered meanings and its relational intent, recog-

nizing that the meanings and uses of voice and silence vary in relation to power (Hurtado, 1996) and by culture (Goldberger, 1996; Gratch, Bassett, & Attra, 1995). Self-silencing does not *always* derive from powerlessness or indicate depression.

In women, silencing the self – that is, stopping certain thoughts, words, and actions – often leads to the outer appearance of passivity and dependence. Because the actions required to silence the self are outwardly invisible, researchers have mistakenly focused on depressed women's supposed passive style of coping (McGrath et al., 1590; Nolen-Hoeksema, 1991) without observing the "cognitive activity required to appear outwardly passive and compliant" with traditional female behaviors expected by certain partners, social contexts, and personal beliefs about goodness (Jack, 1991, pp. 129-139). Whereas from the outside women look passive and compliant, on the inside it requires tremendous self-monitoring and self-inhibition to present this appearance. Depressed women's statements such as "I have learned, don't rock the boat with my partner" and "I won't cause waves, I won't say anything" show their conscious awareness of making themselves appear passive or compliant for an intended effect: to keep outer harmony, to preserve relationship. Self-silencing becomes obvious when women try to change their thoughts and when they tell themselves how they "ought" to feel. Women take the cognitive actions required to adapt themselves to existing structures for many reasons: the fear of retaliation, the desire to keep relationship, or the lack of models for alternative behaviors. Rather than outwardly challenge the forms of their relationships, they take this inward action against themselves.

Entering a person's experience through her or his moral language allows one to analyze how gender ideologies can masquerade as moral precepts about how one "should" behave in relationships. I noticed that moral language most often occurs within a person's inner dialogues. In depressed people, this dialogue most often takes the form of a divided self, with a judging, condemning voice and an answering voice that defends the self, most often on the basis of lived experience. Inner dialogues not only reflect the standards used to judge the self but also reveal a place of dynamism where new meanings and actions coalesce, where a person challenges accepted truths and formulates new perspectives. Culture not only is reproduced in inner dialogues but it is also changed. Given that a person may choose among competing ideologies that specify what a woman or man "should" be like, researchers can learn which ideologies carry the most power for women and men in particular ethnic groups and social contexts as well as which ideologies cause the most inner conflict and self-alienation (Jack, in press-b).

Listening to a person's inner dialogue, one hears how actively silencing the self leads to the inward experience of a divided self – the condition of self-alienation. Living out the images of relatedness, a woman begins to experience two opposing selves: an outwardly conforming, "nice," compliant self trying to keep relationships and to please and an inner, hidden self that is angry, resentful, and *increasingly hopeless about the possibility of genuine relationship or self-expression*. Women describe trying to keep hidden aspects of self out of relationship, with the result of overwhelming feelings of loss of connection, inauthenticity, and loss of self. This experience of inner division, in which one part turns against the other with rage, is a key aspect of depression.

In summary, the obstacles to voice that I have found to be associated with depression in women are described below.

Images of relatedness

These images are experienced as beliefs about how one "should" behave in order to make and maintain relationships or to stay safe within them. Specific attachment behaviors – pleasing, helping, oneness, self-sacrifice, self-silencing – that are *culturally defined as feminine* have been prescribed for generations of women interacting intimately with men who had direct power over them. They contain inequality in the understanding of relatedness, how one resolves conflict, what it means to give and care for another person, and one's own worth and importance. If a woman adopts these images of relatedness based on selflessness, she envisions the most important issues in her life – how to relate to others and protect herself – as an either/or choice that presents her with loss on either side. The choice is either *isolation* (*lose relationships* if she acts on her own needs or speaks her voice) or *subordination* (*lose herself* if she silences her voice) – either loss of self or loss of other. Such dichotomous thinking leads to feelings of hopelessness about the prospects for authenticity and connection. Furthermore, if a woman enacts these culturally prescribed attachment behaviors, they lead to "compliant relatedness" (Jack, 1991, p.

40), a type of connection that appears to offer intimacy and safety. Characterized by restriction of initiative and freedom of expression within a relationship, compliant relatedness looks like dependence or an anxious attachment behavior.

Shame or fear

Many depressed women appear convinced that voicing opposition, anger, or "selfishness" will be met with some type of negative consequence. Behind this fear, which often feels "inner" or uniquely personal, lie specific outer social factors that influence fear, such as violence, sexual and racial discrimination, and poverty, each of which is a known factor for women's depression vulnerability (McGrath et al., 1990). Directed by the belief that voicing authentic feelings leads to danger, and that silence offers safety, a woman will "bite her tongue" or aggress indirectly or with ineffective explosiveness, rather than state dangerous feelings or thoughts directly. Fear of consequences for voicing one's self depends partly on personal history and partly on current social context. When both conspire to reinforce fear (e.g., when personal history corresponds to current critical or abusive relationships), the images of relatedness based on inequality in relationships are reinforced. If a woman's circumstances allow few options, she may see silencing herself as the least harmful choice, far preferable to other possibilities she perceives, such as retaliation, divorce, or suicide. Because silencing does not mean literally an absence of voice, it is critical to examine what aspects of self arouse a woman's shame and are kept out of relationships, directed by what images of relatedness and fears and with what imagined consequences for the person's sense of possibility for authentic, intimate relations with others.

Prohibitions against women's anger and aggression

Women's fears about the negative consequences of self-assertion (which many equate with aggression) appear to be related to the inhibited behaviors and cognitive styles researchers find associated with female depression (Jack, in press-a). The relevance of aggression inhibition to depression vulnerability in women is underscored by meta-analyses of research on gender differences in aggression. Mediators of aggression in women include guilt and anxiety over display of their aggressive behaviors or feelings, anticipated danger to the self, and empathy (concern about harm that aggression causes to the recipients; Eagly & Steffen, 1986). Like other social behaviors, aggression can be viewed as regulated by gender-specific social role norms that traditionally have deemphasized women's aggression (particularly in middle-class White women) and have encouraged their nurturance. Likewise, depression researchers emphasize that women's social roles affect their vulnerability to depression (Klerman & Weissman, 1980; McGrath et al., 1990). Particularly when a woman's background emphasizes nurturance, goodness, and sensitivity and precludes aggressive actions, often defined broadly as "standing up for myself" and "saying what I think and feel," society's prohibitions against female aggression enter to reinforce self-silencing behaviors. I am investigating this hypothesized relationship in a qualitative study of 60 women's accounts of their own aggression, with attention to variations of ethnicity and class (Jack, in press-a).

If a woman thinks aggression is "bad" – unfeminine, pushy, selfish, destructive – she will work hard to inhibit what she perceives as aggressive behavior in herself. On the outside, this can look like a "failure of action and mastery strategies" (McGrath et al., 1990); it may also appear that the woman is ineffectively "ruminating" on her negative thoughts (rather than restricting her initiatory, assertive behavior). Interviews with women about their aggressive actions and fantasies have led me to a different conclusion: Women focus intensely on how to balance their aggressiveness (what many would call appropriate self-assertion, or standing up for themselves) against their wish to be "good," to be safe, and to keep harmony in relationships. Furthermore, as they calculate the social costs of speaking up – the costs to their relationships, their jobs, and the physical safety and security of themselves and their children-they often silence themselves rather than incur feared consequences (Jack, in press-a).

Silencing the self theory postulates that women whose backgrounds or current contexts encourage them to meet their relational needs in self-sacrificing, inauthentic ways are more likely to adopt gender-specific schemas about how to make and maintain intimate relationships. These schemas, or images of relatedness, reflect cultural prescriptions for feminine relationship behavior that are based on inequality. Self-silencing contributes to decreased possibilities for intimacy, to a loss of self-esteem, to the experience of a divided self, and to a heightened vulnerability to depression.

Silencing the self scale

Given the need for multiple methodological strategies, I constructed the Silencing the Self Scale (STSS; Jack & Dill, 1992) to measure the association between self-silencing and depression. Thirty-one scale items, with Likert scores ranging from *strongly agree* to *strongly disagree* with a range of 1 to 5, represent the themes that were heard most often in the narratives of clinically depressed women.

Four rationally derived subscales represent the proposed dynamic of depression: *Externalized Self-Perception* (judging oneself by "external" standards); *Care as Self-Sacrifice* (securing attachments by putting the needs of others before the self); *Silencing the Self* (inhibiting one's self-expression and action to avoid conflict, possible loss, and retaliation); and the *Divided Self* (presenting an outer self that does not express personal, authentic thoughts and feelings; the experience of inner division). Each subscale was conceptualized to be part of a pattern that is associated with a dynamic of depression. Subscales are considered to work together in a dynamic, interactive fashion, so that as one aspect is strengthened, it heightens the other three.

Researchers using the STSS consistently find self-silencing associated with depressive symptoms in different samples of women (Brazaitis, 1995; Carr, Gilroy, & Sherman, 1996; Gratch et al., 1995; Penza, Reiss, & Scott, 1997; Thompson, 1995), with levels of self-silencing varying in predicted directions with differing social contexts (Jack & Dill, 1992). Construct validity of the scale has been affirmed through replication of subscale structures with samples of Asian American, African American, Hispanic, and non-Hispanic Caucasian women and men (Duarte & Thompson, 1998; Gratch et al., 1995; Gratch & Jack, 1998; Stevens & Galvin, 1995). Construct validity has also been affirmed through studies of the scale's association with predicted variables, for example, with eating disorders (Cawood, 1998), "loss of self" (Drew & Heesacker, 1998), lack of mutuality (Penza et al., 1997), marital distress (Thompson, 1995; Whisman, Uebelacker, & Courtnage, 1998), and perceived power in relationship (Cowan, Bommersbach, & Curtis, 1995).

Although silencing the self theory was proposed in the context of women's depression, samples of men score consistently higher than women on the STSS (Cowan et al., 1995; Gratch et al., 1995; Hart & Thompson, 1996; Jack & Dill, 1992; Thompson, 1995; Whisman et al., 1998). Whereas initially this finding appears to create a problem for construct validity, researchers have found that the correlates of self-silencing vary by gender in predicted ways. For example, in Thompson's (1995) study of heterosexual couples, silencing the self was more closely related to depressive symptoms for women than for men, and women's silencing was negatively associated with both their own and their partners' relationship satisfaction, whereas men's was not. Also, the meanings of self-silencing appear to differ for each gender. Cowan et al. (1995) speculated that perceived power is more critical than gender as a variable that influences the level of self-silencing. The STSS appears to correlate reliably with depressive symptoms (although differently) in both women and men; thus, further investigation into patterns, meanings, and

correlates of self-silencing by gender is warranted, with particular focus on genesis and relational intent.

In my view, while both genders endorse a set of social conventions about goodness in relationships, how they translate those conventions into interpersonal behaviors differs and is affected by perceived power and social context. Content analysis of standards used for self-evaluation (Scale Item 31) may further the understanding of high male STSS scores. In the Jack and Dill (1992) scale construction study, responding to Item 31 ("I never seem to measure up to the standards I set for myself"), male college students referred to, in order of frequency, grades and then stereotypical male role requirements, such as sports ability, wage-earning ability, or interpersonal issues revealing problems of socialization to the male role, such as "play it safe in relationships." Female college students also first listed grades and then specified the following gender-based standards in order of frequency: physical appearance, weight, and having good personal qualities that make them attractive to others. Content analysis may further the understanding of how social imperatives translate into self-alienating standards used to judge the self and into images of relatedness that do not foster genuine connection.

Assumptions of self-silencing theory

Silencing the self theory assumes that the images of relatedness measured by the STSS are reflexive, that is, that they interact with the individual's life history and with situational variables, particularly with how the social context and close relationships "expect" a person to behave interpersonally. This "reflexive model" of depressive vulnerability asserts that "the categories of thought that people bring to actively interpret their worlds, guide their behavior, and assess the self are socially constructed and are reflexive with social institutions and contexts. Gender-specific aspects of socialization practices and of material social power are reflected in these social categories of thought" (Jack & Dill, 1992, p. 99). Rather than being permanent and internal, called into use by events in the environment, images of intimate relatedness measured by the STSS are presumed to be reinforced, challenged, and changed by current social contexts. The degree to which women, for example, engage in self-silencing is related to their personal history (their identification with the mother's power in relation to men), their current relationship context (e.g., "their partners" dominating, coercive behaviors or the setting they work in), and their personal functioning (e.g., depression, level of self-esteem) and, reflexively, will also affect their relationship functioning (e.g., interpersonal behavior, intimacy).

Silencing the self theory differs from a diathesis-stress model, including Beck's (1983) cognitive-personality model, Blatt, Quinlan, Chevron, McDonald, and Zuroff's (1982) psychodynamic personality model, and Nolen-Hoeksema's (1991) coping response model, in two respects: (a) stability of trait and (b) location of problem. Regarding stability of trait, diathesis-stress models assume that the trait in question is an enduring, stable aspect of personality that interacts with factors in the environment to cre- ate a vulnerability to depression. Highest risk for depression is assumed to occur with a congruency between negative life events and the personality domain of value. Although these theories attempt to take account of the social context more fully than did earlier cognitive-behavioral models, they still inadequately account for the impact of social context on the person (Coyne & Whiffen, 1995). Furthermore, the personality domains of value seem artificially divided into achievement and interpersonal realms, and they do not take into account how people often construe the achievement realm as an interpersonal field, and vice versa. They also do not consider how norms directing gendered social behavior effect women's and men's interactions both in the achievement realm and in their intimate relationships. In contrast, self-silencing relational images and behaviors are not considered permanent features of personality but rather are susceptible to the affects of changing social contexts and specific relationships.

Regarding location of the problem, diathesis-stress models clearly include consideration of the social environment as it interacts with aspects of personality, but the vulnerability factor is considered to reside within the individual (Coyne, 1992). In silencing the self theory, the focus and conceptualization of the problem differ. The focus is on images of relatedness and their *reflexivity* with social factors. These images of relatedness, open to influence from social contexts, are hypothesized to relate to depressive symptoms through the specific dynamic previously described: self-silencing, loss of self, inner division, anger, and self-condemnation. The problem is not considered to lie in a deficit (such as ruminative coping style) or in a favored personality orientation (dependency-autonomy) that interacts with environmental events to create depression. Rather, the problem is considered to lie in specific forms of unequal, negative intimate relationships as well as larger social structures that demean an individual's sense of social worth. Such specific conditions are assumed to be internalized differentially (depending on personal history and social contexts) and to manifest in images of relatedness that contain moral standards, which then affect the individual's behaviors, self-evaluation, and self-esteem. Endorsement of self-silencing schemas is linked to depression through the mechanisms described earlier (see also Jack, 1991).

Although findings regarding the association of the STSS with depressive symptoms are promising, they do not address which of many causal pathways might account for the correlations. The theoretical assumptions regarding variations of self-silencing with particular social, relational contexts throughout the life span need to be investigated through prospective, longitudinal studies with clinically diagnosed samples of women and men.

Case examples

To demonstrate the phenomenology of depression associated with silencing the self, I present three case examples of depressed physicians. I chose these examples to explore how social contexts are manifest in standards used to judge the self and to offer a beginning illustration of the gender-specific nature of such standards. Women and men from other social contexts will sound very different (Jack, 1991, in press-b); the critical factor is to examine the interaction of social context with experience of self through the images of relatedness that guide interpersonal behavior and that supply standards used to judge the self.

Known factors that put professional women at higher risk for depression are found in medical training and practice (McGrath et al., 1990). Male doctors were assumed to have a "wife" who would take care of family and home; historically, two people supported one career. Currently, even when a partner supports her career, a woman still does more of the household chores and parenting than her partner, if a man (Myers, 1988; Sells & Sells, 1989). Not surprisingly, career-family conflict was cited as a stressor by many more female (46.3 percent) than male (6.1 percent) physicians in a study of perceived stressors in medical practice (Gross, 1991). Studies of medical students have shown that women experience more work-related stress and negative emotional reactions than do men (Coombs & Hovanessian, 1988; Janus, Janus, & Price, 1983) and that women in residency training report significantly greater levels of stress and depression than do men (Whitley et al., 1989); the suicide rate in women doctors is four times that of the general population (Craig & Pitts, 1968; Rucinski & Cybulska, 1985).

Women in professions struggle against a social backdrop that sexualizes and trivializes their work and aspirations. An early study of depression in 111 women physicians and 103 women PhDs (Welner et al., 1979) was undertaken at a time when women began entering medical schools in large numbers; the authors documented the relationship of social stresses, particularly sex discrimination, with depressive onset. Fifty-one percent of the physicians and 32% of the PhDs were diagnosed as having primary affective disorder; depression among psychiatrists was significantly higher (73%) than among other physicians (46%). More than 50% of the women reported prejudice in training or employment, and depressed women reported more prejudice. Onset of depression occurred during training or residency (33%) or during practice (39%) rather than prior to medical school (28%), leading to the easy conclusion that the structures of this profession did not support women. These issues of gender discrimination in medicine continue. For example, in the January 20, 1992, issue of *The Nation*, Dr. Adriane Fugh-Berman highlighted issues of harassment, hostility, and threats throughout her training at Georgetown Medical School in the late 1980s.

How are these social factors manifest through processes described in silencing the self theory? Images of relatedness, inner division, and standards used to judge the self negatively, apparent in the following examples, can help guide clinicians in listening to, interpreting, and intervening with depressed clients.

The following excerpt comes from a taped interview with a physician, Carol (age 41, White, diagnosed with major depression), who is currently taking the antidepressant trazodone (Desyrel). She has been in practice for 13 years. Married to another physician for 15 years, her children are 9 and 11. In this passage, Carol explains her strong agreement with Item 7 (Extemalized Self-Perception subscale) of the Silencing the Self Scale, which reads "I feel dissatisfied with myself because I should be able to do all the things people are supposed to be able to do these days." Her words reveal what, in her mind, she's "supposed" to be doing and how she imagines she falls short:

> You can't be Supermom and can't do it all, and yet we all have this image that we can, and we measure ourselves by the standards of our mothers in terms of raising kids. You know, I feel guilty when I'm not there with the warm milk and cookies and when I'm not putting every Band-Aid on. And then I'm guilty because I'm not enough of a spouse for my husband; and I'm guilty because I'm not doing an adequate job professionally and never quite getting it all right. And there's not a role model of a successful woman doing all this except this illusion of a superwoman someplace. On the outside, people, residents, tell me, "You're such a wonderful role model." And I think, "You don't know the half of it." So there is an illusion of role models, but there's not a real role model of what a good mother is who's working. (Q: *When the residents say that to you, what do you say back?*) Actually, to be honest, I usually don't tell them the truth. I say, "Thank you," or something.

Carol presents, a persona that lives up to role demands – both feminine and professional – while her silenced, observing self thinks that observers "You don't know the half of it." She does not alert newcomers to medicine to her private struggles in managing to be mother, wife, and doctor. Her silence does not indicate an inability to speak; it reveals a choice to hide certain aspects of self. Looking at what aspects of self a professional woman chooses to silence and why she does so alerts the clinician to a number of issues: what she thinks self-revelation might cost her, what images of relatedness guide her behavior and self-evaluation, and how she begins to feel a "loss of self" as she removes key aspects of self from dialogue with others.

The achievement and interpersonal spheres (autonomy and sociotropy) do not stay neatly divided in people's lives but spill over to affect each other profoundly. Carol, the president of a national organization, successful as a physician, is undermined by negative self-judgments that carry from home into work, even though her rational self has plenty of ammunition to oppose such judgments. The phenomenology of the divided self emerges in her self-commentary:

> I feel like there are two me's. There's the successful me that I could never incorporate. I guess that I always felt deep underneath that I wasn't very skilled and so when I would see myself as reflected as being successful it didn't match my image of myself.
>
> I don't have a history of failures and so that's so bizarre, and yet somewhere underneath that all, I don't measure up, and I'm kind of just beginning to come to grips with that. *I feel like I'm too selfish, too self-centered, all those, on a personal level all those kinds of issues that somehow then translate into feeling incompetent on a professional level as well* ... I do more than the average woman doctor by a mile. By 2 miles. And it's kind of an overcompensation proving to myself that I can do this and that I am capable.

Carol's attempts to integrate opposing social expectations translate into an experience of inner division, of "two me's," with the harshly judged self that is "too selfish, too self-centered" covered over by a professional self that tries to overcome these feelings by proving she is capable. Yet her considerable achievements pale next to her sense that she is fading to be a "good" wife and mother; interpersonal issues "translate" into her experience of the achievement realm. The terms *successful professional* and woman each carry specific expectations and images for interpersonal behaviors. How a woman physician "should" fulfill the norms of her profession carries one set of expectations; how a woman "should" interact in intimate relationship carries a different set. The requirements for success in each sphere – the romantic and the professional – are opposed: How can a woman be both lovable and a successful professional if norms for feminine behavior require being deferential to others whereas professional success demands competition and self-assertion? (See also R. Jack & D.C. Jack, 1989, and Westkott, 1986.) For Carol, the beliefs that direct her behavior and self-evaluation appear to be most strongly based on an ideal of selflessness that undermines her in both spheres.

As one might predict, in response to Item 4 (Subscale 2: Care as Self-Sacrifice) "Considering my needs to be as important as those of the people I love is selfish," Carol circled "agree." The standard of selflessness, derived from the feminine role requirement to care for others by putting their needs first, directs her vision of the hierarchy of needs within relationship. Selflessness directs behavior by dictating how she should choose when her needs conflict with those of others she loves; it provides a standard for harsh self-judgment if she veers from its command. Furthermore, the standard of selflessness arouses anger as, following its dictates, she places her needs second to those of others; yet it also commands the repression of anger by purporting a moral basis for the suppression of her own needs. Disguised as moral demands, such role requirements are difficult to challenge. Selflessness reinforces a woman's low self-esteem by affirming that she is not as worthy or important as others, and finally, it legitimizes the historical and still prevalent view of woman's nature as essentially self-sacrificing and maternal (Jack, 1991).

Another depressed physician reveals how this same image of how she "should" relate to others affects her self-silencing and feelings of anger, inner division, and lowered self-esteem. In practice 6 years, Sue (age 36, White) has been married 9 years and has two daughters, ages 2 and 5. Her husband, also a physician, is fully aware of the demands of the profession. At the time of this interview, Sue had been diagnosed with unipolar major depression by a psychiatrist and had been taking fluoxetine (Prozac) for 3 months. Like Carol, Sue agreed with Item 4 in the STSS, "Considering my needs to be as important as those of the people I love is selfish." She said:

> Right now, I'm struggling with the fact that – I keep telling myself, there's this voice in my head that tells me that I'm a bad mother and the reason why I'm a bad mother is because when I come home after working for a day, my husband is lying on the floor playing games with my kids and all I want to do is sit on the couch and read a newspaper. And I feel like then I'm deficient, you know, because I enjoy or I need time to do something – that I would prefer doing something other than being with my kids. I mean I struggle with that. And then my husband wants me to join them, and I do but I don't feel good and I can't tell him. When I'm by myself I don't have to struggle with that – whose needs are more important and whether my needs are valid and okay and whether someone's going to think that I'm silly or stupid or unreasonable or irrational. I can just be who I am.

Like Carol, Sue describes a "voice in [her] head" that tells her she's a bad mother; this voice is directed by the standard of feminine goodness as self-sacrificing nurturance. The voice pronounces self-condemnation ("I'm deficient in my lack of selflessness"), which arouses her anger as she accedes to its demands. Then the voice demands anger's repression. Sue struggles with the dilemma of how to act, how to judge herself, and how to relate within her family. Yet the cognitive activity, the "struggle," required to curb her own needs or voice is not visible to others. What they see is her outward compliance with her husband's wish that she join the family, a demand that coincides with her own images of what a "good woman" does. Sue joins them but does not feel good about doing so. This important issue of how to balance her own needs with those of her family is silenced by the belief that she "can't tell" her husband about her feelings. Sue imagines how her husband would respond to her voice ("think I'm silly or stupid"), blames him for her compliance, and feels resentful.

Of course, silencing one's needs in order to give to others does not always lead to self-alienation and depression. The context within which the giving occurs and the giver's ability to choose when, how, and in what form to care are critical. If a woman experiences selflessness as a requirement because of inner images or outer coercion, she enacts subservience to others' needs and becomes increasingly angry, resentful, and confused.

Both Carol and Sue value being physicians and attempt to live up to ideals about how to be a "good doctor," which contradict behaviors demanded of them as wives and mothers. The voice of harsh self-judgment can align with both sets of norms to critique the self for not "measuring up" to either of them. Sue goes on to talk about how she feels as a physician:

> I think I've always been perceived as very competent and, you know, bright and responsible, but have never taken that in, and all my life I wondered, you know, when somebody was really going to find me out. (Q: *And what would they find out?*) That I wasn't – that I was not competent and – not bright and a lousy physician. I don't think I think the way I imagine physicians should think. You know, the kind of analytical, rational, sort of step-by-step thinking that I imagine physicians do. For me, medicine is very intuitive, it's very creative, there are certain kind of leaps that I make ... I think the whole process of medical education ... is very, very brutal, very dehumanizing, very damaging, especially for a woman. All the attributes that are traditionally womanly are discouraged and belittled. I was even once told by one of my residents to "be a man." You know, be a man. Be decisive. Be, you know, be aggressive. Be a man. And that's essentially what they want you to be. They don't want you to have any womanly virtues. They don't want you to be compassionate or caring, or loving, or humble, or emotional. They don't want you to be any of those things ... And I think part of what I'm really angry about is the fact that I buy into it.

Social factors, specifically Sue's personal experiences of being objectified, devalued, and punished as a woman in a profession designed by men for men, contribute to her inner division. Her narrative reveals how these social factors are structured in thought and work to affect her self-alienation and vulnerability to depression. Sue uses the language of the culture to devalue and deny what, on another level, she values and desires. Listening, one hears how she has judged her abilities against a dominant standard that says one must leave "womanly virtues" aside to be a physician. Sue reflects on her capabilities and strengths not on the basis of who she is and what she needs but in terms of how colleagues in her profession and others see her. Her capacity for creative, intuitive thinking and for listening to people, advocating for people, and seeing herself as a hand-holder go unacknowledged as strengths. Rather than reflecting a shortcoming of the profession, the problem is identified as her feminine style. Listening to Sue's feelings about self-worth, her confusion about what she values and what the culture says she *should* value, one hears that the self-alienation and separation from feelings are reflexive with her social context.

In Sue's inner dialogue, her harsh, critical voice condemns her as "a lousy physician." This voice reflects male values and ordains what a woman "should" be like from a male perspective. I call this voice of the inner dialogue the Over-Eye because it judges the self from the perspective of the culture's Eye, reflecting women through the male gaze (Jack, 1991). She is the "outsider" to medicine, and she is expected to adapt to a stereotyped version of the physician role: "Be a man. Be decisive. Be ... aggressive." Sue adopts a male standard, "how physicians should think," and sees her style as different and *deficient*. These exclusionary practices arouse Sue's anger and contribute to her feeling "like a fake." To succeed, she believes she must present the *appearance* that her values accord with those of the profession, particularly those of commitment, objectivity, impersonal professionalism, and rationality. Doing so requires separating from valued aspects of self.

The other voice in Sue's inner dialogue, the perspective that emerges when she is "by herself," is that of the authentic self. As Sue describes it, when experiencing her authentic self "I can just be who I am" and not struggle over whose needs are more important or "whether my needs are valid and okay." It is a self that does not, worry about "whether someone's going to think that I'm silly or stupid or unreasonable or irrational" if she acts on the basis of her own needs. When Sue enacts the perspective of her authentic self, she does not silence herself (take cognitive actions against herself to create compliance with the perceived expectations of others) nor does she feel self-alienated or self-condemning.

As Sue uses competing personal ("be selfless") and professional ("be aggressive") norms to judge herself, she undergoes a profound silencing of valued aspects of self in both realms. Afraid that honest self-expression may lead to retaliation, loss, or both (as well as violate images of relatedness), she turns her anger against herself rather than against the structures that devalue her: "And I think part of what I'm really angry about is the fact that I buy into it." This anger, arising from her self-enforced compliance to standards she knows are self-alienating, reveals both her acquiescence and her resistance to dominant stereotypes. Such anger and self-awareness offer a point for therapeutic intervention. What is paralyzing and leads to the sense of hopelessness is Sue's belief that if she let the oppositional, authentic self speak, she would not be accepted but would be harshly judged by others – her husband, her colleagues – with negative consequences. Thus, the authentic self remains in hiding and feels increasingly resentful, angry, and hopeless. The Over-Eye takes this angry, nonconformist self as its object and evaluates it as "deficient," "a bad mother," "not competent," and "a lousy physician."

The phenomenology of depression – self-silencing, inner division, and negative self-judgment – appears to be similar in men. However, men often internalize images of "goodness" from the culture that cluster around different attributes of self. As a group, they enjoy different levels of material and social power than women, and they appear to silence different aspects of self. As a result, their images of relatedness – how to make and maintain relationships – appear to differ from women's in terms of some of the "shoulds" that direct behavior and self-judgment. Given more permission from the culture to be aggressive in their own behalf and living in a social world in which their dominance is still most often assumed, their dilemmas appear to have less to do with fears of asserting their voices in relationship and more to do with feeling inadequate in gender-specific roles, such as breadwinner, successful professional, or father, or with revealing vulnerability to others. The following example of Dan, age 48, in a medical practice similar to Sue's and Carol's, illustrates a similar phenomenology of depression, but there is variation in the standards used to judge the self, directed by different images of relatedness.

Married for 25 years and the father of two children now in college, Dan has been in practice for approximately 20 years. At age 48, his episode of major depression remitted after a two-month vacation from medical practice, but it returned gradually after he resumed work. At the time of his interview, he was in combined drug and cognitive therapy.

On the STSS, Dan received the highest possible score on the Externalized Self-Perception subscale. In discussing his agreement with Item 7, "I feel dissatisfied with myself because I should be able to do all the things people are supposed to be able to do these days," he explained:

> A lot comes up about work. I should be able to see more patients more efficiently and have a life, and should be able to adapt to the changes [in medical practice], and should be able to keep up in medicine, do the reading I need to do, and somehow it's a defect in me or a deficiency that I can't do it.

Dan's litany of "shoulds" contains not only an implied perfectionism but also an image of selflessness focused on professional role: He should be "selflessly" married to medicine. His "shoulds" require his adaptation to what he perceives as unlimited claims of medical practice. Rather than question the demands of his profession, he turns against himself, requiring acquiescence to unrealistic standards and condemning himself for an inabil-

ity to keep up. He explains that increasing overhead costs and his role as sole financial provider for his family exacerbate the pressure to continue in his untenable professional position. Professional demands, then, gain coercive power as they mesh with capitalistic competition and the valued roles of husband, father, and economic provider. Whereas Sue and Carol locate the sources of their depression in the conflicting demands of wife – mother and physician, Dan focuses solely on the impossible demands of his professional role.

Dan also explores his agreement with Item 16 ("Often I look happy enough on the outside, but inwardly I feel angry and rebellious") from the Divided Self subscale:

> I think of the office a lot. I really feel stressed or angry about something, but I don't let the patients see that because they aren't coming to me to see that. I feel like I need to put on my professional face and my caring face and something like it, because if I'm feeling like that, it's not their fault. I rationalize it as my issue.

Dan's inner division occurs primarily within the context of the profession. When he thinks of presenting a false face, of hiding his anger, he locates these actions within his work setting.

Dan does not mention feeling silenced by "shoulds" from his role of husband and father, only from his role as physician. Speaking of his relationship with his wife, he said, "I think she obviously looks out for me, and I think other people do." Selflessness does not guide his images of how he should interact within his family, only of how he should behave as a physician. In contrast to Carol and Sue, whose concerns revolve around whether they are focused enough on family members, Dan assumes that others in his family look out for him.

Elaborating on why he disagreed with the statement "I feel that my partner does not know my real self" (Item 25), with which both Sue and Carol agreed, Dan said:

> I think that my wife probably sees me better than most people do, knowing how I act. Even though my mouth may say something, she knows from my actions in the past [the words] may mean something else.

Dan does not feel he has to hide his authentic self in his primary relationship; even if he tries to hide, his wife sees his real feelings because of her extensive knowledge of him.

Although intimate relationships carry emotional importance to Dan, different "shoulds" and images of relatedness, as well as different power dynamics, guide his participation in them. Likewise, although profession is central to all three physicians, fitting into the norms of the profession requires that men and women silence different aspects of the self or judge the self as "deficient" for differing reasons. Both women and men engage in self-silencing; how it differentially affects their lives and their vulnerability to depression remains open to further investigation.

Implications for therapy

Depression is profoundly existential and social, affecting all aspects of a person's felt experience.

Moral themes provide a direct, vital entry into the heart of experiential aspects of depression. Encouraging a client to be more self-affirming, or "arguing" about the accuracy of a person's self-perception, often does not touch the core of negative self-judgments. To challenge these core issues, clients need to explore the origins of their images of relatedness; how they are tied to gender, inequality, and culture; and how they became moralized. Sue, one of the physicians quoted earlier, explained that when a therapist tries to convince her that she's "not dumb,"

> I can carry ore this very involved argument in my head: "Well, you are dumb because of this, this, this, and this." You know, any sort of argument that someone can throw at me, I can think of five things, five examples to counter it.

Sue has been advised to counter "you're dumb" with accurate self-statements and to challenge global thoughts with instances that demonstrate that she is not dumb. Sue finds the advice unhelpful because it misses the point. The issue is not accuracy of self-regard; her struggle is developmental, existential, and moral. It is a struggle about identity: Through whose eyes does she see and evaluate herself? How does she position herself in relation to inner and outer voices that say her perspective is wrong? Feeling "dumb" represents a long-term theme in Sue's life that preceded her depression. This negative self-judgment becomes a critical point of entry into understanding how the social context interacts with her images of relatedness to contribute to vulnerability to depression.

How can therapy help move Sue from spinning her wheels in this rut of self-perception? First, sorting out the different strands of interpersonal history that form the standards used for negative self-evaluation allows a person to gain a perspective on the power of such standards. Such an exploration leads to Sue's awareness of her physician father's assessment of family medicine as a profession in which one has to "know everything. He couldn't hear that you didn't have to know everything ... so he couldn't understand my wanting to go into family medicine." This awareness, then, links back to her feelings of being "dumb," of not being "good enough," in her father's or in her male colleagues' eyes, and an awareness that the vision of her inner authority (Over-Eye) parallels that of her father and the predominately male profession she works within. She sees and judges herself from the perspective of a devaluing male gaze.

Second, helping Sue voice inner arguments about her "dumbness" to an attempt to decide which voice "in her head" she wants to align with can give her a sense of choice regarding self-judgment. According to whose standards is she dumb? How does that judgment render her voiceless and powerless in situations that matter to her? How does that judgment reinforce the authority of those she may wish to challenge – both inner and outer authorities? Her refusal to see herself through her father's or her colleagues' eyes can become part of her ongoing quest to invent herself as distinct from family and professional dictates, and it can support her healthy resistance to damaging self-images. Where can she get support and help from others who are in her posi-tion so that she does not pathologize aspects of experience that have more to do with discriminatory practices in medicine than with "deficits" in an individual personality? This exploration leads Sue to a discussion of the realities of the external difficulties she faces and how she can strengthen her own perspectives on her profession through participation in a support group with other female physicians.

To facilitate a client's movement out of the trap of negativity, therapists may want to direct close attention to that person's inner dialogues. Once aware of the voices of their different selves, individuals can hear and decide which voice (or potential self) they want to align with. Many people have not acknowledged silenced aspects of self or attended to their whisperings; this is a task of therapy. If the therapist is intrusive and suggests, for example, that a woman's behavior is too compliant, that she needs to become more assertive, without engaging with the relational images and prohibitions against aggression, the risks of her outer compliance and inner self-alienation, anger, and despair are heightened. For example, Carol said, "It's kind of like how do you disagree with somebody? Being assertive has felt bad all along and I would intuitively do it, but then what I would feel really was "was that OK? was I wrong? was I ...?"" Again, Carol questions not the "correctness" of her behavior but its moral meaning and its conformity with her images of relatedness.

Third, a therapist can foster a change in self-perception by helping a woman see that her compliance or "passivity" requires a tremendous amount of cognitive activity. As a woman explores how and why she silences herself, she can watch the specific cognitive actions she takes against herself and what her expectations are regarding the interpersonal consequences. Her self-silencing can be understood as a self-defensive strategy instead of as "self-defeating thoughts." She can work with the fears that underlie bringing her voice into dialogue. What would happen if she did not silence herself? What does she consider her own aggressive behaviors to be, and how does she feel about them? What does she expect as a social response to her self-assertion, disagreement, or anger (which she may see as aggressive)? Do these issues figure into her "inhibited mastery and action styles"? For men, explorations can similarly focus on what aspects of self are being silenced, on the activity required to live up to self-alienating role demands, and on what fears accompany change.

The Silencing the Self Scale can be a useful adjunct in therapy with groups, individuals, and couples to explore issues of moral meaning, self-silencing, inner division, and depression. Using the STSS in treatment groups with depressed clients provides a structure for short-term therapy that quickly deepens discussion. In couples therapy, responses to the STSS provide a useful entry into discussion of issues of power and silence. After each person separately responds to the scale, each also writes how he or she thinks the partner would answer. The couple can explore together their responses, and each person can gain a greater awareness of the uses of silence, as well as standards the partner uses to judge the self and find it lacking. Such exploration often leads to greater empathy and understanding for each other concerning issues of gender, "passivity," voice, and aggression. It also makes clear underlying issues of inequality within relationship.

Conclusion

Depression affects a person's sense of self and identity at the deepest levels; its roots lie in the complex interactions between person and social context. Silencing the self theory offers one possible understanding of how images of relatedness and standards for self-evaluation are reflexive with social contexts. Studies using the Silencing the Self Scale have not yet confirmed whether the phenomenology sketched here is a cause or effect of depression. In the meantime, attending to moral themes and images of relatedness offers new possibilities for listening to and engaging with the harsh inner dialogues of depression. Such a dialogue can become a vehicle for change rather than self-blame as a person shifts the focus from the shortcomings of the self to explore how outer social conditions interact with inner beliefs to create alienation and anger. Because silence itself carries complex, multiple meanings, researchers and therapists must acknowledge the complex thicket of power, choice, and intent that surrounds acts of self-silencing while also exploring the contribution of self-silencing to depression.

This chapter was presented in
Joiner, Thomas (Ed); Coyne, James C. (Ed), (1999). The Interactional Nature of Depression: Advances in Interpersonal Approaches, (pp. 221-246). American Psychological Association, Washington, DC, US.

References

American Psychiatric Association. (1994). *Diagnostic and statistical manual of mental disorders* (4th ed.). Washington, DC: Author.

Babcock, J.C., Waltz, J., Jacobson, N.S., & Gottman, J.M. (1993). Power and violence: The relation between communication patterns, power discrepancies, and domestic violence. *Journal of Consulting and Clinical Psychology, 61,* 4050.

Beck, A.T. (1983). Cognitive therapy of depression: New perspectives. In P.J. Clayton & J.E. Barrett (Eds.), *Treatment of depression: Old controversies and new approaches* (pp. 265-290). New York: Raven Press.

Blatt, S.J., Quinlan, D.M., Chevron, E.S., McDonald, C., & Zuroff, D. (1982). Dependency and self-criticism: Psychological dimensions of depression. *Journal of Consulting and Clinical Psychology, 50,* 113-124.

Blazer, D.B., Kessler, R.C., McGonagle, K.A., & Swartz, M.S. (1994). The prevalence and distribution of major depression in a national community sample: The National Comorbidity Survey. *American Journal of Psychiatry, 151,* 979-986.

Bowlby, J. (1980). *Attachment and loss: Vol. 3. Loss, sadness and depression.* New York: Basic Books.

Bowlby, J. (1988). *A secure base: Parent-child attachment and healthy human development.* New York: Bask Books.

Brazaitis, S. (1995, August). *The psychological constructs of voice and silence across racial identities.* Paper presented at the 103rd annual meeting of the American Psychological Association, New York.

Brown, L., & Gilligan, C. (1992). *Meeting at the crossroads: Women's psychology and girls' development.* Cambridge, MA: Harvard University Press.

Carr, J.G., Gilroy, F.D., & Sherman, M.E. (1996). Silencing the self and depression among women: *The moderating effects of race. Psychology of Women Quarterly, 20,* 375-392.

Cawood, R.M. (1998). *Self in relationship in women who engage in disordered eating.* Unpublished doctoral dissertation, University of Florida, Gainesville.

Chodorow, N. (1978). *The reproduction of mothering: Psychoanalysis and the sociology of gender.* Berkeley: University of California Press.

Christensen, A., & Heavey, C.L. (1990). Gender and social structure in the demand/withdraw pattern of marital conflict. *Journal of Personality and Social Psychology, 59,* 73-81.

Coombs, R.H., & Hovanessian, H.C. (1988). Stress in the role constellation of female resident physicians. *Journal of the American Medical Women's Association, 43,* 21-27.

Cowan, G., Bommersbach, M., & Curtis, S.R. (1995). Codependency, loss of self, and power. *Psychology of Women Quarterly, 19,* 221-236.

Coyne, J.C. (1992). Cognition in depression: A paradigm in crisis. *Psychological Inquiry, 3,* 232-235.

Coyne, J.C., & Downey, G. (1991). Social factors in psychopathology. *Annual Review of Psychology, 42,* 401-425.

Coyne, J.C., & Whiffen, V.E. (1995). Issues in personality as diathesis for depression? The case of Sociotropy/Dependency and Autonomy/Self-Criticism. *Psychological Bulletin, 118,* 358-378.

Craig, A.G., & Pitts, E.N. (1968). Suicide by physicians. *Diseases of the Nervous System, 29,* 763-772.

Dobash, R.E., & Dobash, R.P. (1979). *Violence against wives.* New York: Free Press.

Drew, S.S., & Heesacker, M. (1998). *The role of relationship loss and self loss in depression: Understanding differences between women and men.* Manuscript submitted for publication.

Duarte, L.M., & Thompson, L.M. (1998). *Gender differences in self-silencing.* Manuscript submitted for publication.

Eagly, A.H., & Steffen, V.J. (1986). Gender and aggressive behavior: A meta-analytic review of the social psychological literature. *Psychological Bulletin, 100,* 309-330.

Fredrickson, B., & Roberts, T.A. (1997). Objectification theory: Toward understanding women's lived experience and mental health risks. *Psychology of Women Quarterly, 11,* 173-206.

Freud, S. (1961). Some psychical consequences of the anatomical distinction between the sexes. In J. Strachey

(Ed. and Trans.). *The standard edition of the complete psychological works of Sigmund Freud* (Vol. 19, pp. 248-258). London: Hogarth Press. (Original work published 1925).

Fugh-Berman, A. (1992, January 20). Man to man at Georgetown: Tales out of medical school. *The Nation, 37,* 54-56.

Gilligan, C. (1982). *In a different voice: Psychological theory and women's development.* Cambridge, MA: Harvard University Press.

Goldberger, N. (1996). Cultural imperatives and diversity in ways of knowing. In N.R. Goldberger, J.M. Tarule, B.M. Clinchy, 4 M.F. Belenky (Eds.), *Knowledge, difference and power* (pp. 335-371). New; York: Basic Books.

Gottman, J.M. (1994). *Why marriages succeed or fail.* New York: Simon & Schuster.

Gratch, L.V., Bassett, M.E., & Attra, S.L. (1995). The relationship of gender and ethnicity to self-silencing and depression among college students. *Psychology of Women Quarterly, 19,* 509-515.

Gratch, L.V., & Jack, D.C. (1998). *Gender issues and factor structure on the Silencing the Self Scale.* Manuscript submitted for publication.

Gross, E.B. (1992). Gender differences in physician stress. *Journal of the American Medical Women's Association, 47,* 107-114.

Hart, B.I., & Thompson, J.M. (1996). Gender role characteristics and depressive symptomatology among adolescents. *Journal of Early Adolescence, 16,* 407426.

Hurtado, A. (1996). Strategic suspensions: Feminists of color theorize the production of knowledge. In N.R. Goldberger, J.M. Tarule, B.M. Clinchy, & M.E Belenky (Eds.), *Knowledge, difference and power.* (pp. 372-392). New York: Basic Books.

Jack, D.C. (1987). Silencing the self: The power of social imperatives in female depression. In R. Formanek & A. Gurian (Eds.), *Women and depression: A lifespan perspective* (pp. 161-181). New York: Springer.

Jack, D.C. (1991). *Silencing the self: Women and depression.* Cambridge, MA: Harvard University Press.

Jack, D.C. (in press-a). *Facing aggression: Hidden aspects of women's psychology.* Cambridge, MA: Harvard University Press.

Jack, D.C. (in press-b). Ways of listening to depressed women in qualitative research: Interview techniques and analysis. *Canadian Psychology.*

Jack, D.C., & Dill, D. (1992). The Silencing the Self Scale: Schemas of intimacy associated with depression in women. *Psychology of Women Quarterly, 16,* 97106.

Jack, R., & Jack, D.C. (1989). *Moral vision and professional decisions: The changing values of women and men lawyers.* New York: Cambridge University Press.

Jacobson, N., & Gottman, J. (1998). *When men batter women.* New York: Simon & Schuster.

Janus, C.L., Janus, S.S., & Price, S. (1983). Residents: The pressure's on the women. *Journal of the American Medical Women's Association, 38,* 18-21.

Klerman, G., & Weissman, M.M. (1980). Depressions among women: Their nature and causes. In M. Guttentag, S. Salasin, & D. Belle (Eds.), *The mental health of women* (pp. 57-92). San Diego, CA: Academic Press.

Kohlberg, L. (1981). *The philosophy of moral development: Moral stages and the idea of justice.* New York: Harper & Row.

McGrath, E., Keita, G.P, Strickland, B.R., & Russo, N.F. (1990). *Women and depression: Risk factors and treatment issues.* Washington, DC: American Psychological Association.

Miller, J.B. (1986). *Toward a new psychology of women* (2nd ed.). Boston: Beacon Press.

Mitchell, S.A. (1988). *Relational concepts in psychoanalysis: An integration.* Cambridge, MA: Harvard University Press.

Myers, M.F. (1988). *Doctors' marriages: A look at the problems and their solutions.* New York: Plenum Medical Books.

Nolen-Hoeksema, S. (1990). *Sex differences in depression.* Stanford, CA: Stanford University Press.

Nolen-Hoeksema, S. (1991). Responses to depression and their effects on the duration of depressive episodes. *Journal of Abnormal Psychology, 100,* 569582.

Penza, K., Reiss, A., & Scott, H. (1997, May). *Sexual orientation and communication in relationships: Self-silencing, mutuality and power in heterosexual and lesbian relationships*. Paper presented at the American Psychological Society, Washington, DC.

Piaget, J. (1932). *The rules of the game*. London: Routledge & Kegan Paul.

Rucinski, J., & Cybulska, E. (1985). Mentally ill doctors. *British Journal of Hospital Medicine, 33*, 90-94.

Sells, J.M., & Sells, C.J. (1989). Pediatrician and parent: A challenge for female physicians. *Pediatrics, 84*, 355-361.

Stevens, H.B., & Galvin, S.L. (1995). Structural findings regarding the Silencing the Self Scale. *Psychological Reports, 77*, 11-17.

Stoppard, M.M. (1989). An evaluation of the adequacy of cognitive/behavioural theories for understanding depression in women. *Canadian Psychology, 30*, 39-47.

Thompson, M.M. (1995). Silencing the self: Depressive symptomatology and close relationships. *Psychology of Women Quarterly, 19*, 337-353.

Welner, A., Marten, S., Wochnick, E., Davis, M.A., Fishman, R., & Clayton, P.J. (1979). Psychiatric disorders among professional women. *Archives of General Psychiatry, 36*, 169-173.

Westkott, M. (1986). *The feminist legacy of Karen Horney*. New Haven, CT: Yale University Press.

Whisman, M.A., Uebelacker, L.A., & Courtnage, E.S. (1998). *Depression and marital dissatisfaction: The role of marital processes*. Manuscript submitted for publication.

Whitley, T.W., Gallery, M.E., Allison, E.J., & Revicki, D.A. (1989). Factors associated with stress among emergency medicine residents. *Annals of Emergency Medicine, 18*, 1157-1161.

List of Authors

Foreword

Anja Cordes

Is Master from University of Copenhagen (1981).

Broad experience as lawyer and counselor with specialty in family law.

President of Danish Family Lawyers 2004-

President of the Organisation of Family Law Lawyers (1996-2000).

Lecturer in family law at Universities of Århus and Copenhagen.

Senior lecturer on divorce law at Copenhagen University.

Officially appointed defender at the court in Vejle (1998-2003) and in Copenhagen from 2006.

Member of IAML (international academy of matrimonial lawyers.

Trained mediator from 1997.

Qualifications:

Family law: separation/divorce, dividing assets, custody matters, marriage settlement, international family law – Law of wills and succession - Acquiring and selling property – Criminal law and Mediation

Chapter 1

Barbara Wilson

PhD, MSc, CQSW, MCM has been a family mediator since 1990. She became a self-employed practitioner and consultant in 1999, having worked originally in the family, civil and criminal courts, and as a therapeutic social worker. She is particularly interested in theory-to-practice issues and writes for a number of professional journals. She teaches various modules of a graduate conflict resolution course run by the Institute of Family Therapy, (under the aegis of the University of London), and also runs post-qualifying workshops for experienced mediators. Barbara lives in Hampshire, England, and may be contacted at info@questmediation.co.uk

Chapter 2

Robert Benjamin

M.S.W., J.D., has been a practicing mediator since 1979, working in most dispute contexts including: business/civil, family/divorce, employment, and health care. A lawyer and social worker by training, he practiced law for over 25 years and now teaches and presents professional negotiation, mediation, and conflict management seminars and training courses nationally and internationally. He is a Adjunct Professor at the Straus Institute for Conflict Resolution of the Pepperdine University School of Law,

Southern Methodist University's Program on Conflict Resolution and in several other schools and universities. He is a past President of the Academy of Family Mediators, a Practitioner Member of the Association for Conflict Resolution, and the American Bar Association's Section on Dispute Resolution and the recipient of the 2009 John Haynes Distinguished Mediator Award. He is the author of numerous book contributions and articles, including "The Mediator As Trickster," "Guerilla Negotiation," "Strategies For Managing Impasse," and "The Beauty of Conflict," and is a Senior Editor and regular columnist for Mediate.com.

Chapter 3
Joanna Kalowski

Is mediator, facilitator and judicial educator who served eight years as a Member of the Administrative Appeals Tribunal and three on the National Native Title Tribunal in Australia. She has observed judicial officers across Australia in many courts, and runs workshops here and in Europe and Asia in communication, dispute resolution and about cross cultural aspects.

Chapter 4
Henry Brown

Is an English solicitor and South African attorney who has mediated extensively in both the family and civil-commercial fields. He co-founded and is a Vice President of the Family Mediators Association and co-established the mediation programme of the UK's family lawyers' organisation, Resolution, and was its first Director of Mediation.

Henry was author of the English Law Society's 'Report on civil and commercial ADR' (1991) and co-author with Arthur Marriott QC of ADR 'Principles and Practice' (1993 and 1999). He also co-wrote a lawyers' training book and DVD with family therapists Neil Dawson & Brenda McHugh in 2006 on 'Managing Difficult Divorce Relationships'.

He has run mediation training in England, Hong Kong, South Africa, Denmark and Iceland. He holds a Certificate in the Fundamentals of Psychotherapy and Counselling.

Henry is a PIM Senior Mediator Emeritus (Panel of Independent Mediators). Until his retirement from full-time practice, he was on the CEDR panel of mediators; a Member of the Chartered Institute of Arbitrators; a Member of the CPR Institute of Dispute Resolution's International Panel of Distinguished Neutrals; an Advanced Practitioner member of the US Association for Conflict Resolution; and a Practitioner Member of the Law Society's commercial mediation panel. He was also accredited with the FMA and Resolution.

Chapter 5
Lisa Parkinson

Is an accredited family mediator and trainer in the UK with over 30 years' experience in family mediation. She was co-founder and co-ordinator of the first family mediation service in the U.K., set up in 1978, and co-founder and director from 1988-1994 of the Family Mediators Association. A founder member of the European Forum for Family Mediation Training and Research and of World Mediation Forum, Lisa has given mediation training in many countries. She is also a member of the Hague Central Bureau Group of Experts advising on a Guide to Good Practice for International Cross-Border Mediation.

Chapter 6
Dale Bagshaw

PhD, is a past President and Vice-President of the World Mediation Forum, the founding President of the Asia Pacific Mediation Forum (ongoing) and is on the International Editorial Board for the Conflict Resolution Quarterly. Before retiring from the University in 2009 she was the Program Director for the Masters, Graduate Diploma and Graduate Certificate in Mediation and Conflict Resolution and the Director of the Centre for Peace, Conflict and Mediation at the University of South Australia. Dale is currently an adjunct at UniSA, a Visiting Professor at the National University of Ireland, Maynooth, a consultant and a trainer and among other things is researching violence against older people. She has conducted a number of research projects on family violence for the State and Commonwealth Governments in Australia, has published many reports, chapters and papers on the topic and has trained mediators in nine different countries.

Home Page:
http://www.unisanet.unisa.edu.au/staff/homepage.asp?Name=Dale.Bagshaw
dale.bagshaw@unisa.edu.au

Chapter 7
Greg Rooney

Has been a practising mediator in Australia since 1991. His professional background is in law. He has written and presented programs in mediation, dispute systems design and project allianceing at an undergraduate and postgraduate level at a number of Australian universities including the University of Queensland and Southern Cross University. He has practiced as an arbitrator in workers compensation disputes using the med/arb model. He worked for three years as an accredited family and child mediator with Relationships Australia Queensland. Greg has conducted in excess of 300 face-to-face mediations between religious leaders and the victims of child sex abuse in a number of Christian-based religions in Australia. Greg lives in Adelaide, South Australia, and may be contacted at www.gregrooney.com.au

Chapter 8
Camilla Emborg

Is a journalist, an author and an editor – born and raised in the town of Horsens in Jutland, Denmark.

Earned her degree from the School of Media and Journalism in Denmark, 1999.

Employed at DR, Denmark's oldest and largest electronic media enterprise, founded in 1925 as a public service organisation. All 11 years she has been involved in TV – as a producer, editor and host on various tv-programmes.

Has published the book "Idiot" in 2009 (People's Press) about experiences with bipolar sufferings' effect on individuals and on their families.

Chapter 9
Sabrine Mønsted

Works as a journalist. In 2006 she received her MSc Journalism and Sociology from Roskilde University, Denmark. She has written freelance articles for magazines, trade journals and newspapers and currently works at Perspektiv the journal of The Danish Union of Librarians, Information Specialist and Cultural Intermediaries.

Sabrine Mønsted writes about Fay Weldon:
Fay Weldon (b. 1931) is one of Britain's most well-known and successful authors and has published more than 30 novels, a number of short stories, tv series and newspaper and magazine articles. She started writing in the 1960's and published her first novel *The Fat Woman's Joke* in 1967. In 2006 she was appointed professor of creative writing at Brunel University in London in recognition of her more than 40 years of professional writing. The trademark of her authorship is an unorthodox feminist perspective of the relation between the sexes, a sharp satirical wit, and increasingly an involvement of political, ecological and cultural critical angles.

Before Fay Weldon became a full-time writer she studied psychology and economics and worked in the advertising industry. She has four sons and was married for more that 30 years to Ron Weldon from whom she divorced in 1994. Today, she is married to Nick Fox a jazz musian who also work as her manager.

Chapter 10
Tina Bolbjerg Winther-Nielsen

(Born 1982), LL.M., graduated from the University of Copenhagen in 2008. She is currently employed as a Head of Section at the Danish Maritime Authority. She wrote her Master's thesis about 'The Effect of Female Stereotypes in a Negotiation Situation' following studies of Negotiation and Dispute Resolution in Theory and Practice. She has been as a guest speaker at an educational mediation course in Denmark in 2009.

Chapter 11
Dana C. Jack

Psychologist, earned her BA at Mount Holyoke College, her MSW at University of Washington, and her doctorate at Harvard University. She teaches at Fairhaven College of Interdisciplinary Studies, part of Western Washington University in Bellingham, WA. USA. Her research focuses on women's depression and anger in the U. S. and internationally. She was a Fulbright Scholar to Nepal in 2001, and taught in a graduate women's studies program at Tribhuvan University, Kathmandu, and also completed research on gender and depression in Nepal. She was awarded WWU Olscamp Outstanding Researcher in 2002. She has published numerous chapters and 4 books:

Silencing the Self: Women and Depression. Cambridge, Ma: Harvard University Press, 1991. *Paperback*, 1992, HarperCollins; *Behind the Mask: Destruction and Creativity in Women's Aggression.* Cambridge, Ma: Harvard University Press. November, 1999. Paperback, 2001; *Moral Vision and Professional Decisions: The Changing Values of Women & Men Lawyers.* New York: Cambridge University Press, 1989. Co-author, Rand Jack, and, most recently, *Silencing the Self Across Cultures: Depression and Gender in the Social World*, Oxford University Press, 2010.

Behind the project

Pia Deleuran, born 1960 in Denmark

Works as an attorney and mediator in Deleuran Law Firm.

She has an educational background from University of Copenhagen – Faculty of Law, (1979-85) and Faculty of Humanities, (1994-1996). She has been connected to Department of Psychology and Educational Studies, Roskilde University since 1997 where she works on a project concerning the legal profession – i.e. research methods, subjectivity and sex- and gender issues.

Pia Deleuran was authorised by the Ministry of Justice as an attorney in 1990 and is trained and certified as a mediator (1997-98).

She was appointed to The Gender Equality Board, (2000-2003) and has been appointed mediator in the Court-mediation-pilot-scheme, (2003-2007).

She is a member of The Bar and Law Society as well as a member of the The Association of Danish Law Firms and DJØF. She helped to start the Danish Association of Mediator Lawyers and became a board member (2003-2007).

Pia Deleuran has for many years been an external lecturer at University of Copenhagen and has been involved in various initiatives developing mediation. She assisted the Bar and Law Society setting up the mediation-training for lawyers in Denmark in 2002, and has, since then, been involved in designing and running the training-courses.

She gives workshops, lectures and is joining learning-settings around the world.

Other projects:

www.vdc123.dk and www.kamelkaravane.dk

Illustrator Sisse Jarner, born 1946 in Denmark

In 1961 trained as a press photographer at Pressehuset. Employed at the Danish National Broardcast DR-News from 1977-1996. Has worked free-lance since then. Sisse Jarner has exhibited her pictures and photos many places

- Byggeriets Hus, Frederiksberg, DK,
- De Frog Gallery, Houston, US.,
- Kvindemuseet i Århus, DK,
- Humlemagasinets Galleri på Fyn, DK
- »12« Scandinavian Center Århus Festuge, DK,
- guest at PRO ,Charlottenborg, DK,
- Galleri Bastillen, DK
- as well as in art-clubs and at libraries.

Sisse Jarner has created illustrations to books.

The touring exhibition
Mediation as a Way Forward
The illustrations from the book can be seen
www.mediationtouringexhibition.com